Stories of Prayer

Stories of Prayer

Interviews with leading Catholics on their experience of God

Betty and Art Winter

Sheed and Ward

Dedication

To our parents,
Nellie and Henry Denner
and
Teresa and Joe Winter,
who first taught us how to pray,
and
to our children,
Jean, Steve and Tom,
for whom we are grateful.

Sheed and Ward™ is a service of National Catholic Reporter Publishing, Inc.

Library of Congress Catalog Card Number:

ISBN: 0-934134-15-4

Published by: Sheed and Ward
P.O. Box 40292
Kansas City, MO 64141

To order: 1-800-821-7926

Contents

Introduction

We are in the midst of a spiritual revolution. As Roman Catholics, we believe this revolution is particularly strong among members of our church, though it is by no means confined to them.

Revolutions are most often thought of as times of overthrowing, tearing down, or blowing apart. This revolution is different. It is a revolution of putting things together. To varying degrees, Roman Catholics and others have in recent times viewed life and the things of life as separate. Categories and dichotomies reigned: body and soul, secular and sacred, Catholic and Protestant, East and West.

Now these divisions are lessening. There is convergence. We are starting to see the individual human being as one entity, not two as in the days of body and soul. God is no longer confined to the church, but is once again recognized as present and active in the world, even in other churches and religions. Following the lead of Thomas Merton and others, Catholics and other Christians are looking to the East — non-Christian as well as Christian — for ways to help them enrich their understanding of life and faith. And instead of arguing as they have for more than 400 years, Catholics and Protestants are working and praying together.

For Roman Catholics, there are other convergences as well. Largely because of the Reformation and our church's reaction to it, Catholicism has been cut off from modern thought. This separation, too, is ending. Catholics' adoption of much of modern biblical study — most developed among Protestants — is an example. Catholic theologians are beginning to use process thought as a philosophical base for reflecting on faith. Further, Catholics are using psychology, a relatively recent discipline, to enhance their understanding of Christianity.

The convergences are not limited to contemporary thought. There is a rush to find the treasures of Judeo-Christian tradition. Again, the rediscovery of Scripture among Roman Catholics illustrates the point. The flood of books on saints and spiritualities of the past — Christian and otherwise — is another example. Often these treasures from the past are mixed with contemporary thought. For example, books and workshops comparing and blending Carl Jung with Teresa of Avila are common today.

In some cases, this historical research has confirmed modern thinking. For example, contemporary teachers and writers, in drawing on modern psychology, have stressed human love and experience as the basis for spirituality. But historians will tell you this is nothing new. They say that in the twelfth century love and experience were an even richer source of spirituality.

In summary, the convergences are telling us life and the things of life are one. We are a whole. So is our world. "Holistic" is the current word. Health and health care help to illustrate the point. Good health care is more than medicine, doctors, hospitals, and pills. Food, exercise, and environment are also crucial elements. So are the insights of psychology. The religious dimension has entered the health care picture as well, with praying for healing becoming a contemporary phenomenon.

We should note two approaches in praying for healing. One is holistic and fits in with the notion of convergence. It sees prayer for healing as part of the total care of a sick person. All legitimate forms of health care are valued. The second style of praying for healing discounts all other efforts at healing. As a result, it maintains the separation of the past.

Paradoxically, the convergences in spirituality have greatly expanded and enriched our forms of prayer — our way of keeping in touch with God, who we believe is the author of the spiritual convergences. Currently, many forms of prayer are in vogue — old and new, Christian and not. Many are combinations and are producing a convergence of their own. The following is only a partial listing:

Centering, bodily prayer, holistic prayer, mantra prayer, guided imagery, biblical prayer, shared prayer, common prayer, charismatic prayer, praying in tongues, faithsharing, prayer of the heart, prayer of quiet, breathing prayer, yoga and prayer, healing prayer, imagination and prayer, Sufi, journal keeping, liturgy of the hours, chanting, fasting, the Jesus prayer, meditation, contemplation, Oriental meditation, meditation with music, Enneagram, Hesychasm, extemporaneous prayer, affective prayer, discursive prayer, altered states of consciousness.

The convergences in spirituality are great. The developments in prayer are many. Yet the number of people affected remains small. We see this among Roman Catholics and suspect it is true of other Christians as well. Many people are experiencing extreme poverty in the areas of prayer and spirituality.

For Roman Catholics, this came about in large part because of the collapse of traditional spirituality and forms of prayer following the Second Vatican Council. (This might have been the "blowing apart" stage of this revolution. If so, we are now in its second phase, the one of bringing together and building up.) As a result of this collapse, many Catholics have been, and still are, striving for spirituality and prayer. The Reverend Edward Farrell was among the first to note this in his book, *Prayer Is a Hunger*, published in the early 1970s.

Thus, on the one hand, we saw a group — for the most part teachers and writers of prayer and spirituality — who were in the forefront of this exciting convergence of spirituality and the rich expansion of prayer. They were an elite. In the language of economists, they were the "haves." On the other hand, ordinary Catholics were having difficulty finding spiritually satisfying nourishment. They were the "have nots." The situation called for another bringing together — another convergence.

This book is our response. We interviewed leading Catholic teachers and writers on prayer and spirituality. We asked them for their ideas and thoughts about prayer. But we also asked how they prayed — would they share with us their methods of prayer and the experiences they had using them?

This latter was particularly important, we thought. It goes back to the idea of convergence. In the recent past, faith and spirituality were expressed largely in an intellectual way. To oversimplify: From one head to another. In those days, interviews such as these most probably would have concentrated on a person's ideas and thoughts about prayer. What information did he or she have? The interviews would have had a catechism quality. Or, in the language of modern journalism, they would have emphasized the objective side of things — just the facts, please.

But in these days of convergence, more was required. We had to get the experts not only to explain their ideas — to tell what they knew — but also to share themselves, their faith, their methods and practices, their experiences. In this way, the interviews would not only be intellectual presentations, but personal and whole as well. The interviews would be "holistic." The currently popular story theology provides another way of looking at the interviews. The persons interviewed would tell their stories of prayer. They would speak from the heart as well as the head. In this way, you, the reader, could encounter a praying person. With luck and grace — and some prayer of your own — this might produce a little revolution in your own life. The interviews did that for us. We hope they do for you as well.

A cautionary note — sounded by Thomas Merton and others, including some people we interviewed — is in order: Ways to pray and ideas about prayer and spirituality are not ends in themselves. If they are, they have become idols. Prayer must go beyond itself to its object: God. We tried to keep this in mind in our conversations. We asked the persons we interviewed to tell us about God and their experience of God in prayer. Naively, we had expected them to introduce God more or less as one would a friend or a neighbor. They couldn't. At first, this was disappointing and made God seem further away. But after a while, we began to notice how often those we interviewed spoke of God as a presence. Again and again they struggled, often with biblical images, to convey a sense of this presence. Inspired by their efforts, we wrote a prayer on presence. It follows and is our prayer for you as you read this book.

> In the beginning
> when the earth was without form and was void,
> and there was darkness on the face of the earth,

your Spirit moved over the waters, and you created.
Your presence brought life out of chaos.

You walked with our parents in the garden.
You visited, called, and guided our father, Abraham.
You appeared to Moses in the burning bush,
you brought the Israelites from slavery,
leading them as a cloud by day and a fire by night.
You pitched your tent among them,
And they made a place of honor for you in their ark.

You were present to your chosen people
in your law and in your covenant.
You raised up prophets to speak your word
so it might be present among your people.
Through them, you told of another
and special presence to come.

Through Isaiah, you told of the day of Emmanuel,
the day when God would be with us.
Through Jeremiah, you told of a new covenant,
one that would be written on our hearts.
After sending John to make the way straight,
your Word was made flesh.
He dwelt among us
and showed us how to live and how to die.

You raised your son from the dead,
and once again he was present to us, in a new way.
He appeared to Mary,
to the disciples on the way to Emmaus,
to the apostles, to all who believed,
and even to some, like Thomas, who did not.

On the day of Pentecost,
when the apostles were gathered,
there was a wind.
It was you again, in your Spirit,
and tongues of fire came resting
on each one of them,
not just the leaders or a selected few,

but as the Scripture says,
"They were all filled with the Holy Spirit."

Since that time,
your followers have believed in your presence,
and have preached it.
Paul, the proclaimer of the Gospel,
said, in speaking of your presence,
that it was so real to him
that it was no longer he who lived,
but you who lived in him.

We have experienced you in our lives.
We are loved by you,
we are blessed by you.
In our churches, we celebrate your presence.
We praise you.
We thank you.
We worship you.
We glorify you.
In our sacraments, we encounter you.
We are washed by you,
nourished by you,
confirmed by you,
forgiven by you,
healed by you,
and commissioned by you.

We have heard your Word read
and your Gospel preached.
We have adored you over the years
as you were present in our holy of holies,
the tabernacle.
And in these latter days,
we have even learned to find you
in your world
and in each other.

Help us to open our hearts
and see the covenant that is written there.

Send your Spirit now as you did in the beginning.
There is a void in us, a darkness.
Speak your creative word once again,
and bring life out of the chaos of our lives.

We have this long and wonderful history
of your presence among your people.
This is our heritage
as sons and daughters of you, Father,
as brothers and sisters of Jesus,
who is Lord,
and as temples of the Spirit,
who has pitched his tent in our lives.

When your son was on earth,
he said he would be with us always,
especially as we gathered in his name.
With that promise in mind,
we ask that he be present again,
and we cry out,
Come, Lord Jesus, come!

We thank the persons who agreed to be interviewed, and who
shared, in the words of one of them, a relationship "more intimate
than sex." Without them, we would have nothing. We thank the
Reverend Ed Hays of Shantivanam, a prayer farm in Kansas, for
his encouragement as we undertook this project; particularly
valuable was his advice to do the interviews as pilgrims seeking
the Lord rather than as journalists looking for information. This
helped keep the interviews on a "holistic" level. We thank Rich
Heffern, who typed the manuscript. Finally, though he did not
contribute directly to this project, we thank Studs Terkel, whose
books of interviews gave us the idea for this one and the courage
to go ahead.

— Betty and Art Winter

1
Praying Where
You Are

Mary Reed Newland

**Mary Reed Newland has been writing about Christian liv-
ing, much of her work emphasizing the family, since 1954,
when she published the first of her twelve books, *We and
Our Children*. Her writings have shown a strong interest in
prayer in everyday life. This was particularly true in a recent
series, "Praying Where We Are," which appeared in *PACE*, a
publication for religious educators. She was born July 11,
1915, in Kalamazoo, Michigan, and grew up on Long island,
where she went to art school and secretarial school. She
and her husband, William, who is deceased, had seven children, and she is the grandmother of four. She never attended
college. She says she learned theology by reading the
spiritual classics and "everything published by Sheed and
Ward." Her books, she says, are attempts to adapt this reading
to Christian family life. She is consultant on adult and family
education for the Diocese of Albany, New York. She has received three honorary doctoral degrees.**

How do you "pray where you are"?

It's like living with someone. I don't want to sound like a "rip-
roaring saint," as Granny Newland used to say, but I think people
ought to get to the point where prayer is like that. I think it is

possible for anyone, especially for people like me who have had faith since they were young and who have always been curious about God.

I did all the things people do when they are introduced to the spiritual life. I used to do an hour of mental prayer and things like that. I read Teresa of Avila, John of the Cross, Augustine, Therese of Lisieux, and others. I am sure all this was good for me, and I enjoyed it. But I found I got beyond it. I have an enormous amount of energy and drive. It's in my family. I found I was on the run a lot and that if I was to pray, I was going to have to do it on the go. That's part of praying where you are. Another part is the internal "conversation" you are having all the time. And part of it is the awareness — well, that there's someone around.

I believe everything is related to God. Everything that happens is kind of a clue to the mystery of God. God is no longer simple or easy for me. His mystery becomes more immense the longer I live. This is hard to express. There are no words. We use anthropomorphic terms, because in the end we have to. Perhaps the best I can do is to say God is a presence, a kind of knowingness, a kind of rhythm you pick up. You try to listen and watch for it. I find that happening all the time.

For example, driving from Albany to Massachusetts is beautiful. The Berkshires, which you pass through, are unbearably beautiful hills. They are almost too much. I can hardly bear it. I often say out loud, "Oh, thank you!" That sounds silly, I know, but if you see the Berkshires, you would understand. They look one way going and another way coming back. They look different at various times of the year. They are a clue to what God is like.

But God is not to be found only in beauty. I remember reading something a long time ago by Robert Hugh Benson, an English writer, that God was present in even the ugliest part of cities. He hasn't created the ugliness, but he doesn't eschew it either. He is everywhere, not just in beauty, as we are so often inclined to think.

When Granny Newland was dying in the hospital, she had a terrible infection in her leg. I sat up all night with her. I watched her heart pounding and her breath gasping. I remembered how we speak of life being God's presence, and how he creates it. I thought, isn't this a mystery. There was something very, very sacred about this really dreadful business of an old, old woman dying in a noisome condition. It was unpleasant, but nevertheless God was present.

On the other hand, I can go to the museum and jump out of my skin, because it's such a revelation of all the gifts people have been given by this mystery we call God. I can have a more exultant experience walking through the museum than I can many places where you are supposed to settle down and pray. It seems God is addressing me in a museum.

This is not the result of any virtue on my part. I may sound as if I've disciplined myself to see God in everything. Well, it is exactly the opposite! I can't miss him. God is a presence that bears down on you all the time in what is beautiful, in what sounds you hear, in the people you meet. You stand in line at the bank, and suddenly it occurs to you that these people are expressions of God.

If you talk about this or try to write about it, it sounds as though you think you are some kind of saint. Certainly, I'm not. I don't think of my experiences as being anything special. I think people pray all the time, but they don't know they are praying. On the other hand, we don't see the situation that way as a church. We think we have to get people to pray, or help them pray, especially families. It seems everybody is saying, "We have to teach families how to pray. *That's* what we have to do."

I am reminded of the time I was invited to speak on family prayer. The person who introduced me had a pet theory about prayer and had a program that spelled it out in great detail. The problem was that if you did it, nobody would get anything else done. I can't think of a family that wouldn't lose patience with it in a week. This person went on for forty-five minutes telling about the program. After that, there was only fifteen minutes left for me to talk.

That wasn't necessarily bad, because it forced me to get rid of everything that wasn't important. What could I say in fifteen minutes that would leave the audience with something to take home and think about? I finally wound up saying, "You know, people pray, but they don't know they are praying, because we never tell them they are. They learn to say their prayers, and they learn about silence and meditation and all that, but we never tell them that much of the conversation that goes on inside of themselves is prayer. That goes for the agony when things are bad and they pound their fists and say 'Oh, God!' as well as the joyful, happy times."

Here's an example of prayer from the joyful times in my life: I have a new granddaughter who is three weeks old. I look at her, say, in the tub, and something just grabs me by the throat, and I want to weep. I get choked up, because this creature is so beautiful and such a mystery. That's a response to something God has done. It's a response to creation. You don't have to say to yourself, "Oh, I thank you, God, for creating this child." That's what a lot of people think of when they think of prayer. They think you have to put it into words. On the contrary, if people have faith — real faith — it is the frame of their lives from morning until night. I think this forms a kind of stream through our lives. This stream is a relationship with God, which is prayer.

We pray in lots of ways. I say the rosary when I walk around the park in the morning. The rosary is one way of holding yourself in an attitude of prayer. It is a good way to keep yourself from going off on a tangent. The first time I ever heard people praying in tongues, I thought they were saying the rosary. The two are very close. The rosary often becomes an unintelligible sound which holds you in an attitude of prayer.

A woman once told me she had been advised to say prayers while she was working. She said she thought this was "baloney." I know what she meant. A lot of people pray while they work, but they do it by working carefully and honestly and well. Something in them says that's the thing to do. They don't stop to put it in words, analyze it, write about it. Their conscientious work is a response to the mystery of God's presence. I think that's praying.

Once, when I was polishing our dining room table, a friend said to me, "You polish that table as though it were an altar." One doesn't say, "Well, my dear, don't you understand that I consider it an altar?" There's something marvelous about polishing a table, about making this gift in your life a little more beautiful. I like doing things that way. Again, I am afraid that sounds pious and holy, but I am under no illusions that I am.

For example, I recently had a very clear perception of my own mediocrity and sinfulness. A woman I love dearly won't pay income tax, and the Internal Revenue Service towed away her car. She refuses to pay for any more military weapons. I thought to myself, "Well, there you are. You haven't got the guts to do that. You excuse yourself by saying, 'If you didn't have a car, you wouldn't be able to get around the diocese and give all those workshops and teach all that Scripture.'" I think the older I get and see my own limitations, the more I am aware of my own mediocrity compared with the generosity of other people.

How long have you been "praying where you are"?

For years. I learned it from books and from my mother and my grandmother. I think its roots are in the old business of "offering up" and regular prayer. We said the rosary when I was little, and I used to hate it. My children hated it, too, when they were small. One of them said to me, "Oh, mother, it was all so tedious."

In any event, when I was young, we said the rosary every evening during Lent. My grandmother, who stayed with us during part of the year, was a real saint, although she had a bit of a sharp tongue. We used to line up on both sides of the bed for the rosary. One night, I was lying on the bed, and I pretended I had fallen asleep from sheer exhaustion. When they finished, grandma poked me and said, "All right, you can get up now. Nobody thinks you're alseep anyway!"

Another member of my family, an aunt who was a nun, was a wonderful, humble woman. Like my grandmother and my aunt, I also wanted to be a saint. I asked my mother what I had to do to be a saint, and she said, "You mustn't be naughty." Well, that lasted about a week. Unfortunately, that was our approach in the old church. If she had said, as we would today, "You must go on loving God with all your heart, darling, all the time, and you must remember, even when you are naughty, that he never stops loving you." That kind of thinking was not part of the scene then. You

had to *please* God. Nevertheless, I remained curious about him.
I had a hunger for finding out more about him. I had the feeling
I was onto something. And, of course, that was not the result of
virtue. It was a gift.

*What have you found out about this God you have been eager
to learn about all your life?*

I have come to believe in his mercy, and I'm going to throw
myself on it. I don't know if I have any points going for me at all.
I say that laughingly, but I am serious.

An experience I had in Africa will help to illustrate the point.
One Christmas I attended midnight mass in Nairobi, Kenya. A
little Italian priest celebrated mass for members of the local
people, who were Kikuyus. In broken English, he told them that
the sin against the Holy Spirit — the one Scripture says is unfor-
giveable — was to think we have nothing to be forgiven. I thought,
"Oh, wow, I came all the way to Africa to hear that!" I am sure
he is right and, therefore, I am certainly under no illusion that I
have nothing to be forgiven.

I find it humiliating to look back over my life and realize I have
committed all sorts of sins I can't even remember. At the same
time, I can remember the humiliations, the times I made a fool
of myself by doing or saying dumb or stupid things. It's awful to
have the capacity to be sinful and to find that the things that cut
the biggest groove in me were the things I now wish I hadn't
done, not because they were sinful, but because they were stupid
and foolish. If nothing else, that's a clue that I am sinful. But in
spite of that, I am not going around like some scrupulous head
case, because Jesus tells us of the Father's mercy, and he shows
his own enormous compassion in the Gospels.

*Mercy and compassion are the key characteristics you have
discovered about God?*

Yes.

*How did reading the spiritual classics help you learn to "pray
where you are"?*

That is obvious in Therese of Lisieux. She calls it her "little
way." She saw God's presence everywhere. The famous examples

are getting splashed in the laundry and listening to a nun whose rattling rosary beads drove her mad. Instances like that suggest that life and prayer are all of a piece and that you can't take them apart in segments, as we have done for years.

That is one of the primary things I talk about in "praying where you are." You're not taking prayer and separating it from life. Therese said she nearly went mad when she heard this nun rattling her rosary all the time. Then she decided to listen for it and use it as a way of controlling her own orneriness. Having gotten over her resentment of the nun, Therese got to the point where she could say the clanging rosary sounded "like the sweetest music to me, and I welcomed it." It became an experience of God for her.

The same thing was true of being splashed with the cold water in the laundry. She also did some things I thought were extreme. That's the way with saints — they go to extremes in some things. People often mistakenly think — and I made this mistake, too — they have to imitate the saints even in these extremes. They think they have to become replicas of the saints. They don't. They are supposed to remain themselves.

For example, Therese loved pretty things. Someone gave her a pin with a pretty bead or something like that on the end of it. She found herself admiring it. But she decided she was going to reserve all her love for Christ, and she stepped on it so she wouldn't waste time admiring it.

Now, I couldn't do that. I love beautiful things. I don't lust after them, and if you took them away from me, I wouldn't have a fit and pout. But beautiful things tell me about God. For example, the poster on the wall over there is a portrait of God for me. It's just squares and circles, but the colors are simply wonderful. The arrangement makes the colors move. They vibrate against one another. As a result, you don't look at any one spot. You don't see one color. You don't look at a yellow or a red or a green or a blue. It's all color. The artist used the same blue throughout, and yet it looks as if there are six or seven different shades of blue. The different colors around the blue produce the various shades. This amalgam, this beauty, this movement is what the world, life, and people are like. Together, they give us our clues to the enormous mystery we call God and, in this way, the poster comes about as close as we can to describing him.

As Catholics, we used to have a strange attitude toward great artistic geniuses. They were all sleeping with people they weren't married to, and carrying on like mad, and dying of drink and drugs or things like that. But, by God, they were true to their gift! We had no theology to handle the greatness of men and women who had enormous gifts, but who otherwise were living in questionable ways. We thought of them as scum.

There's a problem with that. The gifts these people have give us a clue to God. The rest of their lives, what we saw as their sinful ways, was the artist's weakness, which is human and pretty familiar. But the clue to what God is like is to be found in what these people produced with their gifts.

I think that is especially true with music. I love all kinds of music — romantic, Mozart, Bach. When I am listening to some pieces, something happens inside of me, and I want to say out loud, "I love you" — and I am talking to God.

The same is true of great voices. They are miracles. This funny little box in someone's throat with a set of vocal chords produces something that is indescribable. It's so beautiful! It makes me want to cry, and all of a sudden, I have this aching for God, because these things all hint at him.

The same thing is true of what grows between the cracks in the sidewalk, or what you look at with a microscope. People with children should always give them magnifying glasses, so they can discover the beauty of the crummy little things they walk on all the time. How beautiful they are! Again, that gives you an idea of what God is like. I don't mean he's like an ant. I am saying he is like the infinite variety of creation. Praying where you are is really getting on the track of picking up the clues to God.

That sounds like a definition of "praying where you are." Do you have one?

It is really like living with someone and always being aware of that person's being there. It's like living with a presence. I hope that doesn't sound as if I am walking around in an ecstasy all the time, because I am very short of ecstasies. The ones I have are triggered in me by things. You can have an ecstatic experience of God when you see something. But you don't trigger it. Something happens, and it's triggered in you.

For instance: A few years ago, I stopped at a traffic light in the morning on the way to work, and a bird flew over my car. The bird's shadow passed across the hood. My God, it was beautiful. It was just too much. We have grown up with the idea of the Holy Spirit as a dove. That's one association, but there are many others. These associations set me up for that. The world is full of things that come together like that — sounds, music, colors. Whose are they? They are all clues to the mystery we keep trying to figure out, God.

Do you have any kind of prayer regimen at this time—

I'm writing a book on Scripture, and so I read a lot of Scripture. As I'm doing that, I get caught up in various passages. But, no, I'm not faithful to a regimen, though I go to mass during Lent and say the rosary in the park.

What Scripture passages have you gotten caught up in?

I just finished the chapter in my book on Exodus. A passage in Exodus is one of my favorites. It comes right after the commandments have been given a second time, and the Hebrews have been punished and forgiven for the golden calf. There are eight or ten verses in which Moses and God are speaking. It's like a love scene. It is so beautiful.

Moses says to God, "Let me see your face." And God says, "Oh, no, I can't let you see my face. Tell you what I'll do. You hide in the cleft of the rock, and I'll walk by, and I'll hold my hand over you, and when I'm gone, you may turn and see me from the back." So Moses does, and he turns and sees God from the back. Well, that's like looking back on your life and seeing all the times God was present. If you do that, you'll find yourself saying, "Oh, yeah, we were so fearful, so unsure, so doubtful, and we wouldn't have had to be, because he was there all the time."

You can find yourself doing that again and again and again. The more I think about that, the more it seems true — we see God from the back. He's present all the time in our lives, but we see him only when we look back, and then we realize he was there all the time.

If you look back and see him and repeat that again and again, does that help you to see him in the present?

Oh, yes, yes, yes.

Is there another Scripture passage that strikes you?

I like the beautiful speeches in Job. I can hear God saying to Job, "Were you *there* when I set the limits of the sea?" God goes on questioning him like that, and he's getting very sarcastic with Job. God describes the horse, and how the mountain goat brings forth her young, and so forth. All of a sudden, you realize we take things like that for granted. But in this speech, God is talking about things that are sacred and almost bear the imprint of his hand, and we have forgotten that or have never looked at them that way.

I'd like to ask you how you "pray where you are" in various circumstances in your life. Let's begin with being at home.

I have a nice, little one-room apartment. I love it. I am happy there. I am grateful that it is a pleasant place to live. I am aware there are people who are cold and hungry. I don't understand why they are and I am not. I don't understand why I deserve this, and I probably don't, but I have a sense of being happy and grateful. I have a desire to keep it nice and tidy because order is called for, and order isn't always easy for me. Being there, I feel present to someone. I'm not in an ecstatic state, though I must confess I say "thank you" out loud a lot.

When do you say these "thank you's"?

First, you must understand that I think you are somehow or other trying to be tuned in all the time to this rhythm or energy or mystery we call God. Let's say I am about to go out the door, and suddenly it comes to me that I think I have left the stove on under the coffee. I go back and see and, yes, I have. I turn it off and say, "Oh, thank you." I don't think that kind of thing is unusual. I think people who have a faith-filled relationship to the Father and to Jesus and to Mary and to the saints do that kind of thing often.

How about in the morning? How do you "pray where you are" then?

I always talk to God in bed.

You are sleeping with him then?!

That's right! I think a lot of people do. And I think they talk to him when they turn the lights off at night, and when they wake up in the morning. In the morning, I am often struck by the fact that I'm still alive. I don't wonder what's going to happen during the day. I am aware that there are still things I'm useful for. My prayer is not so much a matter of words. One gets past that. The mystery is so big, you can't describe it in words. You get beyond saying, "Now please help me do a good job today, and please help me get my work done well." Once you get past that, you wake up, and there's the presence again.

Getting beyond words in prayer is quite common, I think. Granny Newland used to say, "Oh, I'm not much for praying. I start the rosary, and then all of a sudden it seems to me I have wandered off for the longest time, and I never finished my rosary." I said to her, "Granny, in case you are interested, some people see your wandering off as a superior form of prayer."

When you wake in the morning and find yourself in the presence again, it has an effect on how you act, talk, look at yourself, and so forth. It affects everything. That doesn't mean you don't remain human and fallible. But if you give it half a chance, the mystery, the presence of God, bears in on you, even the likes of me. The presence is there, and when we begin to see it and pick it up and sense it and connect, it seems to me that's legitimate prayer. That's "being with." I guess that's a good definition of prayer: It's being with the One that is present.

How do you "pray where you are" as a mother?

I had a sense of the vocation. I loved it. I had seven children, and I had a sense they were really sacred. They are God's, they belong to God. Their gifts are a mystery to you as parent, and your work is to help them be whole and sound, and come to know God, and love the teachings of Jesus. I am afraid that sounds sentimental and smug and pious, but I think it is true. You try to take the long view. You try to remember they are unique. You try not to have overwhelming ambitions for them, but realize you must be patient and allow them to develop. With this long-range view, you go through the daily routine, which often includes a lot of unpleasant stuff, such as harangues about noise, cleanliness, slamming doors, being irresponsible, or banging each other over the head.

This will show you how much I was into being a mother: It never bothered me to clean up messy diapers. Now that sounds unbearable. What kind of person wouldn't say "yuk"? Well, it didn't bother me. And I am sure that came from the spiritual reading I did and spiritual training I had. I used to think, "Isn't this something? This lovely, lovely creature. Everyone of us is like this, and we have certain functions that are annoying and unpleasant, but that is human, too." The next thing I knew, I was aware of the mystery of God and what he was up to in my life and the life of my family.

Not being bothered by dirty diapers was more than a question of having a strong stomach?

Oh, yes. It came out of a point of view about people and babies and life. That point of view was formed by Christian teaching about the nobility of a child. This funny, irritating little creature, this messy little creature who was driving me out of my mind, had such nobility. That's part of the mystery.

How does one "pray where you are" as a citizen?

Praying where you are as a citizen is constantly confronting what you think of as important politically, and what you ought to do about it, and testing how far you can go with it. For example, I first brought the Nestle boycott to the Albany area and helped organize it here. The boycott concerned Nestle's promotion of infant formula to Third World mothers, who then bottle-fed their children in cultures where breast-feeding had always been before. It resulted in a dramatic increase in infant mortality.

I didn't originate the boycott. I just heard about it from the people who did and brought it back. I was a link in the chain — we all are. Later, Nestle said the two cities that gave them the most trouble were Minneapolis and Albany. If you care about the Gospels, you must act on the public, political, and social things that seem relevant to the Gospels. You can't remain aloof. The problem is always, am I doing enough?

How does one begin to "pray where you are"?

You go back to what you believe about God: That he is all love, all good, all present. You remember you are in relationship to this Presence. You hold that in place and let the day happen.

2
Our Friend
the Bible

Carroll Stuhlmueller

The Reverend Carroll Stuhlmueller has combined his interest in prayer and Scripture by writing four books of biblical meditations. He has also written a two-volume work on the prayers of the Bible, the psalms. In addition to writing, he edits. He is editor of *The Bible Today* and a series of books, "Old Testament Message," published by Michael Glazier, Inc. His primary work is teaching Old Testament at the Catholic Theological Union in Chicago. Father Stuhlmueller has a doctorate from the Pontifical Biblical Institute in Rome. He is a Passionist, and first came into contact with that community in his native Hamilton, Ohio, where he was born April 2, 1923. His books include: *Psalms 1* and *Psalms 2,* and *Biblical Meditation for Advent and the Christmas Season, Biblical Meditations for Lent, Biblical Meditations for the Easter Season,* and *Biblical Meditations for Ordinary Time.*

In a U.S. Catholic *interview, you said a crucial moment came for you when you were a senior in high school. "Our religion teacher," you said, "got sick one day, and a substitute came in and gave a talk on the Gospels. Now I don't want to make a public confession, but I really didn't know a word of the Gospels and had never really looked at the Bible in my life, but I was caught*

*by that talk. I started reading the Gospels every day and started
writing down favorite passages of the day, on my own." What
happened to you during that experience?*

Before that, I was devoted to reading such books as the *Imitation of Christ* by Thomas á Kempis. One of my sisters sent me a
copy. It rather fascinated me. I don't know why, but once I got
onto the Scripture, I put aside the *Imitation of Christ*. It didn't
seem to have the verve. As I look back on it now, I think the
Imitation of Christ tended to have a very passive spirituality. It
was like another old classic, *Abandonment to Divine Providence,*
by Pierre de Caussade. I don't want to speak against either book,
but after discovering the Bible, they didn't strike me as something
I wanted to build my life on.

There could be a human explanation for what happened during
this class, but I am inclined to think it was God's hand, although
I didn't feel any Spirit breathing down my back. It just happened.
In regard to reading the Scripture at that time, I was innocent of
any concern about the historical background of the text and its
literary form. I knew nothing about any of that. Luckily, I was
also preserved from the stereotyped, literalist reading of the Scripture. In that approach, people are rather rigidly determined to
prove their point by quoting the Bible. At the time, I think if I
was going to prove anything, I would go outside of Scripture to
other courses, such as the old, Catholic-style apologetics. The
Scripture turned out to be a very liberating and window-opening
experience for me.

*In the interview, you went on to say you went through the
Bible seven or eight times in that manner.*

Yes.

*And even though you didn't have the background of modern
Scripture studies, you avoided literalism and proof-texting and
were able to make it a religious experience.*

Yes.

*Based on that experience, would you say the same is possible
for the average Catholic who is unschooled in the Bible?*

Yes, I believe that firmly. I believe Bible learning and Bible classes are excellent, but it's not necessary in God's plan. My only requirement for reading the Bible for prayer is to read it as you would contact a friend. If you are with a friend, there are times he or she will say something you don't quite understand, but the conversation moves on. And you drop the matter you didn't understand; there's no big problem. Other times, friends may say something you disagree with, but it's not a big deal either. You don't argue with them or fight about it. You let that drop, too. I think life is too short to have to settle every problem that comes up and refute every statement we disagree with. I recommend that we read the Bible in the same friendly way. At least, I have found this helpful for myself.

That's how I would explain now what I did when I first started reading the Bible. At the time, I wasn't trying to explain anything. If I came to passages I didn't understand, I kept going and dropped them. A certain amount was of human weakness or laziness in it too, I suppose. If I found a stretch in Numbers or Leviticus with a lot of names across the page, I'd glance at those and be done. I believe that as long as we read the Bible as a friend, read it with the faith that God is speaking, and try to see what God is saying to us in our daily life, we can use it effectively for prayer.

As you became more learned in the Scripture, did that affect the way you prayed with the Bible?

After learning the background of the Scripture, I didn't center so much on particular texts or verses as I did at first. I think now I can experience better the larger impact of an entire psalm or a whole episode in the Bible. I now find it helpful to reflect on two or three passages of Scripture together. That is particularly true of the liturgical readings. That's what I tried to do in the biblical meditation books I have written. In doing this, I usually find some major theme will connect the readings.

I was noticing the readings for today, Easter Sunday. In the reading from the Acts of the Apostles, the major religious leaders of the Jewish people and the members of the Sanhedrin refused to accept that a crippled person was brought back to life in the name of Jesus. And then in the Gospel reading, when Mary Magdalene and the two men on the way to Emmaus came back to say they had seen the Lord Jesus and he had risen, the official eleven apostles refused to believe.

Something is linking these events. The reflection that begins to form in my mind is that if we are religious leaders — teachers, parents, priests, etc. — we probably have a lot to learn from the unlearned. Something can burst into our lives suddenly — without our programming it — that can tell us a whole lot. I find by connecting readings in this way, then re-reading each passage, I begin to see other aspects of the readings and other ways God is present in them.

How do you pray daily, and how do you use the Bible in that prayer?

I usually pray in the early morning, because so much can happen during the day. I like to take an hour. I read the three psalms in the first part of the liturgy of the hours. Then I read the Scripture for the day's mass. Maybe I will jot down a particular insight that joins the readings. Often, I don't write it down anymore, but keep that thought in my mind. And I spend the rest of the time in silence. One of my principles is that prayer is not a time to learn anything or solve anything. It's not the time to prepare a sermon or put the final touches on my next class. It's time spent being with God. I think a first principle in prayer ought to be one of being absolutely non-pragmatic. You ought to enjoy the time and be with God, and let what happens happen.

Can you cite a favorite scriptural passage you have used in that way?

Certain ones, yes, might summarize or synthesize my spirituality. I think one of my favorites would be in Chapter 55 of Isaiah:

> As the rain and the snow come down from the heavens
> and do not return without watering the earth
> bringing forth food for the eater and seed for the sower,
> so shall my Word be.
> It does not return to me without
> achieving that for which I sent it.

So you go to Amos and his criticisms of the wealthy of his time with, say, the problem of world hunger in mind. You find what God said through a prophet regarding feeding the hungry. Does thinking about today's problem of hunger help you to understand what God says about it in the Bible?

I think what you are saying is the result of prayer and not prayer itself. I would place that in the category of preparation, say, for teaching or preaching. I think I would limit prayer if I "used" it to settle the question of hunger. I would use the problem of hunger and what the Bible says about it in this way for prayer: On the one hand, you have hunger. On the other, you have the Scripture that gives a perception into world hunger, particularly the hunger of the powerless and the defenseless — what the Bible calls the orphans and the widows. For prayer, I would try to reflect on the idea of living with a God who also experienced hunger and deprivation. As far as prayer is concerned, I would leave it at that.

In one of your books Biblical Meditations for Lent, *you say, "This book grew out of several years of personal prayer during the early morning hours of Lent, with a small missal, pencil, and pad of paper at hand." Can you tell us about that experience?*

At that period, I used to read and I still do to a certain extent — the Scripture selections for the liturgy of the day. I would write down what impressed me at the moment in each passage. Then I would be silent for a while and see, almost through the subconscious, what link emerged to tie the readings together. I would write that down, maybe two or three or four lines, and that was it. That would be enough of a discipline to keep out distractions. It was enough of an intellectual stimulant for my mind to continue in one direction. Then, I would simply be silent in God's presence.

Could you tell us about the God you have come to know as a result of your prayer and study of the Scriptures?

That's hard. God is most understanding, not in the sense of solving the riddle, but in accepting, and in accepting, mysteriously enough, enabling me and others to be at peace with whatever is happening.

The first thing that appeals to me is the image of rain and snow. It's a gentle image, yet a vigorous one. It's cold when the snow falls, yet the snow comes very lightly upon the earth. On one hand, winter is a tough time, a barren time. But the Word of God does not stay in mid-air like the clouds, but soaks the earth. I think that means that when God's Word reaches us, it does so in an earthy way, in people, in their events.

As a result, we never have the pure Word of God. It's never that quintessence of exactly what God would want to say. It's mixed with the earthy and the human. That means different points of view and sometimes human prejudice and bullishness and ambition. You have that whole mixture of what we call human nature, good and bad together.

This is the situation in which the Word of God comes. Once it starts to grow, it reaches back to God, toward the heavens. I like that passage very much, because it shows a certain cycle. It emphasizes the human aspect, the total human environment. At the same time, the earth would be barren without the rain of God coming. The earth doesn't dictate what happens, either. Through the sun, God draws things back again. A passage such as this directs a lot of my thinking and attitudes.

Another favorite passage of mine is from Jeremiah, in Chapter Twelve. Jeremiah is arguing with God. In that passage, what seems non-negotiable is Jeremiah's faith in God. He says, for instance, "You are just, O Lord." Even though that is an absolute as far as Jeremiah is concerned, he has a question, "Why do the ways of the wicked flourish?" God's response never answers the question, but insists on more faith from Jeremiah. I guess what appeals to me is that often our questions lead us to God, not in the sense of getting the answer, but of increasing our faith in God.

You can see Jeremiah's faith in God is not something he would negotiate with God about because, even if the ways of the wicked are flourishing, he still begins the passage by saying of God, "You are just." In effect, he is saying, "I can't figure out how you are in view of the circumstances, but you are." It does make this point: I believe a big part of prayer is allowing ourselves slowly to become adjusted to the God who is living with us moment by moment. Rather than adjusting God to our life, I think, it is a case of our life getting in tune with God. We don't, however, become adjusted to God by turning to him, purely, or in an isolated form, but rather by developing a sense of God's presence always in our life.

Do you feel a sense of God's presence and, if so, what is it like?

It's a sense like this: I am not really thinking about a chair being over there across the room, but I have an awareness of the chair being there. I think the same happens with the presence of God. There is an awareness of God being in the atmosphere or of God being the atmosphere. This is not explicit. A writer might say the presence is between the words of the sentence.

How does the Bible help you with the sense of God's presence?

A passage such as the one from Isaiah is meaningful to me. I think it shows God in moment-by-moment events. In this way, there is no part of life where I would feel God is not present. In fact, one of the explanations I find for the violent scenes in the Bible — and I am not trying to justify violence — is to realize that somehow or other, God is present in those wrenching moments. God is present even in moments where no truly spiritual-minded person would draw up a drama of how God might be present.

I think the same point can be made regarding our faults, failures, and sins. These have to be viewed over the long stretch of life, but somehow, in the mystery of it all, they help us, too. They help us to learn and, I think, eventually we find that God was present while they were occurring.

I would be willing even in a sophisticated academic setting to contend that to understand the Scripture as the word of God, one must include within the elements of interpretation the immediate context of one's life. The reason: that God is the living God.

As I look back upon the movement of Catholic Bible scholarship before and since the encyclical letter of Pope Pius XII *Divino Afflante Spiritu* in 1943, I would look upon the critical historical study of the Bible as a passing phase. It is important and will

always sustain itself as an essential aspect of investiga Scriptures.

But I would contend that what God is saying to us in a passage cannot be acquired simply by knowing what th writer intended to say. Nor would the Word of God b simply by what church authority says it is. Another im ingredient would be the way the spirit of God is movin my life and environment. A further one is the question by the world today with regard, for example, to the pro providing food for all the hungry people. There is also the threat, the problem of national security vis-a-vis oppressiv eous governments. These questions are unique to our least in emphasis.

I think if I want to know what God is saying in a pas Scripture, it is necessary to blend these ingredients. Go God of creation. God is the God of history, even the histor made today. God is the personal God of each of us indiv God is the God of our ancestors — Abraham, Isaac, Jac onward. God lives within my church. To hear this one Go his mystery and grandeur, I cannot limit God to any one o aspects.

How might the world situation — and your relationsh — affect your reflection on a particular passage at a par time?

That can be answered better by saying it probably will what parts of Scripture I gravitate toward. If I am conc about world hunger, for example, I will probably gravitate toward the Jerusalem psalms — such as Psalms 46, 47, 48, speak so much of the grandeur of Jerusalem and the enth ment of God. Or perhaps I will gravitate less toward Psalm 15, which are about the requirements for purity of heart. R if I am immediately involved in this kind of wordly issue, find myself moving toward prophetic literature in the Bible, as Amos or Micah. They wrestle with the problem of a re that is not necessarily false, but one that is phony, becaus not interacting and helping people find God in the most auth questions that come from their lives.

Let me tell you about a notion I have of God that I find in the Book of Exodus. When I first read it, I was really struck by it. It was a totally new experience for me. Until that time, I had a completely different idea of God than the one I thought I had found in Exodus. There I found a God who was present with his people, who was involved in their daily lives and not off in a church somewhere, who was down in the mud with them where they were making bricks, and who finally led them out not so much of spiritual slavery as of physical captivity. From that, I got an image of God as a liberator I had never had before. From that, I came to think of and believe God was leading and guiding us. And when I tried to look at my own life, occasionally if I would let him, it seemed as though I could find him trying to free me, too. I like that a lot. It seems real to me. How does it sound to you as a Scripture scholar?

My emphasis would be somewhat different. It's probably a question of different spiritualities. Each spirituality is genuine, although each would emphasize one or another aspect. In the sense of liberation and liberation theology, I can talk about it and write about it — and I hope it is genuine — but it is not where I live in my deepest person. It's not an ultimate emphasis for me. I suppose because my life has been more surrounded by books than, say, parish ministry or foreign missionary work, I think my vision of God from the Book of Exodus would come from chapters 20, 25, and 34, in which Moses is on the mount with God and sensing the vision of God. In Chapter 34, God says of himself: "The Lord, the Lord, kind and merciful, just and compassionate, showing loving kindness and steadfast love to a thousand generations." That sense of a quiet, contemplative moment appeals to me more. It doesn't mean one is right or holier. It means there are different types of people, of spiritualities. It makes life interesting.

How do you, as a Scripture scholar, image or picture Jesus?

The scenes that would speak best to me would be the silent moments of Jesus, whether he is alone in prayer, or in agony in the garden, or on the cross. These moments, the more contemplative ones, appeal to me. They are not the most active moments of Jesus' life, and maybe not the most important, and not much space is given them in the Scriptures, but that's where I would find myself.

You have written a two-volume book on the psalms. How would you recommend that they be prayed?

I always insist in class that one must read and reread the text of the psalm. Know it backward and forward. After a person is at home with a psalm, I think it is helpful to try to spot the general style or atmosphere or spirit. Is it a hymn of praise or a prayer of supplication? A prayer of confidence or thanksgiving? I think that as a person reads more and more of the psalms and reads each several times, this becomes second nature. So, for example, in one psalm, you may get a feeling of wanting to shout with joy. In another, you may feel God has forsaken you. In another, you sense your soul is thirsting for the Lord. Or, you develop a sense of sorrow or lamentation.

I also suggest another step, which I do in class. Look for key words, repeated words. In Psalm 22, a key word is *distance.* The psalmist is saying, "Why have you abandoned me? You are distant from my cry." In verses 12 and 20, it repeats, "Do not be distant."

Or, in Psalm 132, a key word is "to go up." Israel "comes up" out of Egypt. The ark "goes up" to Jerusalem. We "go up" to worship the Most High. God is "going up." Often, the key word will be an authentic part of the psalm but will also be somewhat specific to the person reading the psalm. I think when you go for the key word, you almost always go for the center of your spirituality. When you find the key word, read the psalm again and see how it expands and enriches the key word.

I think, for example, a true aspect of spirituality is the "distinct God." Professor Samuel Terrin calls him the "elusive God." Isaiah calls him the "hidden God." Job talks of God "speaking from the whirlwind." In all these, there is a sense in which God is distant. And that is a real aspect. If God were as evident as that chair I referred to earlier, you probably wouldn't bother with these interviews.

Let's take the notion of "going up." How would a person use it in prayer? Would one use the image of lifting or being lifted up?

Yes, although a lot would depend on a person's character and immediate circumstances. On a particular day, "to go up" may reflect a liberating moment. All of a sudden, great burdens or obstacles are lifted, and the person is going through the Red Sea, as it were, and there is a kind of "going up." Or "going up" could mean going through the wilderness experience for a period of time. The theme has different aspects for different people at different times.

It seems this method might be helpful in telling a person where he or she is on a particular day. Let's say a person feels "distant from God" on a given day. Maybe the person would rather not be "distant," but that's the way it is at the moment. At least the person knows what the situation is. It becomes a kind of map, doesn't it?

I think so. Another dimension of the key word is that we tend to gravitate toward key words that are also keys to unlocking ourselves. I think that's the way human nature tends to be. The other side is that in the Bible, these key words are usually crucial words. They are not like trinkets scattered around. They are usually central themes, and I think they are central to the Bible because they are central to life. They aren't the little piece of parsley, they are the meat and potatoes. I think a method like the key word helps to keep people rooted in themselves and in God. The person isn't tinkering around but is at the heart of life.

Besides Jesus, what biblical figures come to mind as people of prayer?

Jeremiah, Isaiah, Hosea, Job. I think, for instance, that Jeremiah comes across as someone in the mainstream of life and yet as someone who seeks depth in prayer. He reflects the desire and the necessity of long periods of silence with God. Usually any of the things I have given a lot of time and attention to — like Jeremiah — have been things I got pushed into by somebody else. And as I look back on my life as to what has been worthwhile, I find I am more on target when that happens. The booklet on Jeremiah that was part of the "Old Testament Reading Guide" fell into my lap because someone else wasn't getting it done and

finally pulled out on it. Unplanned occasions like that have turned
out as great graces, or blessings, or insights for me.

*You dedicated one of your books to the Passionist community,
saying it was "where I learned to love the Bible and prayer." What
did you learn in your community that might be helpful in praying
with the Bible in local church communities and parishes?*

I don't want to be too judgmental, but I find that too much of
Catholic liturgy is too active, too busy for me. Our new liturgy is
also too demanding intellectually for me. Oh, I understand the
Scriptures; they come fast to me. There's no problem with the
readings. But when everything is in English, when everything is
spoken out loud, and when I am supposed to interact with everything that is going on, I find that is too much. I find that incom-
patible. I could not survive on that.

As I have said, I find the liturgical cycle of readings important.
To appreciate these readings, I think we need much more space
or silence. And I am referring here not only to the liturgy of the
word. The same is true of the whole eucharistic liturgy as well.
With the preface, the canon, the offertory said out loud, the whole
thing occupies me too much. I'm not passing judgment on what
others find helpful and not helpful, but my instinct or my desires
would say that if the mass is to take thirty or forty minutes, we
should make sure we have fifteen minutes of silence at various
times.

A lot of that silence can be programmed in. For instance, after
the first reading, you could have several minutes of silence. You
can also do that with the responsorial psalm. Another idea is to
have a quarter of a minute or so of silence between each verse
of the psalm. But it shouldn't drag. What's said or sung should
be done with normal rhythm, but there has to be space between
things.

I think too, the celebrant should simplify the amount of themes
or key words or material that should be pondered. Whether he
is introducing a penitential rite or some other prayer, there ought
to be a simplicity and sameness so intellectually, a person is not
being pulled in many different directions. I would favor having

the celebrant say the words in silence in a number of places —
such as the offertory and certain parts of the canon.

What has been the effect of prayer on your life?

As I look back on it, I think the greatest thing it has given me
is a sense of peace, a sense of tranquillity. Also, it has helped me
to realize life is worth living. It wasn't wasted. No matter where
we are in our life in the sense of major vocation and major work,
I think to do that major work well, we have to do lots and lots
of itsy-bitsy stuff. And I think whatever we do, if we are going to
do it well, we have to be on top of all these details. When we are
facing the reality of having to do all these little things, we can
legitimately wonder, is this why God created me? To do this little
thing and that little thing? It can seem so useless. Prayer helps
me to see that these little things are worthwhile. It also helps me
to realize I am living with a God who is as personal as I am.
Perhaps even more so. What more need be? What more need I ask?

3
A Storyteller's Story of Prayer

John Shea

The Reverend John Shea, a priest of the Archdiocese of Chicago, is the leading U.S. Catholic exponent of storytelling theology, which has rediscovered that the truths of faith are passed on more effectively in stories than in abstract thought. He has written seven theology books, including *Stories of Faith, Stories of God* and *An Experience Named Spirit,* and two books of poetry, *The Hour of the Unexpected* and *The God Who Fell from Heaven.* He has also published audio tapes and speaks extensively. He was born in Chicago September 3, 1941, and was educated there, receiving a doctorate in theology from St. Mary of the Lake Seminary, where he is director of the doctor of ministry program.

I started telling stories as a camp counselor. I had to tell stories every night to keep the kids from ripping the cabins apart. After I was ordained, in giving homilies, I found people would remember the story you told six weeks ago but had totally forgotten the clear and distinct idea you lucidly portrayed twenty minutes ago. It became obvious the story form had a certain immediate interest and fascination.

Another way I became interested in stories was sitting in kitchens listening to people talk. People would relate the significant experiences of their lives in story form. Within the narrative format, a couple of clear and distinct images would pop out. Often these images would show the people's religious personality. In ministry, you listen to many people. They are always telling the story of their lives, one way or another. Most people use narrative language to talk about the deeper meaning of their lives. The more educated ones will use analytic language, but not often.

The narrative language is much more powerful, much more effective, much more unfolding. I found story as a language form of human expression and communication was central to understanding people. If it was that central to them, then ministry, which tries to live at the most important juncture of people's lives, should know about it and learn how it works and be able to use it effectively.

As a storyteller, how do you pray?

I guess I pray in different ways at different times. I don't have a set time to pray. Prayer for me is being responsive when I feel things beginning to move me in some way. It begins with a kind of stethoscope on myself. A lot of experiences I undergo, or events I am part of, have a tremendous impact on me. I could be in a hospital talking to a woman suffering from cancer. I could be trying to help a teenager who has been caught stealing and is going to court. I could be dealing with a group of people who are doing some reflection on their lives, say, during Lent. When I am in such events or experiences, often something in them will jolt me or fascinate me. Later, in solitude, I will check out what happened.

Basically, I pray off an action-solitude dynamic. After an experience, I will wait for a while. I never write anything down. I remember the experience at certain times. A time will come when I pull the plug on the phone, and I'll be alone with that experience. I will bring it to mind again, and I will replay it and ponder it until the grace in the experience surfaces. What I am trying to do, I suppose, in theological language, although I usually don't talk about it this way, is to decipher a divine voice within all the human voices I hear. Something is speaking to me, something is being said. It could have been a harsh word. It could have been a kind word. But I don't know yet what it is. When it surfaces in solitude, I address it. In my prayer, I often do not address God directly for a long, long time. I only do that when the divine makes an appearance in my mind or memory. I don't sit down and address God. I wait until God addresses me, then I talk back. That's basically how I pray.

If my prayer is slow, it is often because I have not had enough action. It is not that my solitude isn't good enough. My active life has been too mundane. It hasn't been deep enough. I haven't been with people in critical enough moments, both for them and for me. I haven't been at the core of anything. I never pray when I am writing a book, for example. I never see anybody then. I'm just sitting in my room. I'm not getting any action. I don't have an action base off of which to pray.

I used to do spiritual direction with college students. Many of them were praying in a vacuum. They hadn't been touched deeply enough to pray. How could they pray? All they could do was rehearse the prayers from their bedsides when they were little kids. It was really tough for them. You had to teach them to be sensitive to their encounters before they could have any depth in prayer.

The solitude part of my prayer is like a storm. I can feel it coming. I know then that I have to get away. It wasn't always that way. For a long time, I was sort of awash. I don't have any standard prayer forms. I meditate on the Scriptures once in a while. I will read all the scholars say about a passage, then I'll sort of dwell inside it. I'll wait until the scriptural passage begins to interpret me, and then I'll move with that.

One of the funny things about this process is that time doesn't seem to mean much. You can go back to experiences you had a long time ago, bring them forward and have them yield grace in the present. For example, here is an experience from my camp counseling days, a long time ago. The camp served as a place to screen kids who wanted to get into a military school. The people who ran the school thought parents who had troubled kids would send them to the school for discipline. They ran the camp during the summer, in part at least, to look the kids over. The idea was that the best way to determine if a kid was a sociopath was to watch him play baseball. You could see if the kid could work with the other kids, then you could either take him or not.

I was the head counselor. On the first day of camp, a kid lost his baseball glove by noon. By three o'clock, another kid had lost his hunting knife. At canteen time, someone had lost five dollars. We had a thief on our hands.

I caught the thief the next day. It wasn't very hard. Eleven-year-olds are pathetic thieves. I asked him, "Why did you do it?" He said, "I didn't do it." I said, "We found everything in your locker. You did it, why did you do it?" He said, "I didn't do it." I said, "Okay, let's wipe the slate clean. This is the second day of camp. No one knows you took it. I have returned all the stuff. Let's forget it ever happened." He said, "I didn't do it."

A day or two later, he stuck a fish hook into a kid's leg while they were in a boat. So, there we were again. I said, "Why did you do it?" He said, "I didn't do it." I said, "Two other kids saw you do it." But he still insisted he didn't do it. I went to the nun who was head of the camp, and she said we couldn't send him home because his parents were on vacation, but she said we would give him to Sister Ruth Ann, an old, retired nun who worked around the camp.

For the next two weeks, the kid was running around the camp helping this nun. She would be planting stuff and painting stuff and plumbing stuff, and he would be with her all the time. She ate with him. She brought him to the cabin at night. She wouldn't let him out of her sight.

At the end of two weeks, the parents came, and they asked what parents from the dawn of time have asked, "How's our son doing?" The head nun, who was the most direct person God ever made, told them, "You lied to us. This boy is very troubled. And you pawned him off on us. We'll keep him another two weeks, but I want you to know he is not going to be playing baseball with the other kids. He's going to be working with Sister Ruth Ann."

So, we kept him another two weeks. The other kids started asking him if he wanted to play baseball. He would look at the old nun, and she would say, "You go play baseball, and when you get back we'll paint the benches." During the next two weeks, she gradually let him out and then reeled him back in. She let him out and reeled him back in, let him out, reeled him in. By the end of four weeks, the kid was integrated back into the group, playing baseball and doing other things with them. And he was no longer acting out the sociopathic tendencies he obviously had.

Even though that happened long ago, there is one image from it I remember clearly. On the day the kid left camp, he and the old nun were coming up the path. She was sort of hip hugging him, pulling him against her as she walked. I can still see them moving toward the car that way.

When I bring that experience to mind now, it says a lot to me. Besides the meanings I pull out of it, it is sort of a mini-experience of what I consider grace. People change, or destructiveness in human life can be changed, but at tremendous cost. This old nun had the time and the ingenuity and perseverance to pay the price for this aberrant eleven-year-old. Now, I sort of see her in this story as God. When I move off that experience and pray, I critique my own life in terms of giving up on people, of not paying the price to bring about some kind of redemption in their lives. This leads me to pray off other experiences from the point of view of perseverance, ingenuity, and the cost of bringing about change.

A lot of times, prayer for me is discernment of sin. During solitude, I try to discern how I am cooperating with destructiveness in the situations I'm in. That can either be implicit or explicit. I may be fostering it deliberately — maybe not in a malicious way, but in some self-serving way. Or, I am battling it. A lot of my prayer concerns strategies for change, at least in my thinking and I hope in some of my behavior. I guess the old cliche, "I'll pray over it," is true. I guess I do that.

Last week, for example, I was giving grades of my students. After you teach for a while, giving marks is old hat to you. And yet you are dealing with the egos of a lot of people. You can become very flippant and destructive about it and be insensitive to what it really is: It's a terrible social divider. It dictates futures, puts people in classes, limits possibilities, squelches hopes.

I wound up giving six failing marks. How do I hang in there with the six kids who flunked? That becomes a big question for me after reflection on the experience of the old nun. In this way, in my moments of solitude, the experiences of the past and the grace in them are brought forward to judge parallel experiences going on now.

In the introduction to one of your books of poems, The Hour of the Unexpected, *you say, in writing about prayer, that "first something happens. . . . In these moments, and many more, we are thrown back on ourselves. More precisely, we are thrown back into the mystery we share with one another. These moments trigger an awareness of a More, a Presence, an Emcompassing, a Whole within which we come and go. This awareness of an inescapable relatedness to Mystery does not wait for a polite introduction. It bursts unbidden upon our ordinary routine, demands total attention, and insists we dialogue. At these times, we may scream or laugh or dance or cry or sing or fall silent. But whatever our response, it is raw prayer, the returning human impulse to the touch of God." Can you tell us about a couple of instances when you screamed or laughed or danced or cried or fell silent?*

The book is filled with them. So is my other book of poems, *The God Who Fell from Heaven.* They contain mainly personal experiences cloaked and retold so the people involved would not be embarrassed. One poem comes to mind. It is about loss. The poem actually has two parts and is called, "Two Prayers of Loss." The first part is about a guy I knew in a parish. The second is about my grandparents. The first part goes like this:

> Thaddeus Edward Bornowski
> would not be at the lathe today.
> It was the twenty-fourth of June
> and he was angling his kitchen chair
> down the narrow back stairs.
> It slid perfectly into the trunk
> of his car. It had been there before.
>
> It was seventeen minutes to St. Adelbert's
> and three winding, five mile-an-hour minutes
> to the Holy Rosary section
> and just a moment past

the stone bead of the Annunciation
to Rosemary Dorothy Bornowski
       1909-1968

He set the chair on the side
leaned over with kitchen intimacy,
and talked downward
past the plaque and grass,
the settled dirt, cement casement,
and the copper casket with the crucified God
to the listening memory within.

And the second part, about my grandparents is as follows:

For Daniel and Mary O'Malley
after supper came the beads.
He would Hail Mary the first part:
She would Holy Mary him back
       and the rote prayer rose to chant,
       word ran upon word, a marriage sound,
       the Catholic trick for ecstasy.
Every evening for forty-seven years.

Now she was gone.
The family agreed their father
had held up well
but every night after supper
in the den of his daughter's house,
he would Hail Mary
and wait.

From *The Hour of the Unexpected* by John Shea © copyright 1977 Argus Communications, Division of DLM, Inc., Allen, Texas 75002.

I think death is the experience that most throws us into mystery. It's the key one. And the response to that mystery of loss is usually silence and tears. Seldom do you have a lot of words, especially if the death has been premature or tragic in some way. Language fails you. People sit there, and they usually cry. And that's the response. That's the prayer. What words there are, are always inadequate. Years later, you may be able to talk about it, but at the time, it is too deep an experience for words.

When I say the tears are prayer, I am saying they are coming not only from loss but also from the encounter with the evanescence of human life. The mystery of human life, not just the loss of one person, is causing those tears. It is the loss of ourselves, too. The tears are a response to the inbreak of that mystery, and, in this case, a brutal inbreak that is very diminishing.

On the other side is birth. Think of the laughter that goes on around babies. Think of how people watch babies crawl around the floor and just sort of wonder. People can stare at a baby for long periods of time and get totally immersed in the baby. They can let the baby play with their fingers. They talk to it. Through the baby and through all their carrying on, people are coming in contact with the wonder and mystery of a life that is continually reborn.

Their prayer comes from the fact that they are not just responding to the baby but also to the mystery of life through the baby. And so they laugh. That laughter is being caused by God, just as the tears were caused by God. And the laughter is prayer, because it is a response to the touch of God, the same as the tears.

We construct worlds of normalcy, worlds of predictability, for ourselves. That is absolutely necessary. They are new wombs we form to comfort and protect ourselves and to make life stable and coherent. Those worlds of normalcy, while protecting, often become monotonous. They are frequently untouched by passion or beauty. And because they are self-constructed, they are fragile. There are times they are broken down. Sometimes, they are broken down in a bad way, in a tragic way. Sometimes, they are broken down in a beautiful way. At moments when the unexpected breaks into the world of normalcy, with a grace you didn't think was possible, no matter what the response is at the time, it is prayer.

What do you do when the unexpected happens?

It depends whether the unexpected is a good unexpected or a bad unexpected. If it is a good one, you relish it. You go with it, you respond to it. You play it out. And you might want to store it away, too. There is a hoarding instinct in prayer experiences. You are a hoarder of good experiences. You are like a squirrel with nuts. You might want to stack an experience in your memory and bring it back. I think that is legitimate. We do that with liturgy.

I think part of the prayer of praise is to allow your spirit to soar with the good times. A lot of people fear soaring; they fear their spirit. They can petition and they can repent, but they can't praise. They can never really get into Francis of Assisi's canticle to the sun. That's too much. Most people can deal with prayer out of experiences of diminishment, but not out of experiences of power. One of the things necessary in prayer, as W.H. Auden says, is that "when grace enters, you have to dance." You have to allow your spirit to soar and not be afraid of the joy, because it can get dizzying at times, terribly dizzying.

The baptism of my nephew was a very soaring experience for me. It was for our whole family, and I put it into a poem. It's the first one in *The God Who Fell from Heaven.* It was really a great experience. There hadn't been a baby in our family for a long time. His name is Johnny. The poem is called "A Prayer at Baptism."

> I must remember, Johnny
> to tell you —
> perhaps on some teen day
> when your loneliness
> is as loud as a rock concert —
> how
> fresh from the bent space
> you came among us
> in a new womb of blankets.
> You belched and laughed and wailed,
> your face as friendly as a dog's tail.
> We did rites over you
> with all the ceremony of a primitive tribe
> painting their babies.
> Your grandfather,
> his thumb the trunk of a tree
> winter could not break,

traced a cross on your forehead
like a man signing a will.
Your parents held you
under a waterfall of grace,
and your sleeping eyes
suddenly sat up and stared
into the funny faces of our love.
We made you our own
by making you God's.
Your uncle Len played paparazzo
and has the evidence of all this
in a box somewhere.

Afterwards
you slept
and we ate and drank and laughed
and knew
our love would outlast diamonds.

I must remember, Johnny,
to tell you.

We were all high. And it was obviously God who was making us high. Catholic theology today places heavy emphasis on mediated presence. The idea is that the divine comes mediated through people, events, and situations. Becoming sensitive to the mediated presence of God in human life enables you to respond. I sometimes respond in solitude after the experience has cooled by trying to write it down in poem form to crystallize all I felt.

I guess that comes during what you might call mini-highs. The situation becomes luminous, and then you take off your shoes. Then you know something is going on. It happens in all sorts of different areas, but it doesn't happen, at least for me, unless I am with people. For the great mystics, I guess it did. If you read them, they seem to go into a cell and find it. That has never been my experience.

In addition to our experience, you say we also pray with the

Scriptures. "We place our personal stories within the Spirit-created story of Jesus," you say. "In this placing, in the interaction of the two stories, the deepest meanings of our lives unfold. We discover ourselves in dialogue with the events generated by Jesus. . . ." How do you do that?

I am able to move in the Gospel stories and events and monologues and proverbs that sort of illuminate the situation I am looking at or dealing with. Many times, if I am reading the Scripture stories, the connection will not move so much from my experience to the Bible story, but from the story back out into my experience. Theologically, this is the way it works. Jesus is the fullness of revelation, and you also have revelation continuing in human life. You take the partial revelation of human life, and you bring it to the fullness of revelation in Jesus. In prayer, that is what you are supposed to do; I think and live out of the mix.

You have written and spoken a lot about the parable of the prodigal son. As you have reflected on it in your prayer, what has it come to mean to you?

It has meant different things to me at different times. It's a story of radical acceptance that leads to the possibility of change. The radical acceptance is by the father, and he extends it to both his sons, not just the younger one. This radical acceptance leads to the possibility of change for both of them. And yet the story doesn't tell us if either does change. The younger son goes into the feast, but the father puts the clothes on him, because he cannot do it himself. But we don't know if he wears the clothes well or not, whether he accepts sonship or not. The older brother is even more reluctant.

The parable means this to me both in my personal life and in dealing with other people: The possibilities of life occur out of a real, radical, foundational acceptance that allows the defense and frantic protection of our egos to relax long enough so we reach out to each other.

I try to understand that acceptance in my own life so I can relate to other people more freely. I try to extend that acceptance as best I can to other people, so they can find that type of freedom, too. I think this was close to the core of the religious experience of Jesus. It was a radical intrusion of love into people's defensive selfhood. This enabled people to reach out, and they could join the human celebration in a new way.

This radical acceptance is necessary if you are continually criticizing yourself, because you have to have a foundation. If the criticism cuts to the core and destroys the self, you are going to fear criticism. You can incorporate criticism and change in your life only when you are grounded in an ultimate, unconditional acceptance in love. That is what the story means to me.

It also means: Don't be too quick to exclude. Work at inclusion, not exclusion. That's a relevant ecclesiological principle these days. The party is big. We have to figure out how to get everybody in, despite their resentments. We have to work beyond resentment in human life. The parable talks to me about these things. I am sure that in five years, it will say other things to me.

Did the idea you got from the parable about inclusion and exclusion come to mind when you were doing the grading and gave the failing marks?

Sure. Grading is a source of division. It may be a necessary source of division, but so much of what we do is divisive. The question that flows from this parable and the other stories of Jesus — and this becomes your question in prayer — is: How do you use power in human life? That was, I think, Jesus' core question. And in my little world, the question is, do you use knowledge to bolster your own position over against other people? Do you use knowledge to put down other people? Or, does knowledge contribute to the well-being of all involved by sharing the knowledge.

I have seen this situation in many classrooms: After ten weeks, the students know two things: The professor is smarter than they are, and they are dumb. That's all they know. The use of knowledge in that way secures the professor's privilege, status and class over against the students. When you read the stories of Jesus, you see knowledge shouldn't work that way. His great line against the lawyers is, "You hide the keys of knowledge." They have taken the knowledge that can liberate people and have locked it up for themselves.

That's what everybody does in this country. The people who run the stock market, for example, do that. They know, and they are going to use their knowledge over against other people to secure themselves. The stories of Jesus raise a major question related directly to this kind of behavior. How does a person use his or her gift or talent? Is it used for chronic self-aggrandizement — and that self-aggrandizement means others will be oppressed — or can it be unleashed to contribute to the good of all? When I read the stories of Jesus and reflect on them in prayer, that kind of question comes to me over and over again.

How about the parable of the workers in the vineyard?

That is a terrific story. I like to tell that story at union meetings. I love that story, because it points up the problem of envy and resentment. The first set of workers get exactly what they bargained for. And the last line of the story is terrific. The owner says, "What's the matter? Can't I be generous?"

The story suggests that at the core of our makeup, there are chronic envy and resentment. And we live out of that. That is true in large part because we have not appropriated our own originality. We do not understand ourselves as originals. As a result, we judge ourselves only in relationship to other people, usually the people who have what we really want — the husband who is more attentive, the home with the extra bedroom. We always judge ourselves in envious and resentful ways. The workers feel cheated, because their only way of evaluating themselves is in comparison to the good fortune of others.

I had an interesting experience with a young woman who came to me for instructions. She didn't know anything about the Christian faith and had never heard any of the stories. When I told her this one about the workers in the vineyard, she reacted as we all do. "It's wrong, it's wrong," she said. That is the reaction Jesus wanted, because nothing is wrong except that we live in a world of comparison rather than in the world of our own originality. That makes us envious and resentful. This is also part of the refusal to rejoice theme in Jesus' stories. Jesus lived out of his own originality, which is captured in the image of sonship. He is the loved one, and that is enough.

When you get inside the parable of the vineyard story and meditate on it, you begin to focus on your own life. How does resentment work with you? How does envy work with you? Some people are in such a chronic state of envy that they don't even know it anymore. The story isn't a program for anything, but it focuses on sin and then asks: What's it doing to you?

The story works in this way because it gets everybody ticked off. People hate the story. I have never told it where people liked it. And they all try to rationalize it. One common rationalization is that the men who worked only an hour worked real hard. No, that ain't it. The question is: Why do you respond to the story by getting mad? You have to go back and look at the reason.

It's a great story to use in a group and ask people what they would do if they were in the story. You get the most creative responses. A lot of people say, for example, that the next day they would come in last and work for only an hour. That's very sharp. That's how we work. We figure out the situation and how we can maximize it for our own gain. From that point of view, this is a good response, but that isn't what the story is trying to uncover in us.

The story has been used in countless ways in the history of Christianity. It has been used as the story about the Jews and the Gentiles. It's been used as a story about young people dying; when a child died, people would say the child worked only an hour in the vineyard and yet received its reward. Martin Luther used it for the theological point that it was not works that brought about salvation, but the free generosity of the vineyard owner, God. But these interpretations do not capture its impact as a mode of oral storytelling. It is supposed to get you mad, and it does.

You hear the story and you are judged, but also you are hopeful, because you now know something is working within you. You're hopeful that maybe there is a new way, and that you don't have to live in this type of resentment. In the middle-class parish where I work, resentment and envy are among the most selfdestructive vices of the neighborhood. Many live in resentment because of promotions or lack of them, money or lack of it, and the injustices they experience. I'm not saying the injustices aren't real, but that isn't the point.

The parable also has another meaning for me. You only know who you are when you know who somebody else isn't. You only know you are somebody when someone else is on the bottom. You only know you are more valuable when someone else gets less pay. As a result, you have a vested interest in someone else's oppression. And, you also have a vested envy when they supersede you. This type of thing goes on when you get inside a story like that and meditate on it.

In literary analysis, the purpose is to get at the meaning of the story. But from a religious viewpoint, the purpose is to allow the story to influence your life, to allow the story to question you, then to think through some questions it proposes to you. The hope is that this will lead to change.

This I call praying off Scripture. You move inside the story and allow a conversation to go on between yourself and the story until, finally, in that conversation, according to the current jargon, the text is interpreting the interpreter. The story is interpreting your life.

At that moment, when the story interprets your life in prayer, it becomes the Word of God. Then if you begin to think through, say, the question of envy and resentment and how they work in your life, you might come upon the word of judgment and hope, and at that time, within yourself in your solitude, you might address the source of this criticism and possibility in you, and then you might pray directly to the God who is causing this to happen.

4
Two Become
One and Three

Gene and Mary Lou Ott

Gene and Mary Lou Ott have been active for ten years at the national level in developing marital spirituality and fostering prayer among married couples. Most of their efforts have centered on Retorno, a sister program to Marriage Encounter. Its purpose, according to Mary Lou, is "to help people get in touch with their own married spirituality and enter into a life of couple prayer." The Otts helped form Retorno in the mid-1970s and were its first coordinating couple. Their Retorno work has taken them to forty states and to Ireland. They give workshops and retreats and have taught in a summer spirituality program at the University of Notre Dame. Gene was a family physician for twenty-two years and now teaches at the University of Minnesota Medical School. The Otts have ten children. They live in Edina, a Minneapolis suburb.

What is couple prayer?

Gene: To start, it's Mary Lou and I sitting down and inviting the Lord to enter our presence, then being attentive to whatever occurs. We usually pray with the Scriptures. Sometimes we use other readings or reflect on what is going on with us as individuals or as a couple. I look at this prayer as a listening rather than doing, although saying prayers is certainly part of praying. But to me, couple prayer is primarily listening to each other and to God.

Mary Lou: It's also a way of life. The time we spend together in prayer is not the most important aspect of it. Living out the prayer is. Looking at it this way, couple prayer is more of a response in faith. As such, it colors everything you do and reflect on. Because the term "couple prayer" is relatively new, people often ask what it means, what we do. I feel embarrassed, because I don't have a list of ten steps for doing it, but it's not complicated. Just begin. Each couple develops its own style.

Prayer is the most intimate area a married couple shares. Yet over and over again, couples will say to us they just can't pray together. They say they'll try a few times and quit. But our experience, as well as that of other couples, tells me prayer for a couple is more intimate than sex. When a couple enters into a commitment to grow together in prayer, the process becomes pretty serious. The outcome is going to be a certain kind of continuing nakedness in front of each other.

When we are talking, even about something important, there are parts of ourselves we can hold back. But praying together is like taking a step into a mystery in which you can no longer say, "I am going to hold back, or give myself only in bits and pieces." That doesn't mean a married couple who pray together know everything about each other, but if they continue, they will become more and more — well, naked is probably the best word to describe it.

Gene: Couple prayer has helped us to become aware of something we didn't understand early in our marriage: that when Mary Lou and I married, something new was created, our married relationship. Couple prayer comes out of this new creation. The uniqueness of this new creation in relationship to God is a reality, even though we do not fully understand it. We even named this new creation.

Mary Lou: It's like a third self, different from the two of us alone. We like to speak about it in images. One image is that when Gene and Mary Lou got married, we gave birth to a third self, and this becomes like a child. It needs to be nurtured. You have to spend time with it, just like a new child.

Gene: We not only nourish the relationship, the third self, but we also draw upon it. Couple prayer is a process partly of nourishing and feeding ourselves and the third self. The first step toward that is to acknowledge its reality. When we married, nobody told us we had anything like that. And it took us time to realize it. But as we started looking at our own experience, we had to find some way of defining what was going on. This third self seemed the best conceptual way of talking about it.

You say you named this third self. What did you name it and why?

Mary Lou: The name came, in part, out of letters from our names. We used "ML" from my name, Mary Lou, and "EU" from Gene's full name, Eugene. That gave us "MLEU." At the time, we were also influenced by Pierre Teilhard de Chardin's book, *The Divine Milieu,* in which he speaks of milieu as the center and the environment. We borrowed the word "milieu," because we liked the concept and because it sounded MLEU.

Gene: In coming up with the name MLEU, we noticed that if you take the word *milieu* and remove the two "i's" from it, you have MLEU. That was meaningful to us, because we had to take the "I's" out of milieu in order to become the third self, MLEU. The "I's" are nourished by MLEU, and at times MLEU has to be more important than the "I's."

Did the "I's" fade into the background?

Gene: Not always. I think rather you have a triangle in which the dynamics are going three ways. It's like a three-legged stool. There has to be a balance. If I spend too much time taking care of myself and don't give enough time to Mary Lou or to MLEU, the situation will be out of balance for us.

What do you do in couple prayer? How do you do it?

Gene: We have gone through a lot of trial and error. Our basic format is one in which we use Scripture. For us, the best time to pray is in the morning. We'll sit down together. We'll invite the Lord into that moment. Then we will talk. In the process of talking, we will usually identify what is going on with each of us.

I'm tired, I'm angry, I'm joyful, whatever. Then we will usually read Scripture. We might take a Gospel and read it in segments, or we might follow the daily readings.

After we have read Scripture, we sit and allow whatever is going to occur to occur. In this period of reflection, we concentrate on the Scripture. That isn't always easy. Sometimes I am focusing on work or problems I am trying to process. After a time, we share whatever occurred during those moments of quiet. Our whole day will be conditioned by what we shared.

Do you try to do this daily?

Gene: Yes, our usual routine is to take prayer time between six and seven in the morning.

Mary Lou: I know that sounds to people like a terribly long time, but it's our time. We are parents of a big family. We don't have much time when we can go off by ourselves and not have the kids banging on the door. The children have always known this is our time, a sacred part of the day for us. Never again in the entire day are we able to have moments like this. I'd get up at two o'clock in the morning if that were the only time we had for prayer, because it is so vital to my entire life.

I feel like I am going to a well to get a drink of nourishment that gets me through the day. We have gone through periods when we didn't pray. For example, we recently went almost a year without praying on a daily basis. There was a big difference in our relationship. It was so obvious that we finally started again. It was OK, too, that we stopped because of cycles one goes through, but there was a wonderful difference after we started again. I'd describe it as vitality.

Do you pray in the same place?

Mary Lou: Yes, we think that is important. There has to be a kind of sacred spot. We learned many elements of prayer from the Ignatian method, and one is the place of prayer. We started on the Ignatian way of prayer in the early 1970s. Gene and I made what is called a nineteenth annotation. It is for people who can't make a thirty-day retreat. It consists of a weekend of introduction followed by daily prayer with Scripture and follow-up visits with a spiritual director. That was our initial training. It was good. We needed to grow in communication. That drew us into a deeper spirituality. After listening to each other for a while, and sharing our individual lives, we felt that wasn't enough. We wanted to go beyond that, and when we did, we moved into what we call couple prayer.

Do you use the place you pray for prayer only?

Mary Lou: No. We always pray in the same room, but it's not like a shrine. We also use the room as an office.

Gene: There are trees right outside the windows and a large open area beyond where you can watch the four seasons. As the seasons change, you can sometimes relate what is going on outside to what is going on inside in your prayer.

Mary Lou: We feel safe there. It feels comfortable. But I don't want to give the impression that we are some kind of levitating couple in an upper room. We go to prayer because raising a big family is a helluva lot of work, and we can't do it any other way. We have as many problems with children as anybody has. I don't want to come across as being better than other people, as set apart somehow. We pray out of a need to pray.

Prayer has made a big difference in our family. It has made a big difference in how we respond to the kids. That has been an important part of our prayer. We spend a lot of time praying for our children. A married couple has considerable power to pray for their children. It is awesome. According to Scripture, we as couples are the living image of the relationship God has with us. As a married person, I am going to know the love of God in the way Gene loves me and in the way I love him. That's holy.

Couples have a tremendous power, but we don't realize it. We are too busy living and surviving. We are like people with our fingers in the dike, trying to hold back crisis and chaos. We don't have to live that way. The power and the gifts and the grace and reconciliation are all there, in marriage. All we have to do is ask for them.

Gene: The church commonly uses the Scripture passage "two shall become one" for marriages. But I don't think we understand the depth of that passage. We relate to it only in the physical sense and forget the spiritual dimensions. This spiritual oneness is part of what we are talking about. It is a resource. Mary Lou speaks of it as money in the bank that we can go and draw from as long as we keep making deposits. When a crisis comes, that's the strength we draw from.

Our relationship is the strongest thing we can develop as far as survival is concerned. That must be a priority. You build such a relationship by becoming vulnerable, intimate, and by making a commitment. If you do that, the relationship will be filled and strong. Then, if I feel down, or Mary Lou does, we have something to draw on. At the same time, we can feed it when we are feeling good.

Can you take an instance or crisis you have dealt with and show how you have worked with it in prayer and tapped the power you say exists in your relationship?

Gene: Let's begin with a relatively safe one. About three years ago, I was going to a meeting in Boston. Now, Mary Lou loves Boston. If she were going to move anywhere else, that would be the place. I was being sent there by my department for a meeting, and I had a heavy schedule. I planned to go to Boston by myself, concentrate on this meeting, then meet Mary Lou in New York, where we had a couples' meeting to attend.

Mary Lou had another idea. "Why can't I go to Boston?" she said. I can't recall all the details, but it became a major conflict. A barrier went up between us. I soon realized that unless I could say, "OK, Gene, all your reasons may be right, and they may make sense to you, but are you accepting what is happening to you and Mary Lou? What is happening to MLEU?" MLEU wasn't being nourished. It was suffering.

That meant we each had to see that our "right" reasons weren't so right. Our focus had to be on what was going to give life and strength to the relationship. Are we in good space as Mary Lou *and* Gene, not just as Mary Lou *or* as Gene? When we started looking at it from that point of view, we negotiated what was best for MLEU. Mary Lou came to Boston midway through the meeting, and we made certain we spent some time together, and it was good time together. When we went to the couples' meeting, we were revitalized.

And you worked this out during your prayer time?

Gene: Yes. The starting point was that in the prayer time, we were confronted with the reality that we couldn't pray, because we weren't in good space as a couple.

Mary Lou: When we have a decision to make, we ask ourselves if it will be good for our relationship. Sometimes the answer is easy, especially if the choice is time together or one of us taking classes. At other times, the choices are harder. For example, through my prayer, I personally feel called to active involvement in the peace movement in a way that calls for civil disobedience. Before I moved in that direction, we looked at how our relationship would be affected. For example, what were Gene's concerns? His biggest fear was whether I would become so involved that I wouldn't have time for our relationship. When we talked about that and agreed that the relationship would come first in spite of what I might choose to do, it was OK. I would stop being involved in civil disobedience when our relationship started to suffer. In other words, the relationship comes first.

How has couple prayer helped you with raising your children?

Mary Lou: I'm sure that if you listed any major crises parents have with children, we have had them. I can't think of anything we haven't had. We have to live through these crises the same as anybody else. But they didn't split us apart. I think the fact that we spend time together in prayer is a major reason for that. In the first place, it gives us some quiet, reflective time. Second, we have time with each other. Third, you can't pray together if you need a lot of reconciliation, so we try to keep the lines open in that regard. Fourth, we look at the problems, whatever they may be, together.

As a result, we keep conflict, which is always present in a relationship, to a minimum. With prayer, the two of us are together. Somehow, when we go to the Lord and say, "We need some help," it always comes. I can't tell you how it happens. I just know it does, because it has.

Gene: In any marriage when a crisis occurs, especially one relating to children, there is a certain amount of blame and guilt and shame. I know sometimes, that is expressed in anger at the other person. I may feel guilty, but that is uncomfortable, so I unconsciously blame Mary Lou, which then makes her feel guilty. But if we acknowledge our negative feelings, own them, and share them, a positive result occurs. That nourishes the relationship. You are being open to one another. You are being vulnerable to one another. The relationship grows in the process.

This is how you experience the power of the relationship?

Gene: Yes, and that doesn't necessarily just come while we are praying. We may sit down to pray and find we can't, because we haven't talked over problems. That comes out loud and clear when you are sitting there and trying to reflect. One of us may have to say to the other, "Look, I can't pray, because I'm angry at you right now. So, let's talk about it."

Mary Lou: I suppose the bottom line is that praying together makes you honest. I don't think anybody could fake going to prayer and pretending, when there is a whole pile of unresolved feeling. In that respect, it keeps our relationship up-to-date.

Gene: It keeps us from building up a lot of garbage. We get the junk out quickly if we are honoring our time together.

When you get the junk out on the table, what happens to it?

Gene: It depends. Sometimes the situation may call for outside help. That was the case when one of our boys had a problem with drug abuse. We wound up going to family counseling. We couldn't deny the problem. We had to name it and do something about it.

How did prayer help you with that?

Gene: I have a tendency to deny unpleasant things, to pretend they aren't real. But prayer makes you more reflective about what is going on. That makes it harder to deny things. In prayer, you also find yourself asking, "What are we called to do?" In this case, it meant putting our son into a treatment program.

It sounds as if prayer helped you to face facts.

Gene: Partly, yes. Most important, it helps you to identify and begin to change attitudes.

Mary Lou: If prayer doesn't help you to face reality, it is not prayer. It's escapism.

Mary Lou, how did prayer help you with situations like this?

Mary Lou: Through prayer, Gene and I have become more open to looking at our family systems. A family system might be described as a process that occurs in families and is conditioned by all the parts or the individuals making up that family. This involves looking at all components of a family, including its history — the individual members and the interactions between them. So we ask: Where did we come from? What did we come into the marriage with? How are our children growing up? What are they inheriting from us? What rules exist in our family? And much more. When you are dealing with issues like that, you can see that couple prayer is not confined to the time you are praying.

As a result, a few years ago, we approached the kids with the notion of some family systems therapy. It was a time nobody needed it. We didn't wait until someone had a problem. The approach was more like this: Hey kids, you are growing into young adults. A deeper understanding of where you came from can be valuable to you. It can, for example, help you make a good choice when you marry. We were in this kind of counseling for about a year and a half.

And that grew out of your prayer?

Mary Lou: Absolutely. To me, change is a key element in prayer. If the family isn't getting healthier and holier — and to me, the two are the same — prayer is not an escape from reality. People must know that. Prayer is serious business. If you are going to face reality, it isn't always fun.

My ears perked up when you said prayer is the most intimate activity a couple can share, more intimate than sex. It sounds a little scary. Could you explain what you mean?

Mary Lou: Generally, people who live a religious life, say in a rectory or in a community of some sort, rarely pray together. I think that's because it is too intimate, too scary. Oh, they will gather for liturgical kinds of communal prayer, but those are safe. In the same way, families will pray together at meal time, or they will read the Scriptures. Those are wonderful things to do, but they, too, are safe. I think these are indications that the whole world knows serious prayer on a personal level is different. It's awesome, revealing, and scary, although it isn't as scary for me anymore.

Gene: It was scary for me, because it meant being vulnerable and acknowledging parts of me I did not like looking at.

Mary Lou: And it is intimate. A husband and wife can have sexual intercourse every day, but their minds, hearts, and souls may not be in it. It can be purely physical, and I think in some cases it is, even in the best of marriages. When that happens, you really aren't giving yourself. You are just a body. But in praying together, I am saying I will open my mind and my heart and my soul to everything. Somehow I am inviting the Lord's life to come in and show things about me I may not want to see, or I may not even know about. These may be things Gene knows but I haven't given him permission to talk about as yet.

What kind of things?

Gene: In my own instances, it was acknowledging a temper and an anger. Praying together called for sharing that. I wasn't proud of it, and I didn't really want to talk about it. But I shared with Mary Lou. It meant sharing some of the shame. I asked her to help, to tell me if she saw it was building up and if I wasn't acknowledging it.

This was risky, because I often saw her as the cause of my anger. It was risky for Mary Lou, too, because we had dealt with anger in a very eggshell way, saying, in effect, don't tread on that area. She was able to say, "Look, Gene, what's going on? Are things piling up? I think I see some unresolved anger and frustration." Not uncommonly, that would come as we sat in prayer. I would probably sit boxed in, very tight, very heady, but I had to respond to that. I might not like what I was hearing, but the challenge for me was to say, "OK, I need that. I want that kind of feedback. Let's sit a while and then talk about it." That's healing.

How would the Scripture help with a situation like that?

Gene: The reading that comes to mind is the one in which the crippled man was lowered through the roof on a pallet. Once, when we were praying with that, I became aware of my anger at the way people were responding to my handicap. I have a birth injury called Erb's palsy or paralysis. I was a breach delivery. During birth, the nerves and muscles in both my arms were damaged. I don't have full motion with them. I can't do anything above shoulder height. Putting on a hat, for example, is a very difficult task for me. I became aware that I had negative feelings toward people when they reacted to my handicap in ways I was not comfortable with or in ways I had not given them permission to react. They might do things for me I could do by myself or give me the impression I should be different.

As I reflected on the reading, I saw myself as the person lying on the pallet. We had learned to put ourselves into the Scriptures and identify with the characters through the Ignatian method of prayer and, as I did that, I felt anger and frustration, and I was thinking, "What the hell are you doing to me? Why are you lowering me to this guy down below who is supposed to heal me? I didn't ask you for that."

The first step in dealing with this anger was to identify it. A lot of the anger was coming from not being able to do certain things, especially common tasks around the house. Dad was supposed to be able to do everything. I had to be honest and say some jobs required more energy and resulted in too much frustration. It also required me to ask, "What are you going to do about it?" Eventually, I went to Mary Lou and said, "Look, this is what happened, and the result is all this turmoil inside me. I need help with this. Will you help me?"

And Mary Lou became, in a manner of speaking, Christ for you? She became the "guy" you were being lowered to for healing?

Gene: Yes. It was a moment of change for me. I experienced acceptance, acknowledgment, being heard. I received what I needed from Mary Lou. "I hear that," she said. "I'll respond to that. I'll try to meet what you are asking." Again, there was healing for me. It is another case of couple prayer being an example of living out the marriage relationship differently, because of my being naked and sharing something difficult.

Mary Lou: Also, as a result of this, I could confront him, say, in ways which had not been open before — for example, concerning the children. And the kids could tease him about the fact that he couldn't do everything around the house. And it was in good humor. But I am not sure they could have done that if we hadn't had our encounter in prayer on this initially. Prayer sets in motion change that affects the rest of the family. This may not be earthshaking to other people, but it is very important to the family. You have a freedom you didn't have before.

Mary Lou, what would be an example of you experiencing healing as the result of couple prayer?

Mary Lou: Being able to face chemical dependency — that is, alcoholism — in my family. I come from a chemically dependent family, one that has a history of it. Through being able to be more open to each other in prayer, we have been able to view my family history in a way we wouldn't have been able to do otherwise. I don't think I would have wanted to own it.

What keeps couples from experiencing prayer together?

Gene: Fear. Uncertainty. Lack of understanding or awareness. Another reason is what I call "giving themselves permission." Couples seem unsure it is for them. They seem unaware not only that shared prayer is possible for any couple, but also that it is a promise to them as Christians. They do not think it is a reality for them. To such couples I say, "Try it, you'll like it."

Mary Lou: I think time is a major problem. It is hard to form a new habit, and prayer is a habit.

Gene: It requires commitment. It requires making prayer a priority. Married couples haven't been told they should make it a priority. They are given all sorts of other priorities in their married relationship, but not that one of the priorities is prayer together as a couple.

Mary Lou: Nor have they been told that if they pray together, life will change. They must be told it is worth sticking to. They also need support. We have a couple of support groups we pray with.

You mentioned time for prayer. What do you say to couples who say they don't have time for prayer? This is one of the most frequent comments one hears in connection with lay people praying. They say they are too busy making a living, paying bills, raising children, and working in their communities.

Mary Lou: I think the important things are to tell them to begin and to be easy on themselves. They don't have to take a great deal of time. They need to be faithful to it for a long enough period to make it something they want to do. If you go to couples and say they should take an hour for prayer in the morning, they will turn away. They are turned off by that, they don't have an hour. I say to couples, "Pick a time period, say, ten minutes a day, and start with that." As it becomes more important to them, they will make more time for it.

Do you ever say, "We had ten kids, and we found time to pray?"

Mary Lou: Not in the sense that if we can do it, they can, because we all have different ways of spending the same amount of time. Frankly, we don't have the active social life we had years ago. We have changed a lot of the ways we lived the first ten to fifteen years. We now have more time for each other and for prayer, because that has become more important.

Also, I would say we pray *because* we have ten children. We can't raise them without it. So, it is not a case of telling people we have ten children and we prayed anyway. It is the other way around. Because we have the children and because we have a life commitment, we need to pray. We need time. Otherwise, I don't think we would be nearly as effective as parents. I think we are pretty good parents, but it comes from having grown into it through prayer.

Gene: There is another reason, too, that couples have trouble praying. When we first entered into prayer together as a couple, we experienced turmoil. I believe this turmoil came from the fact that there is evil in the world, an Evil Spirit. This Evil Spirit, I believe, is going to do his utmost to keep couples from growing in their relationship with each other and with God.

I remember when we started, we fought and argued about minutiae. We would argue about whether we would read verses nine to eleven or nine to twelve of a Scripture passage. We argued about whether we would sit left to right or right to left. After a while, the experience became humorous, but it wasn't funny at the time. I think this was the result of the Evil Spirit trying to keep us from prayer. I think he is trying to do the same thing to other couples who undertake couple prayer. As a result, they experience turmoil, and, because they don't understand why, they'll say, "We can't do it. It isn't for us."

Mary Lou: There's also the fear of change. As I said, prayer produces change if you are open to it. For example, in our prayer, we began asking the Lord to show us how to live a simpler life-style in a more Christian way. Out of that, Gene changed jobs, left a good position with a good income and took a position that reduced his income. Life changed around this house. Yet we did that out of our prayer, and it was the right thing to do.

How did that happen?

Gene: When I went into medicine, I already had the idea that some day I would like to teach. But there were no departments in medical school for teaching my specialty, family practice. Later, when a department was started, I got involved on a part-time basis. As we started to pray, the thought kept coming to me, "Do I want to do this full time?" It was a nudging I kept getting. Finally, I said, "OK, Lord, I don't know if I want to leave practice and teach full time. You show us. You give us some sign." Mary Lou and I also shared what it might mean in terms of change in income and activities.

Some time later, I got a call saying a teaching position was open, and would I be interested. We spent more time in prayer before I gave an answer. Through our prayer, we entered into it with the idea that no matter what happened, it wouldn't be a bad decision. I have had a lot of second thoughts about it, but I was able to rely on the belief that it was the correct decision.

That was nice to be able to do. When there were doubts or difficulties, we would turn to the Lord and ask, "What should we do next? Where do we go from here?" It changes your whole frame of reference. For one thing, I didn't have to do it all by myself. I have my relationship with Mary Lou and with God to help me.

Mary Lou, besides your civil disobedience, what other changes or activities have you undertaken as a result of couple prayer?

Mary Lou: My involvement in the Catholic Worker movement. Part of me has wanted to be involved in some form of the Catholic Worker since I was a child. The impetus came from a weekend of prayer, specifically an Ira Progoff workshop. We were "journaling," as you do at a Progoff workshop. We were to pick a word and us it as a mantra.

I started praying with the word "courage." That moved me to call a friend who had just gone to work at the Catholic Worker in Minneapolis, St. Joseph's House, and, yes, they could use me. The first time I went there was a profound experience. It has affected our entire life. We became part of the Catholic Worker community, and we had a Catholic Worker farm for a while. We began praying and sharing experiences with a different community than we were used to. Through the Catholic Worker involvement, a group of us opened Incarnation House, a home for women and children coming out of battered relationships. My peace activities also came out of this involvement with Catholic Worker.

What is the key thing you have learned from couple prayer?

Mary Lou: That the purpose of marriage is reconciliation. Those of us who marry do so to be reconciled, to be healed — that is, to be healed ourselves and to be reconciled with the Lord.

Gene: That marriage as a sacrament truly is a mystery. Couple prayer has been a way to discover that aspects of all the sacraments are present within the sacrament of marriage. Couple prayer has enabled us to experience the healing and reconciliation Mary Lou mentioned, but also we have found union, community, and ministry. And there is always more. When I rely on this "more," I know there really is a God.

5
From Prayer
to Community

Richard Rohr

The Reverend Richard Rohr, a Franciscan, is founder and pastor of the New Jerusalem Community in Cincinnati, Ohio, one of the most successful local church communities established in the United States during the renewal following the Second Vatican Council. The community, which grew out of retreats Father Rohr gave to young people, began in 1971 and has about 300 committed members. In addition to his duties as pastor, Father Rohr gives retreats, primarily to priests in the U.S. and to communities in the Third World. He is widely known for his audio tape series, including *The Great Themes of Scripture, Jesus and His Church, The Spiritual Family and the National Family, The Price of Peoplehood, Days of Renewal,* and *Broken and Blessed.* He was born March 20, 1943, in Topeka, Kansas, where he first encountered members of the Cincinnati province of the Order of Friars Minor, of which he is a member.

Prayer has been different every period of my life. It's a journey. To say praying is the same all your life isn't true. It's so radically different that what is prayer at one period would hardly be called prayer in another. My first experiences of what I now call prayer — I would never have called it prayer back then — came during my grade school years in Topeka. I now see these as deep religious experiences. It sounds so old-fashioned Catholic, but they came when I was an altar boy in Assumption parish. I'd get up early in the morning and serve the masses. I became comfortable with the church, and I remember going there Saturdays, or after school. It was pious and individualistic by current standards, but I remember kneeling in that church as a boy and having a deep sense of presence, of security and warmth.

I had the feeling that life was centered, not a scattered, meaningless reality, that something was pulling it together. I feel this centered me at an early age, before I moved out into the disparate world. This disparate sense of life is primary for so many young people I have worked with. Their major effort is trying to pull things together. I didn't have to do that. I can think of half a dozen different times I had these experiences. I would say I was between the fourth and eighth grades. They happened not just in church, but in nature as well, in the back yard, for instance. I'd be alone. I don't want to give them an unreal, mystical sense, because they didn't have that, but everything would sort of stop. And I would know life was trustworthy. I would know life was good. There was meaning to it. It was not absurd. Joy always came from these moments.

One time — and I don't think I have ever told this publicly — I was in a field. I was going to a Cub Scout meeting, and I was in my uniform. It was night. I had such a sense of the presence of the Lord that I remember kneeling down. I had the sense that God was there and that he was good. And then, after a little while, I jumped up and went to my Cub Scout meeting. There was no one around I could share these experiences with, nor even talk to about them. That wasn't the age of religious experience. It was the age of law and structures. But they gave me security. Because God was real to me, I wanted to be a priest. During my seminary years, I never had any serious doubts about the priesthood. The God experience of my youth was so certain in my mind that it took away a lot of the usual anxieties. I had had a centering experience that made everything else, including the law, seem like window dressing.

About 1957, I read Felix Timmerman's book, *The Perfect Joy of St. Francis*. It was one of those popularized lives of St. Francis, yet sort of a classic. I saw what everyone sees in Francis. As a young guy looking for a sense of freedom and adventure, I found my star in him. He was my hero. He risked everything and found a way to happiness in this world. The joyful beggar, the free man who wasn't captured by the systems of this world caught my attention. About the same time, two Franciscan priests gave a mission at Assumption. I had never seen a Franciscan, but when I saw them walk out in brown robes and white ropes, I said, "That's what I want to be." So after the eighth grade, when I was fourteen, I went off to Cincinnati to join the Franciscans.

When I was nineteen and a novice, I experienced an overwhelming sense of the unconditional love of God. If I were to use charismatic language, I would say I was baptized in the Spirit. All the legalism we were going through — this was 1961, right before Vatican II — faded into the background. There was a preoccupation with rubrics and laws and endless chanting of the office in Latin. It was dry and in many ways sterile, at least for me, and I think for most of my classmates. At the time, I was still trying to be this perfect little boy. I can see myself as a pharisee, trying to do everything perfectly, perfectly, perfectly. By the middle of the year, it had become a burden. And I can remember, one day I was kneeling in the church, and I was overwhelmed by "I'm Love, I'm your Father. It's OK. All the rest of this is not what's important." After that, I was amazingly free. It was a continuation of those first religious experiences, but on a much deeper level. There was a sense of lavish, unconditional love and deep centeredness.

I think the next great opening up took place in my first year of theology at St. Leonard's in Dayton, where I began to study Scripture. I have had a love of Scripture ever since. As I studied the Gospels — I read the bible at least twice from cover to cover in those years — I was enamored with what I saw happening. And I was upset, because I thought most people had missed the point. This must be a terrible kind of arrogance, but I still think most people have missed the point. I was sure my inner experience was matching the experience of the Bible. Therefore, I trusted my interpretation of the Scriptures. It was matching my inner journey of a movement beyond the law into the inner life of the Spirit. I saw the Bible going in that same direction. So, the

Scripture ws my second great freeing experience. That's when they used to call me "Happy." And I was. I was so happy. I couldn't wait to be ordained a priest, because I wanted to tell other people what I knew was true — if that doesn't sound too self-assured. I knew my heart had been freed by God and my head had been freed by the Scriptures.

Can you explain how the scriptural message resonated within you?

First, I looked at the whole pattern of the Bible, and I saw it was talking about a journey of faith. It wasn't talking about "religion·" As I read the Bible, it was very anti-religion. It is constantly iconoclastic. That's true even in the Old Testament. For example, you have the people preoccupied with building the temple or with liturgical forms. And the prophets, speaking for God, come in and say, "That's not it. I want mercy, not sacrifice."

I knew that was similar to what happened inside me. I began as a religious, Catholic, conservative boy in Kansas (which is a good way to begin, by the way), then made a kind of breakthrough. Religion is just the shell. Religion is just the scaffolding, but the scaffolding has to fall away. I saw most people holding onto the scaffolding, as the pharisees had done. And I saw Jesus breaking in with his teaching of the kingdom. This breakthrough never seemed to happen to most people. They weren't making the journey beyond religion into faith. To do that, you have to go through the second great thing I found in Scripture: A deep experience of the unconditional love of God.

Unfortunately, we don't talk journey language in the church. We talk conclusion language. It's not growth language. It's not going somehwere. We were given the conclusions in the first grade. Our language is perseverence language. We must persevere in the conclusions we have been given instead of surrendering to new experiences as we move along on the journey.

Also, I sadly discovered — and this is why the charismatics made sense to me — that a lot of people were not God lovers. In my probably harsh judgment, they were God fearers. I discovered most people were mainly afraid of God. They were trying to prove themselves to God, trying to win the love of a God who did not really love them. They were not conversant and comfortable with a loving Father-Mother. People who so often were afraid didn't really believe God liked them. And, when they were honest with themselves, they admitted they didn't like God. They would say they "loved" God, if I can put quotes around it. This "I love God, and God loves me" rhetoric was going on. But if you got involved with them in spiritual direction, you found they were damn angry at him and were afraid of him. The only way I had broken through that was with the contemplative element in my life, which enabled me to experience the presence of God. I don't want to glamorize this too much, but it was always an experience of faithfulness and unconditional love.

After breaking through, after getting beyond the scaffolding, you were, or were close to, entering a mystical point on your journey. What was that experience like?

A sense of intense inner vitality dominated, because *I knew this was it.* But there is a thin line between that and righteousness, especially when you think you see people settling for forms and religion and laws. Often, I crossed over that thin line, and I still do. It's my sin. I fall into righteousness, judgmentalism, anger, and cynicism. But you want to shake people who are hiding behind the forms. I know it's not conscious, but I want to say, come on, come on, come on. They put up tremendous resistance when you talk about intimacy and love and breakthrough and growth and journey and unconditional surrender. That is the language of passion. It frightens them. They want a passionless God. When I experienced a passionate God, a God who could be trusted as liking me, a God who "felt" somehow, if I can use that anthropomorphic word, it was an experience of intense inner life, vitality, excitement, and I wanted to tell everyone about it.

You are a charismatic and, if I understand correctly, your home parish is located where pentecostalism began in the United States. Did this connection with pentecostalism's history have an effect on you?

I was ordained in 1970 in Most Pure Heart of Mary parish in

West Topeka, where my parents live. By coincidence, it is located on the spot where pentecostalism is supposed to have started. A big house, called Stone's Folly, was on the corner of Seventeenth and Stone. That is now the corner where Most Pure Heart of Mary is. That house, they say, was the fanciest and biggest house built in Topeka in the turn of the century era. A Mr. Stone built it as his mansion.

In 1900, after he no longer lived there, a group of evangelicals gathered in the house. They were called Charles Parham's Bible School. They gathered in 1900 on New Year's Eve, the last day before the beginning of the new century. They committed themselves to a year of prayer and study to try to discover the gifts of the Holy Spirit. The story is that on New Year's Eve the next year — 1901 — they began to speak in tongues. It sounds almost too dramatically placed — the timing and all — but that's the story. Many credit the pentecostal movement with beginning there.

I knew nothing of this history until the day I was ordained, June 13, 1970. At the ordination, while we were in the receiving line, a woman came up to me and said, "You are going to be used by the Holy Spirit." I said something like, "Yeah, I know." I had this self-assurance, because I had just been ordained and all. She said she wanted to talk to me, and later she told me this story. She was a Catholic charismatic, as it turned out, and she said the Lord had told her I was the first Catholic priest ordained on the spot where the pentecostal movement had begun seventy years before. Like so many charismatics, she had the years figured out, and the seventy years were a symbol to her. My ordination, she said, was symbolic of the institutional church taking in the whole charismatic experience.

I had not had contact with the charismatic movement at that point. And I even thought she was a little strange, but a year later in Cincinnati, extraordinary things began which led to the formation of New Jerusalem. I don't repeat the story the woman told me much anymore, because I don't want to make too much of it. Some people say it was a prophecy that I would be used in a special way. Well, I have been used in a special way, but so have a lot of other people.

After ordination, I went back to Cincinnati and began teaching in the Franciscan high school. I found the prayer in our community rather dry and dead. I heard about the charismatics praying not far from there in a Catholic church, in the basement. I went several times. I didn't consider myself a charismatic, and I didn't trust all the manifestations and emotional displays. But I still sensed it was real. I never doubted it. These people had experienced what I had experienced — centeredness in the love of God. They knew God is love. They had had experiences of him. I didn't align myself with them because of the sophisticated Vatican II theology I had received in the seminary. What these people were doing seemed filled with inconsistencies and lacunae. It wasn't together, in my judgment. But I still never doubted the experience or the goodness of the people there, and I prayed with them periodically.

Then I was assigned to take over youth retreats for the Cincinnati archdiocese. I gave the first boys' retreat in November 1971, and while I was preaching to them about the unconditional love of God, they began to weep. These were macho, eighteen-year old boys, high school seniors. There has never been a retreat quite like that first one. That is why my theology now has to make a place for the surprises of God, for God being sovereignly free to do his thing. I believe that was the beginning of New Jerusalem by an action of God. I have given many retreats since then, and preached much better, but that first one was a special outpouring of the Spirit. Those boys stayed up all night singing and praying around the altar in the church. I came back early in the morning, and some of them were praying in tongues. I did not pray in tongues then, and I hadn't taught them that.

I remember standing in the back of the church and watching them. My first reaction was fear. This was the Franciscan church, and I already had rumblings that some friars who lived next to the church were upset because kids were singing and making noise in the church all night. I remember saying, "Oh God, what do I do with this?" But I was also excited, because I thought we were really onto something. These boys had experienced what I had experienced. So, there was both excitement and fear, inner vitality and outward concern. I would say that continued for the next two years, as I saw this thing mushroom out of my control. And I was supposed to be the leader. It made me circumspect and cautious. I was my own worst devil's advocate. Is this for real? I developed a "yes, but" attitude.

I think you can see that in my attitude toward speaking in tongues. For me, tongues are a movement into the right brain, our non-rational side. While they are important, tongues are the least of the gifts of the Holy Spirit. But they are especially important for Western civilization, because they are an experience that denies one's total reliance on the left brain, the rational side. They get you to the right brain, where you are much more open to spiritual experience. The important thing is once to have had the openness in which you give up your verbal, logical, rational left brain and surrender yourself to the world of incoherent babbling. You surrender yourself to the mystery of the presence of God and to the fact that your little mind and your little mouth will never be able to explain this reality. That is why surrendering to the gift of tongues is significant.

But tongues are not necessarily a sign of holiness. Other people have broken into the mystical part of their mind without receiving the gift of tongues. I don't want to say you have to speak in tongues to do this. I don't believe that at all. I know too many neurotic, screwed up, and selfish people who have the gift of tongues. So, I don't take tongues as a sign of anything. No, I take the receiving of tongues as a sign of breaking through. I think that happened to me through the boys on these retreats and through the growth of New Jerusalem. The experience changed me, because I had to let go when I saw the God of surprises moving sovereignly free. He'd do some things, some he wouldn't. Some prayers he would answer, some he wouldn't. Some people would be healed, some wouldn't. Some people would receive the gift of tongues, some wouldn't. Some would be baptized in the Spirit, some wouldn't. There was no pattern; you could never predict. This forced me to let God out of my theological cages. It forced me to let God be free, to expect the immediate action of God, but never to try to program or plan for it.

The first retreat ended Sunday, November 8, 1971. The boys asked if they could come back Friday and pray together again. When they came back, they brought some of their friends and girl friends. We had the first prayer meeting. That night, a lot of the girls were baptized in the Spirit. It never stopped after that. There hasn't been a week since that we haven't met. Within the first three months, we grew to 300 people. Through 1972, 1973, and 1974, we had 600, 800, up to 1,000 people. Adults were coming, religious were coming, and priests too. Everyone had to come and watch. In that time, we moved to a huge gym. Normally, mass would last about three hours. I would preach for an hour. It was a phenomenon. Kids were sitting all over the place.

I saw a lot of power, energy, excitement, joy, and breakthroughs, but frequently there wasn't much depth. There was power, but only the power youth were capable of. They didn't know themselves yet; they hadn't journeyed anywhere yet. That made us want to move toward community. But the energy was there. One meeting a week wasn't enough. They wanted a second meeting, when I would teach Scripture. The first set of tapes I made was the fruit of those years of teaching. Those tapes changed my life, because they went national. We were given a mansion, and I gave retreats there every weekend for young people. Some of them came to the prayer group, too. But we saw that the experience wasn't going deep enough. We saw, too, that to add this depth, we had to find a way of committing ourselves to one another. That's when we started moving consciously into community. The group named themselves the New Jerusalem Community in May 1974.

What was the role of prayer in the formation of the community?

In the first years, the community's prayer was largely charismatic. It has great power to energize you, to invite you, to tell you there is a spiritual reality. But if you remain at the level of shared prayer, charismatic prayer, or group prayer, you don't go very deep. You must be willing to take that experience and process it alone, to take responsibility for it alone, to nurture it with other disciplines. You have to become an individual before God and not just as part of a group consciousness. We had strong group consciousness. The Lord was there when we prayed together. But a lot of the young people, I feel, didn't go very deep. It became a sort of new consumer item.

Now, some did go deep. There are still ten people in New Jerusalem from the first three months. To develop depth, they had to work out a relationship with the Lord that they took responsibility for. They had to personally walk a journey in which their own ego was challenged. Their ego had to go through death stages. Those are the only ones who remained and the ones who had a deeper faith experience. The communal experience and the personal experience fed one another. But you had to balance the communal with the personal. We·started with the communal, and I'm glad we did. Evangelicals and fundamentalists might have an experience at church, but it is usually couched in highly individualistic, Jesus-and-me language: "Accept Jesus Christ as your personal savior." We never used a phrase like that. We used very communitarian, body of Christ language. We started with a communal experience, and some rich individuals grew out of that. I never regret that we started with the communal, because if you start with people's individual soul trip, they don't want to give that up for the sake of the community.

Specifically, how did you relate the community prayer experience to the daily religious experiences individual members were having in their lives?

The prayer meeting format was helpful. There was testimony, witness, and shared prayer. By doing that, it became clear to people that their religious experience mattered. As much as I love liturgy, it still reflects the pyramid structure of the church. It suggests an official religious experience, from the pulpit to the people. There isn't much chance for the body to feed on itself, to enrich and nurture itself. The priest's religious experience is the only source. This gives us a limited view of the Scriptures. It is a celibate, male, clerical, sometimes academic view. Part of the reason our community grew strong is that we had formats for sharing faith and prayer other than priest-led liturgy. I think the church of the future will have to discover these forms. You see the power for this, for instance, in the *comunidades de base,* or base communities, which began in Latin America. They have sharing of lay religious experience. What is Jesus saying to them through the Scriptures and their daily life? There is an opportunity for this to come out, and it's non-academic, non-male, non-clerical. It's much more homey and folksy, and, therefore, is much more alive.

In some of our community gatherings, especially in the early period, there was so much spiritual reality that people wouldn't feel the need for anything else. The private, personal failed during that period. We're in a period now in which some people have developed such inner authority — by listening and coming to know the Lord — that in a lot of ways, they don't need the community. It's not that they are rebelling against it or leaving it. They just don't feel the need for it. In fact, the community is sometimes a bother to their inner movement. I experience that myself. There's a sense of inner aliveness. There's a lot going on, a lot being processed as a result of people you have talked to and things that have happened.

Celebrating the liturgy with the community may not be where you are at all. You don't need a celebration, because you don't need any more stimulation right now. This has resulted in a desire for simpler liturgies. I can see why some groups went toward monastic-style liturgies. You don't want show, you don't need extra readings, extra songs. You need space to help you process the stimulation you already have inside you. You don't need something to divert your inner life from the direction it has already taken.

Once you develop an inner life — an ability to listen, let's call it — you find there is too much stimulation. You find yourself trying to cut down — fewer tapes, fewer books, fewer liturgies. Some of our more mature people have felt the freedom not to go to masses on some Sundays. They need to spend quiet time at home processing their inner experiences of the Lord. They don't need another sermon, three more readings, and fifty-five hellos and hugs.

How would you describe the format of the prayer groups?

Faith sharing is common in our small groups. You might begin by asking people to talk briefly about their first religious experience. Another would be to have people reflect on their religious experience since the last meeting. Or you might have readings from Scripture, with people responding by saying what the message means in their life. A dialogue homily is another format. Some groups say the rosary, or have a communion service, or shared contemplation in which people are together in silence.

All these formats are ways of hearing the Lord together. There's a mutual respecting and expecting of the Spirit in one another. I hope more of these formats emerge. The temptation from the Protestant side is to always make them Bible studies. This often moves people too much into their head and too much into the left brain. I'm much happier with the ways it is done in the *comunidades de base*. There the emphasis is not on study but on sharing — Bible sharing, faith sharing, and prayer sharing.

Faith sharing has allowed me to see that God comes to people through weakness and brokenness and pain and failure and rejection. It doesn't happen through our strengths. A man sharing about his alcoholism will often open a group to prayer. St. Paul says that in sharing our weakness, "power reaches perfection." He is right. This is beginning to allow the Western church to see an aspect of the Gospel that was pretty much forgotten: That God comes to us through our wounds, even our sin. I think that is almost the biggest revolution happening in spirituality in the church today. And we are learning this through faith sharing. In case after case after case, as people faced their shadow, their darkness, the broken part of themselves, they found that was the avenue to God. And the same is true of sinfulness. God uses our brokenness and sinfulness in our favor. And through faith sharing, we see we are all in this muddy, messy human flesh together. That's where God is meeting us.

Besides alcoholism, another area of brokenness where people find the Lord meeting them is in problems in relationships with their parents. Many people feel rejected by their parents, or were never hugged by their father, or never shown deep affection by their mother. They may have been bitter and neurotic for years as a result. Or their marriage may have broken up because of it. But as they get in touch with that, it turns out to be where God touches them most deeply and where they experience deep conversion. Divorce, sexual failures, and homosexuality are similar areas. There is a broken part of almost everybody, some areas where we have experienced our radical insufficiency. Faith sharing helps people recognize that, accept that, even use that.

Is death then the final brokenness through which God comes to us?

Exactly. As we learn that God uses the darkness and brokenness in our lives, we gain the faith to trust that he will use the final brokenness, death. Then, like St. Francis, we'll be able to say, "Welcome, Sister Death."

What role has prayer played in keeping the community going, especially with regard to determining direction and decision-making?

Prayer both holds the community together and explodes it apart. When people really gain the inner authority I spoke about, they don't need the community. They develop an inner ego strength — in the good sense — that makes the community superfluous and even bothersome at times. But, at the same time, a community is only as strong as its individuals. When you have created healthy individuals who freely can come back to the community by grace and surrender themselves to the body of Christ, you have a powerful community. These people come back to the community because they want to.

It's like you raise your children, and if you love them right, they don't need you after a while. You may want them to need you forever, but they don't. It's the same with community, they don't need the community after about five years.

Your most powerful leaders have reached this stage. They have self-knowledge and an honest relationship with the Lord. This enables them to see that community is a call, a vocation. Even though it is a pain and a bother at times, they can see the gift and grace community is. People who are in community in this way cannot stop growing. They feel called back to community, because they feel God is forming people in community to minister to the church and to the world.

We have various formats for holding the community together. The natural one is our weekly eucharist, on Wednesday nights. Periodically, especially with me on the road a lot, that will be a communion service or shared prayer of some type. We're trying to open that and find better ways for the community to hear itself. But when you have 300 people, as we do, it is hard for people to hear. I think that probably happens better in our small prayer groups, which have six to ten members. During our goal setting process, which we do every year after Easter, we have formal nights of communal discernment. We may pray for a week about a particular issue or section of Scripture.

Last fall, I gave a quotation from Scripture and said I wanted us all to live with the quotation for a month. Then we would come together and share our experience of trying to do that. A faith community must be held together by shared prayer. Otherwise, you are going to create an institution rather than a movement of power. New Jerusalem is an institution, unfortunately, because in many ways you can't avoid it. But there's still a movement of spiritual power present, because our primary gathering point is to pray together. I don't want to say our prayer is what it should be. I think we have become rather formalized, and we must get back to some of our charismatic freedom again.

You recently spoke in a talk you gave of the importance of common memories for communities. What common memories do you have of the Lord's presence and activity in your community life?

First, there's the myth of the foundation, of the powerful gathering of these young people, of the gift of the mansion, of the number of healings. This continues, although not with the sense we had in the first years, the firecracker years, when it seemed as if we got everything we asked for. We sometimes ask, have we lessened in our faith, have we lessened in our prayer? I hope we haven't.

This year, we had a classic moral case. A young woman discovered right after she became pregnant that she had Hodgkin's disease. I never thought I would have to deal with anything like that. Everybody was praying. We asked the Lord for a full healing. She had conservative Catholic doctors who had never advised abortion, but they said either this child goes, or you are going to die. For someone raised in the church, there would seem to be no question. But when it is your life, there is a question. And she had a little girl to raise.

For several nights, most of the community gathered and prayed over her. When she had gone for the first tests, the disease had moved into her spleen already. They had to take some of the spleen. But shortly after that, the disease was eighty percent gone. She went back a couple of weeks later, and it was ninety percent. And the child was born healthy. At this point, the disease is almost completely gone.

It is our most recent miracle in the community. We have had wonderful little gifts like that periodically. I think one reason is to call us back to expectant faith and to believing the Lord still does his thing. He didn't just do it once. That has been a great help. At the same time, you are expected not to need all the signs and wonders you once had. We do seem to have to live a lot more by faith. Not everything we pray for happens, not everyone is healed. A community has to go beyond the signs and wonders stage and live by trusting in his presence, his faithfulness, and his loving, quiet involvement in your life.

6
Creative Beauty

Matthew Fox

The Reverend Matthew Fox, a Dominican priest, is developing a spirituality emphasizing the blessing and beauty of creation rather than the more traditional one stressing the fall of humankind and redemption. To help disseminate his ideas, he has started two major projects: a teaching institute and a publishing company. He began the Institute in Creation-Centered Spirituality at Mundelein College in Chicago in 1978. In 1983, he moved west and started the Institute in Culture and Creation Spirtituality at Holy Name College in Oakland, California. The publishing house is Bear & Company, Inc.

He was born December 21, 1940, in Madison, Wisconsin. After joining the Dominicans, Father Fox decided to get a doctorate in spirituality. He asked Thomas Merton where to study. Merton suggested the Institute Catholique in Paris, where he studied under Father Marie-Dominique Chenu, who introduced him to creation centered spirituality and whom he describes as "my mentor in every way." Matthew Fox has written a number of books, including *Whee! We, Wee All the Way Home* and *On Becoming a Musical, Mystical Bear.* His most recent is *Original Blessing.*

Prayer for me is experiencing depth, a depth that is many things. We are a well that contains flowing energy. Prayer is getting in touch with that energy. It's being able to sustain one's work and one's relationships. It's also the energy of pleasure, the depth of pleasure and ecstasy. It's getting in touch with the depths of pain and suffering.

For me, it's also a sinking, not only into my experience of depth, but also, as I sink, I sense the experiences of others' depth, and I know that deep down, there's probably one place where all the wells flow together into the divine depth. I am at home with Meister Eckhart's imagery of God as "a great underground river that no one can dam up and no one can stop." It's his imagery of sinking I am using. He got it from Mechtild of Magdeburg and the feminist spiritual tradition.

In thinking about prayer, I have to ask myself: What are my ecstasies? Study and ideas are tremendously prayerful for me. They were for Thomas Aquinas, too. He had a big argument with a monk about a special liturgy on a feast day. The monk wanted Thomas to go to the church and pray. Thomas, who was working on a special article for the pope or somebody like that, finally got infuriated by the guilt trip being put on him — about how he wasn't praying — and he swore and said to the monk, "Get out of here, my study is my prayer."

I have to make that clear in my case: My work is my prayer. I am not always comfortable with that, because my work — and therefore my prayer — comes and goes. I know when the "coming" happens, when the ecstasy happens. It's brought about my birthing ideas. I love to write. I love to teach an exciting class. These are moments of the deepest prayer in my life.

You'll have mystical experiences in your work, if it's sensual to you. That's the case for me with lecturing, writing, and teaching. They are experiences of prayer for me. On the other hand, I hate administration. It takes all the faith in the world for me to believe my administrating is prayer. But I know how necessary it is. That is my pain, my *via negativa*. There's my cross, my asceticism, my fasting. But even though I hate administration, it's part of my prayer too, isn't it? It's the pain. Going to faculty meetings is my stations of the cross.

Solitude is another form of prayer for me. I love nature. For years I have lived out in the woods, on a lake, with ducks, my dog, and a friend or two. I need nature, and nature is so much a part of my prayer. And I don't mean prayer with words. I'm talking about being in nature — as my dog is. That's why he's my spiritual director, in a way. He takes me out to nature just to be there — being, listening, smelling, hearing, feeling. Being is more important than saying. Basically, prayer to me is not saying, but being.

Music is also important to me for prayer. I am blessed in that I live with a musician, so there's always music at my house. I would distinguish between what I call depth music, which is spiritual, and most music at Catholic liturgies today. I do not find it prayerful. I do find Mahler, Beethoven, Mozart, Bruckner, Debussy, and Verdi prayerful. They take me on journeys of depth, depth of pain and depth of ecstasy.

I had a wonderful experience a year ago here at the institute. We had a day in extrovert meditation. That's our word for describing art as meditation. I went to the day on opera. I was lying on the floor listening to Maria Callas. I said to myself, "What am I doing here? What's the connection between Maria Callas and the spiritual life and prayer?" Then a phrase from Teresa of Avila shot through my head. She said, "Our soul is a mansion with a million doors, most of which are never opened." And then I realized the connection between Teresa of Avila and Maria Callas. We need opera to open doors, doors of passion and pain, doors of ecstasy, doors that are not ordinarily opened.

Friends are another important dimension of prayer for me. It's important for me to be with depth people, with whom I can share my depth and who can teach me something, because they are different from me. I think one reason I like living with a musician is that I'm not a musician. I love music, but I don't play an instrument. I want to learn to play the piano as extrovert meditation, to pray by playing the piano, and some day I am going to take time out to do that.

Another dimension of prayer for me is the struggle for social justice. This takes me into depth, the depth of my pain, my complicity in evil, the depth of other people's pain. God is where there's depth and pain. God is where there's anger. Entering into such anger, or moral outrage, is at least fifty percent of my prayer — and probably ninety percent — insofar as all my work, all my writing and teaching, is directed, in one way or another, toward the liberation movements, developing spiritualities for the oppressed.

I include the people of the First World as well as the Third World among the oppressed. I think the slavemaster as well as the slave is oppressed by slavery. Liberation for me is not just the liberation of the literally poor. It is also the liberation of the spiritually poor, because they lead superficial lives of power and materialism. The spiritually poor can be in the church or in the world.

Recently, I did a retreat for the first time for homosexuals, for members of Dignity in Minneapolis. It's profound prayer to hear the confessions of these people, to hear how they have suffered at the church's hands, at their parent's hands, at society's hands, and above all, in their own self-image. First, an experience like that causes you to question your own homophobia, then your society's and your church's.

All this comes together. Giving a retreat for homosexuals leads to study. Writing leads to clarifying your thought and allows others to criticize it. There is a unity in this. And the key to it is depth, the depth of people's pleasure, including my own, and depth of people's pain. I think that is the prayer circle.

As far as liturgical prayer goes, that's special and wonderful when it happens. But being stamped "Sunday morning" or "Roman Catholic church" has little to do with authentic prayer. The real liturgical experiences in my life in the past few years have been with Native American people, with women's groups, with blacks, with gay groups, and with people at our institute. These authentic experiences of liturgical prayer have come with people who are moving into depth because they are waking up to their pain, to their capacity for ritual, to their capacity for celebrating.

As a priest, I find it impossible to read prayers during the liturgy. If I can't pray from my guts, I don't know what I'm doing leading others in prayer. Polishing texts, getting the right prayer, having the latest prayer book from Rome or anywhere else isn't the point. If we can't throw away our books and pray the eucharist out of our guts, out of our depths, we are not praying. We're reading. You go into most Catholic churches, and during the Scripture reading, everyone is checking in the missalettes to see if the reader gets every word right. That is literalism. That is reading. Jewish and biblical prayer has to do with hearing.

I cannot, frankly, read mass out of a book. I respect priests who can do that, but I can't. It's not authentic form. If I am going to pray, I am going to pray with people, and I am not going to read someone's else's prayers. There is energy in a group that prays together. That energy comes out of the group. It wasn't manufactured in Rome or Washington, D.C., by a committee. Either it comes from the group or it's not there. And if it's not there, you shouldn't be praying together. That's how I feel as a public pray-er. Intellectually, I can step back from that position and say, yes, there are occasions, such as large gatherings of Christians, when it is good to have a common form of liturgy that people can recognize.

We did a beautiful liturgy at the institute recently for a baptism. We used Gregorian chant, because that's what the parents wanted. We trained some of our students in chant. It was beautiful. I sang the preface in Latin, and I enjoyed that very much. I'm not saying there is no room for tradition in liturgical prayer. I am saying that in praying the liturgy in the vernacular, the prayer should come out of the group assembled and not out of books, however holy.

I would like to say one more thing about music. I am embarrassed by the Barry Manilows in Roman collars who are making it as liturgical musicians. I am embarrassed by their sentimentalized music and their privatized words, except when they stick with the psalms. There's no *via negativa,* there's no depth, there's no pain, no suffering. You have such depth in Gregorian chant and in Mozart and Mahler. What we should be doing liturgically is awakening the people of God to the saints he has given us — the fine musicians of the last three centuries. You might call it raising the cultural level, but that would really mean recognizing that God gave us incredible spiritual gifts for prayer in Mozart, Beethoven, and Mahler. What passes for liturgical music today too often kills the spirit. It's part of the sentimentalizing of religion. I can't stomach it. It kills prayer.

When you are experiencing natural ecstacies that you describe as prayer, what is going on inside you?

Letting go. I love to walk on the earth out in the country, feeling the earth under my feet. It's so pacific. It's so right. It's so gentle. I was in a serious auto accident five years ago, and my knees were greatly affected. For a couple of years, walking on concrete was very painful. My knees were sensitive to what was under my feet. Being able to walk on the earth was such a return to gentleness. It really raised my consciousness about what a gift the earth is. It is firm, yet it gives. When I die, I will return to it. The realization of my unity with the earth — my origins and return to the earth, the gentle earth — is important for in-depth prayer.

So are sunsets. I live right on a lake, and the sunsets are so beautiful. It's a small lake, but it's to the west. Every night, the sunset is different. It's glorious. I love the colors. I think the universe is colors. Colors and music, music and colors. Prayer is entering in. It's not only entering into pain but also entering into pleasure, entering into the beauty of the colors. Prayer is entering into the sunset, being with it. No words. It's letting go and letting be — to let go while letting the sunset be the sunset.

Prayer is being with my dog. He's so ecstatic. He's so capable of self-expression and spontaneity. He is so at home in the universe. He has dignity. Being with him is a way of simplifying my life, letting go, and living the simple life.

Yesterday, I was giving a lecture with a physicist. He was talking about how we now know for the first time that the world is fifteen billion years old. And he was saying we share the same protein molecules as monkeys and moths and all living things. Eckhart called this the equality of being of all things. This kind of thinking shows you the interdependence and interconnections in the cosmos. All this happens if you can let go in any natural ecstacy. We are nature. So part of the ecstacy of nature is human nature, and being able to love our nature, our sensuality, and our passions, instead of fighting them as Augustine teaches us. Eckhart says, "The soul loves the body." What does that mean? What does loving our passions and our sensuality have to do with prayer? It has everything to do with prayer.

You talk about natural ecstacies and prayer, but so far you haven't mentioned God. How does he fit into the picture?

I think it is arrogant of the human race — and Christians especially — to feel it is our task to "fit God into the picture." God is already here, it is God's creation — not ours, not the church's, not mankind's (and I use the word "man" advisedly here). Consider that two books in our Scriptures — Song of Songs and Esther — never mention the name "God" once. Does that mean they are not sacred books? Jesus said, "Not all who say, 'Lord, Lord,' will enter the kingdom/queendom of God." We need to let go of projecting our names and our images — for example the masculine "he" for God present in your question — onto God. We need to let God be God. As Eckhart says, "Quit flapping your gums about God."

How do we find God? We find her through these ecstacies. Creation, unlike what the fundamentalists try to tell us, didn't happen "back then." That debate is the fundamentalists' big concern. On the contrary, creation is ongoing. Yes, there was an immediate burst of creation fifteen billion years ago, but God is continually creating. God is creating every sunset. God is painting the sky with colors. Every time we hear Mozart, God is co-creating with Mozart. She is co-creating with the people who invented the stero that makes it possible for me to hear Mozart. She is co-creating with my ears. God is co-creating this ecstatic union of beauty.

The key word for me in this is beauty. It is the middle term between God and human beings. Aquinas said, "God is beauty." St. Francis of Assisi said, "God is beauty." When you enter into ideas that are beautiful, you are entering into God. God is everywhere. We have overdone the idea that God is a person. What that really means to us is that God is in one place. That's absurd. Everything is in God, and God is in everything. That's orthodox pantheism. Eckhart says, "Enter so fully into pleasure or beauty that you come to its source." The source of all pleasure is God, and the source of all beauty is God.

All you have to do is let go. Eckhart says, "God is at home. It is we who have gone out for a walk." The key to experiencing God everywhere is letting go, returning home, simplifying. Letting go means adopting a simple life-style, and that includes a simple prayer life-style. Some prayer life-styles are anything but simple. Bill Callahan, the Jesuit, is great on this. He calls the religious orders "religious multinationals." He points out that only religious can afford thirty-day retreats and all the burden of religious exercises that some traditions teach are necessary for prayer. Eckhart has none of that. All you need for prayer is to let go. Simplify, simplify, simplify. And that includes letting go of religious exercises.

Letting go is simple, but it's not easy. There are times you have so many problems that it's hard to let go. At times like that, a more formal meditation may be helpful. But I use very little of that, very little.

You've mentioned pain several times. What is the connection between pain and prayer in your life?

Traditionally, this is called the *via negativa*. The ecstasy is called the *via positiva*. You need both, a dialectic. What has been so sick in so much of the spirituality of the last three centuries is that we have ignored the *via positiva*. You don't find creation in Thomas á Kempis. In fact, he says, "Everytime I go into creation, I withdraw from God." So the *via positiva* — pleasure — is not part of recent spirituality.

But what about pain? I think the first step is to be where the pain is. It's like the first step in pleasure: You have to be where it is, be with it. In our culture, we have this myth about controlling pain. Valium does it, and we use it for a lot of different things. I sometimes use the expression "praying pain." By that I mean being with pain or the person suffering the pain. If you are talking about the pain of sexism, for instance, you should be with women and listen to their stories. This turned me into a feminist — listening to women's stories at Barat College. There I ran into women thirty-five to forty years old who had to beg their husbands to finish their B.A. degrees. And they were married to men who had M.A.s in business and were running the city of Chicago. I heard incredible stories I wouldn't have believed if a third party had told them to me.

One also has to "be with" one's own pain. I have to admit my own pain vis-á-vis the Catholic Church, vis-á-vis the American government, vis-á-vis academia, for example. I have to listen to my own pain that comes from the institutions I am part of. How are they tearing me up? How are they killing me? How are they ruining the quest for beauty? Where is the beauty in these institutions?

Then, there is physical pain. My accident was important to me. I think everyone's physical pains are important. I had to live with a severe back pain for two or three years. When I got rid of some of it, I realized I hadn't slept well for two years. Pain is a school of wisdom and compassion. I'm not talking about wished-for-pain; that's masochism. Not made-up pain; that's asceticism. I'm talking about the pain of living.

The deepest pain I have experienced is in relationships. A year or so ago, I had a severe break in a relationship that was very important to me. It sent me into a *via negativa* I had never experienced. I dealt with the pain for months. It was very difficult. Finally, I had an image, and the image began to heal it. I was able to name my pain. The image was that I was falling down a well, a bottomless well. It was dark and dark and dark. Utterly dark. And there was nothing to stop my fall or to slow it. The only sense of hope in the whole fall was that a few people smiled at me. Their faces were like pictures on the side of the wall, and they kind of smiled as I fell. Eckhart was one of them. But they couldn't stop the fall. They just provided a slight ray of hope. Then I was able to fall, to sink, to be with nothingness, and to let the pain be pain.

I think that has everything to do with praying pain. It has nothing to do with asceticism. Eckhart is explicit about this. He says "asceticism is not of great importance," because it creates more self-consciousness instead of less, more ego instead of less. The *via negativa* has nothing to do with making up a set of practices. It has to do with being in tune with life's deep rhythms. When you love deeply, you are going to hurt deeply. When you believe deeply, you are going to hurt deeply. When you believe deeply, as when you write and publish something, you're going to make enemies. When you are stirred by moral outrage that is deep, you are going to step on people's toes. There is going to be pain.

Living with pain is part of prayer. The good news is that the *via negativa* isn't the last stage. For Eckhart, for instance, creativity is next. Creativity comes out of nothingness for him. Creativity comes out of pain. All pain is labor pain. All pain can be rechanneled for creativity. I have learned that. All pain, all emptiness, precedes birth. Without these great plunges of pain that lead to birth, we aren't part of God's creative universe, we're not co-creators with God.

Eckhart has a most incredible image that means a lot to me. He says, "I once had a dream. I dreamt I was pregnant like a woman, pregnant with nothingness. And out of this nothingness, God was born." He's saying God is the fruit of nothingness. That is an incredible image. In a way, it summarizes the spiritual journey: You move from *via positiva* to the *via negativa* to the *via creativa*. By going through the pain, you can begin to create. It also helps you to identify with other people in pain. That's the beginning of compassion.

You are an exponent of a spirituality that you say is creation centered. What do you mean by that?

It's a tradition, the oldest tradition in the Bible. The Yahwist author, who is the oldest author in the Bible, is creation centered. So too is the wisdom literature in the Scriptures. The prophets in great part are creation centered. I distinguish this tradition from the fall-redemption tradition, which begins its theology with original sin. Augustine is the key to this. The creation tradition doesn't begin there. It begins with the pages of Genesis that say creation is "very good." It's in the Hebrew Bible, in Jesus, and in the New Testament. There's a lot of it in Paul and in the Gospel writers.

You'll find it in St. Irenaeus. It's a tradition that Eastern Christianity has kept alive, but the West, insofar as it has been influenced by Augustine, killed it, because Augustine was not creation centered.

The creation tradition, instead of beginning with original sin, begins with original blessing. Blessing is one of the most pregnant and fruitful theological themes for Jews. But for us Catholics, blessing has come to mean something we do *to* things. But blessing really means the blessing creation is, the blessing our existence is, the blessing life is, the earth is, our animals are, music is. This is where our spiritual life begins. We must recognize that we too are blessings, original blessings. We are unique existences in the history of the world. Creation-centered spirituality begins with trust.

This is a prophetic tradition. It does not end with contemplation. Contemplation is not a biblical word. Jesus never used it. His word is compassion, as he says in Luke's Gospel and in the Sermon on the Mount. And compassion for the Jew, as Eckhart says, means justice. So, it is a justice-making spirituality. It deals with sin and pain, but it begins with pleasure and culminates in the pleasure of celebration and justice making.

Some creation-centered mystics have been declared heretics, because of the people doing the judging. That's why Eckhart was condemned. He was prophetic. He backed the women's movements and the peasants' movements of his day. In addition to St. Irenaeus, you had other saints who were creation centered: Hildegarde of Bingen and Mechtild of Magdeburg. Many women were creation centered. Why don't we know these saints? They are women, and they are creation centered. The patriarchy has buried them. Others, who are known, are St. Francis of Assisi, St. Thomas of Aquinas, Julian of Norwich, Eckhart. John of the Cross is creation centered, but he has been misinterpreted by ascetics or would-be-ascetics.

Creation-centered spirituality is a lay spirituality. In recent centuries, the musicians I have referred to, many poets, and other artists have carried the creation-centered banner. You have not heard creation-centered spirituality in the novitiates, seminaries, theologates, or pulpits for centuries. Father Chenu, who was my mentor in Paris, woke me up to the creation tradition. I visited him when he was eighty-four years old. He said this incredible thing: "The greatest tragedy in theology in the last three centuries has been the divorce of the theologian from the painter, the dancer, the artist, the musician, the poet, the dramatist, the moviemaker." This he is saying at the end of a fully prophetic life. He was silenced by Pius XII for twelve years and forbidden to write, because he was a worker-priest-theologian. The connection between art and justice matter in the creation tradition. You won't find the word *justice* emphasized in the fall-redemption theologians. You can read Thomas á Kempis, and you won't find justice mentioned. There's no belief in beauty or in art, or anything that is extroverted as such. He's introverted.

What kind of Jesus have you discovered using this creation-centered spirituality?

Jesus is creation-centered. He was Jew. Jews are sensual in their spirituality. The earth and earthiness and passion are blessings to the Jews, not hints of original sin. For the gnostic, who has so influenced Christian spirituality, original sin is in our sensuality. Matter is original sin. But that's not true for the Jew. Remember, too, John the Baptist was the ascetic. His followers came to Jesus and were scandalized, because they called him a glutton and a drunkard, as it says in Matthew's Gospel. Jesus went to parties, and when they ran out of wine, he did something about it. He ate with the poor and the rich alike. He is always eating in the Gospels. He knew how to enjoy life. And people were scandalized.

When they asked Jesus his message, he didn't say go back and tell John the Baptist everyone's fasting and everyone's taking vows of celibacy. He told them to go back and tell John what they heard and saw: He told them to trust their senses. Jesus told John's disciples to tell them the blind see again, the deaf hear again, the lepers don't smell bad, and the lame leap like deer. And, I think, he said the impotent are making love, but that was censored some place along the line. He also said the dead are raised to life, and the person who believes in him is happy. This is the good news: Awakening to our senses. This makes Jewish spirituality different from Hellenistic, Greek spirituality. Through our senses, we find God in the world, in matter, in creation. We also find him in his acts of creating and co-creating, not in flights from matter.

I have to emphasize what Rabbi Abraham Heschel says about the prophets. The prophets, he says, were not ascetics. They were passionate people who appealed to the passions of other people. That's what Jesus did. He is out of the prophetic line. There's no way to be a prophet and an ascetic. Prophecy has not been a developed category in Christian spirituality, because the ascetic trip has caught our fancy instead. Of course, it has caught the fancy of empires, too. You can expect that, because there's a tremendous political investment in asceticism as opposed to prophetic spirituality. If you can turn a person inward, you've solved the problem of criticism of the way things are.

Jesus, like every good Jew, was a profoundly sensual person. Let me stress this too; The fall-redemption tradition is docetistic. It's all Christ, Christ, Christ. There's no sense of Jesus as human, Jesus as Prophet. Therefore, it is a heresy against the incarnation. What does it mean that God became flesh? It means God became fleshy. Julian of Norwich is brilliant on this. She says God is in our sensuality, and that the meaning of Christ becoming human is that God became the glue between divine and sensual existence. She uses the word "sensuality." That's important, because it shows what the incarnation means. Docetism reigns in Christian spirituality still. We have identified it with the neo-platonic trip of purgation, illumination, and union instead of the creation journey of pleasure, suffering, creativity, and justice.

Let's say a more or less typical, middle-class couple who have two or three children, lives in the suburbs, and go to church on Sundays come to you and say they would like to do something about improving their prayer life. How would you help them, using creation-centered spirituality?

One question I'd ask them is: What are the natural ecstasies that mean a lot to you, and do you take the time and space to do them? Do you like to go camping? What happens when you go camping? What do you feel? I'd do this to get them to talk about their pleasures, their ecstasies. I'd ask, what music do you listen to? What poets do you read together? What do your children mean to you? What things do you do with your children? Do you folk dance? Do you camp with your kids? Do you learn to play a musical instrument with your kids?

All prayer, as I've said, is a matter of letting go. Can the parent let go of being a parent? Can the parent become a child again? I often find this: If the parents and children can do something together, that's the key to whether there's any letting go going on. If you have that, you have celebration and real prayer. I don't even like the expression "prayer life." It is dualistic. Our language is all messed up on things like that. If you're living, you're already living *in prayer*. The real question is: How deep is your life?

I would also ask such a couple: What about your prophetic life? Living an everyday, middle-class life — I say that's impossible. You must protest something. You must feel strongly about something. What do you stick your neck out about? What do you say "no" to? What do you refuse to do? How mad do you get at your parish when it doesn't provide liturgies, the adult education, or the good preaching you and your children need? What are you organizing? What kind of citizenship do you express? How are you educating yourself about America's military budget?

Waking up your consciousness — that's prayer. A holistic doctor I've had for the last year has gotten me off processed sugar, and it's made a real difference in my life. In addition to *what* you eat, there's the question of how. Do you share the cooking? Is it just mom's job, or do the kids cook sometimes? Does the man of the house cook, too? Is eating together a delight, an art, an art of conversation? Or do you have the TV on as one-third of Americans do when they eat dinner?

Prayer is a simple thing. It's not going around asking: What retreat am I going to make, what exercise should I get into? How many new prayers should I learn? That's immature. Growing up spiritually is letting go, simplifying. It's recognizing what Eckhart says, "God is already praying in us, but we don't know it."

Prayer is deep living, radical response to life. Whenever we are responding radically — whether out of joyful ecstasy, out of prophetic anger, or out of pain — that's prayer. We just have to get out of its way and let the Spirit move.

7
Praying
as a Family

Dolores Curran

**Dolores Curran writes and speaks about what she lives —
Catholic family life. From her home in Littleton, Colorado, a
suburb of Denver, she writes a weekly column, "Talks with
Parents," that appears in about eighty-five Catholic diocesan
papers in the United States. It has twice won the "best syn-
dicated column" award of the Catholic Press Association.
She has written ten books, including *Family Prayer* and
Traits of the Healthy Family. Her articles have appeared in
nearly 100 magazines, and she has also done filmstrips and
video tapes. She gives family retreats and has lectured widely
in the United States as well as in other countries. A native
of Edgerton, Wisconsin, she is married to Dr. James F. Curran, director of instruction in the public schools of En-
glewood, Colorado, another Denver suburb. The Currans
have three children: Teresa, Patrick, and Dan.**

We have always been a spontaneous prayer family. We pray
before meals each night, and once a week, we have a family prayer
ritual. We call it our liturgy, because that was a word we used
when the kids were little, and they learned what that meant. I
think ritual would be a better word to describe it. We usually
have our ritual on Sunday night when we have a nice meal. Dan,
my son, says I cook "new" on Sundays. That means we eat off it
the rest of the week!

After we eat, we pray, reflecting on the past week and thanking God for it. We pray for what is coming up in the week ahead. We also have special prayers. If we are in a special season in the church year, we'll include that. We have developed a lot of prayers out of things that happen in our family. For example, when Teresa, our daughter and our oldest, left for college in California, we wrote a family prayer. Every Sunday night, we say that during our ritual here. Teresa also says it on Sunday night at school. If I'm gone, as I sometimes am now, I say it wherever I am. That's important, because we don't see Teresa from holiday to holiday. The prayer goes like this:

"Oh God, our Father, thank you for the great good gift of one another as family, Although we are separated in distance, bring us together this moment in memory, spirit, and love. Help us always to love and support each other, even though we may be far apart. Keep us healthy, safe from harm, and always in the palm of your hand. For this, we praise and thank you, Our Father, Amen."

We wrote that as a family during a family retreat. It is appropriate for our family right now, as the children are going off in various directions. I got the idea from a woman whose husband had been in the military. They ended up dropping kids all over the world, one living in Hawaii, one in Germany, and so forth. This woman said they used a family prayer like this to help them stay together. Our family prayer is now in its fourth year.

We had a sending forth ritual for Teresa when she left. Everybody picked a scriptural passage to read to her, and everyone wrote a sending forth prayer we gave to her and which she couldn't read until she got to school. We let her have her favorite meal, her "last meal," as she called it. We did some silly little things, too. From the time the kids were little, when they were too small to write, we had drawn pictures for various family and religious occasions. So we drew pictures of what Teresa would be doing in school. Those were good for some laughs. One of the moments that was most meaningful was Jim's reading of the scriptural passage on Moses sending the people forth. It was a powerful one, especially because he was the father and she the only daughter.

So that's the kind of thing that has grown out of our Sunday night family ritual. As part of it, we get out our calendars, because we are a busy family, and we go through the week seeing who has what on which days. We see when during the following week we can have our next ritual. If we can't have it Sunday night, we plan for another time. We figure if we can't find a half hour a week to pray together, we don't have much business calling ourselves Christians. And we miss it when we don't do it. This is not a structured situation. It is spontaneous. We have family reconciliations at least a couple of times a year.

Some things we do — like the family prayer — I have learned from other families. Some families are doing wonderful things in the area of prayer and spirituality, but as with most things in the church, this is a time of change and crisis. Today's parents grew up with a rich, pre-Vatican II symbolism and prayer style in the home. They value that, especially in retrospect. But with Vatican II, much of it was lost, so there were no sacramentals, no rituals, no family prayer. The kids roll their eyes at the rosary and that kind of thing. Families are confused as to what to do. Through movements such as Marriage Encounter, Charismatic Renewal, and Cursillo, many families have learned new symbolism and new rituals. I think many families get turned on through these movements. If a couple gets excited through Marriage Encounter, for example, it spills over into the home.

Families can also support each other through these movements. That is important. You feel so lonely. When Jim and I first started, nobody was doing this, it seemed. When I wrote the book *Who, Me Teach My Child Religion?* in 1971, I was advised by several priests not to write it. One said, for example, "Dolores, parents won't do anything; they don't care." I don't agree. I think they care, but the situation is confusing. They don't know what to do. They need ideas. In many parishes where I work with parent groups, the only two things they know how to do are the rosary and the advent wreath. I show them how to do other things — for example, how to take a birthday celebration and give it a religious dimension.

You say parents need ideas. Besides a family ritual, what others would you recommend?

Family blessings are wonderful. Parents can bless their children, and children can bless their parents. I recommend doing it once a day. Bedtime is a good time for it. In my family retreats, we do a little family blessing in which the kids sing a song to the tune of the Oscar Meyer weiner commercial. The kids hold their hands with the palms up and the parents with the palms down, and the parents bless them. It's a simple thing. Parents can go beyond that and bless them when they are in bed, for example. They can even do it with their teenagers. You can say, "God bless you tonight, son." It is a loving thing and brings in the religious dimension without being too hokey or formal.

The younger families start praying together, the better. I encourage families that can't pray together to begin with the traditional grace. If that is all they can do, fine. After they begin that, I encourage them to add a couple of phrases of their own, such as, "And thank you today that Mary did well on her test, and that we had a safe trip over the weekend."

Again, I would encourage the special family meal, when everyone can be together. I can't say enough about that, although it is getting more and more diffcult for families. The importance of this kind of thing was clear, for example, in a survey I did. I surveyed professionals who work with families, and they picked table conversation as one of the fifteen key traits of a healthy family. This kind of communication is the basis for much of family life, including family prayer.

Sunday brunch after mass is often a good time for the special family meal. Whenever it is, there must be time for some sense of relaxation, so you aren't rushed as you are the rest of the week. All you have to do at the end of the meal is clear the dishes, light some candles, and bring out the Scripture. Name days are another wonderful opportunity for family prayer. A lot of families add this to a birthday celebration. A religious dimension can be added to anniversaries, to Mother's Day, or to Father's Day.

How would you do that? Let's say we are going to have a birthday party. How would you add a religious dimension to it?

I wouldn't try to add it to a big birthday party, but rather to a celebration that is pretty much limited to the family. Let's say you have the family and a few small children. Let's say you have had the cake, and you have blown out the candles, and the gifts have been opened. Then you go and get the baby book, and the parents could begin by recounting things from the child's life. An obvious place to begin would be when they first learned they were going to have this child. They could talk about how excited they were, and how they told other people, and how they reacted. A key point is showing how pleased they were to be having a child.

They can talk about picking the name. In our family, that is very funny, because Jim and I had a terrible time agreeing on names. Our children love to hear what each of us wanted them to be named. We also tell how we picked the godparents. We tell the story about the first sign of labor that the baby was about to be born. For example, for one of our children, Jim was at a football game as a high school administrator when I had my first labor pain. I thought, what am I going to do? Kids don't hear this kind of thing often enough. And it's their story.

Then there's the excitement when they were born — how thrilled we were to see them, how we brought them home, how we had them baptized. You can show the little footprints and pictures. You can talk a little about faith, perhaps by beginning with the child's saint. For example, our daughter Teresa is named for Teresa of Avila. And she was born on the feast of Teresa of Avila. We like Teresa of Avila. She's one of my favorite saints, because I think she was a right-on woman. We agreed on the name Teresa, and, without our being aware of it, our daughter was born on her feast day. That kind of thing makes wonderful telling when you are adding a religious dimension to a child's birthday celebration. Incidentally — and this was a real thrill for us — Teresa was studying in Madrid on the 400th anniversary of Teresa of Avila, and she was able to go to Avila for the celebration.

Teresa of Avila has been a continuing part of our daughter's life. When Teresa made her first communion, we got her a statue of Teresa of Avila. We continued to talk about Teresa of Avila as our daughter was growing up. She knows the wonderful little stories about what Teresa of Avila said to some of the bishops, and what she said to God. For example, when Teresa was stuck in the middle of the river with her donkey, she said to God, "It's no wonder you have so few friends, when you treat them this way." Teresa loved that story. This kind of thing gives kids a feeling of kinship and relationship with their saint.

We usually conclude with all of us saying a little prayer for the child having the birthday. In that prayer, we include what we like best about him or her. We go around the table doing that. It can get really funny. I encourage families to let the humor flow. Pat, our son, who just had a birthday, has a wonderful sense of humor. He is always able to make us laugh, especially when things get tense. In my prayer, I said what I like about him is that he's our laid back, easygoing one.

On Mother's Day, each member of the family will write a prayer for me. They'll say what they like best about me as a mother. We do the same with Jim on Father's Day. Occasions like that can have really touching moments. There's a funny story about the first time we had an anniversary celeberation. The kids wanted us to repeat our marriage vows. We had been to a wedding, and they asked us afterward if we had said the same words in front of a large group of people such as the one at this wedding. Wasn't that scary? they wanted to know. You don't ever expect to say your wedding vows in front of your children, but we said, sure, we would do it.

They baked a cake. They had me wear my wedding veil — it was the only thing that still fit! They picked two Scripture readings from the little *Purple Liturgical Bible,* which has always been a staple in our home. The second one they picked was about Samson and Delilah, because they wanted a love story. Well, Jim and I couldn't even look at each other. Then we repeated our wedding vows. That was tough in front of your kids. They giggled all the way through in a nervous but meaningful giggle. Afterward, we talked about marriage, and how people can take the vows and then get divorced. That interested them, because they are touched by every divorce of their friends' parents.

This kind of thing is family prayer. Parents think they have to get into a narrow, formal type of rote prayer. They don't. Prayer is taking ordinary family celebrations and adding a religious dimension. I know from working with families that once they experience the richness of this kind of prayer and ritual, they are not afraid of it anymore. But the first time is often difficult. Getting families together in groups, such as in a family retreat or at a Marriage Encounter, often makes it easier. This dilutes the situation. They can have experiences with their families that might be intense and embarrassing if they were alone.

What else would you suggest for other family occasions? Let's take Mother's Day, for example.

With people living longer, there are lots of intergenerational things you can do if grandma, or both grandparents, are living nearby. When you can get the extended family together, rituals can be meaningful. You can ask grandma, for example, to tell about the toughest time in her life. It might have been when she lost a baby, or when she was told she couldn't have a baby, or when something happened in the Great Depression. I love to get older people to tell their story. In the early church, older people were the sages. They would tell the story and pass on the value of faith in their life. We can get grandparents to do this by asking them. They will be happy to do it.

A parish in Minneapolis, St. Joseph's, has old people tell their story every year on the first Sunday of Advent. The parish sets up locations with rocking chairs and rugs. They rope off the areas, and the kids come and listen. Then the old folks tell their story of what life and the church were like for them. When a bell rings, the kids move to another grandparent. This has been popular.

We can do the same kind of thing in our families. Kids love to hear that. What comes through is this: Hey, things aren't so tough now. Then the kids won't buy into the idea that everything is going down the drain, because they have heard about hard times. They also have models of faith and how faith helped get people through crisis. These old folks often say things like, "God helped us through it," or, "We'd never have made it without the good Lord."

*This is an example of the storytelling emphasis in religion that
some theologians are talking about and which is becoming popular, isn't it?*

Yes. I think in today's families, we don't take enough time for
that. We don't tell our stories to one another, because we haven't
been told it's important. Sometimes in working with families, I
get them to start by reading other people's stories. After that, I
will get them to tell their stories. Parents have a hard time telling
their stories if they have never read to their children.

There's another reason telling stories of family life is important.
It is the first step toward telling the story of our larger family life,
the Jesus story. Families might have some immigrant stories.
There might be some weird characters or strange things that
happened in the family. Perhaps the family gathers at certain
times in certain places and does certain things. Christmas is an
obvious example. These occasions provide a time for telling
stories. And things that happen on such occasions can later be
told as part of the family story. Families with many rituals and
traditions like this are able to teach their children — and they
do it in a non-educative way — that they are part of a bigger
family that includes a relationship with God.

*Can you illustrate that with a Curran family story of tradition
that helped you relate to the Jesus story?*

Let me take one from my childhood. My dad was a farmer in
Wisconsin. There were seven of us kids in ten years. And these
were Depression years. Every Holy Saturday, he would go to town
— he would make a special trip — to get the new holy water
that had been blessed. He would come back, then he and the
seven kids would bless the farm. My mother never went along. I
suppose she was just glad to be free of us kids for a little while!
We would go from field to field. Dad would take the holy water
and bless each field, and we would say an Our Father and a Hail
Mary.

Then he would do something I thought was part of the prayer.
He would reach down and pick up a handful of dirt and run it
through his fingers. And behind him would be seven little hands
doing the same thing. We laughed about this later, because we

all thought it was part of the prayer. Actually, it was just part of being a farmer. It's a thing farmers do.

This blessing of the farm was a significant religious experience. It probably meant more than a whole year of religion classes. Dad was saying to us, "It's out of our hands." Asking God's blessing on the fields, the weather, and the crops was a simple act of trust in a larger being. That was passed on to us children. My parents gave us such a richness.

You have written about one of the ways you have tried to pass on one traditional prayer, the rosary, in your family. How did you do that?

The only time the rosary has worked for us has been in the car, while we have been on vacation. We always say it the first thing in the morning. We have lots of time then, and nobody is rushed. Last summer, we went to New Orleans. I was teaching at Loyola, and we made a family trip of it. The first days we did the joyful, sorrowful, and glorious mysteries.

Then one of the kids said, "These are boring! Can't we come up with some new mysteries?" My first reaction was, oh, no, you can't do that. How can the mysteries of Christ be boring? But my second reaction was, why not find out what he is talking about. "Like what?" I said. He said, "Let's do the miraculous mysteries," so everybody picked his or her favorite miracle, and we said the rosary that way. That was super. The kids had ideas I never would have thought of. For example, the big miracle to Dan was the miraculous catch of fish, because he is a fisherman. One of us picked the face on Veronica's veil. We got to talking about the miracles. What was this or that one all about?

The next day I said, "Does somebody want to be creative again?" Someone suggested using favorite parables. Our older teenager picked the prodigal son. I suppose that would be predictable. I liked the woman at the well. Of course, the good Samaritan was picked. Nobody liked the workers in the vineyard. I think there's a basic feeling of injustice that may be operating in it.

Another day, we did our favorite character in Scripture. If we could have met someone in Scripture, who would you pick? Surprisingly, someone picked Simeon in the temple. The reason was he had waited for so long. He was seen as a good example for the times we have doubts about faith. I learned a lot about my family by doing this, because it gets personal. Picking someone reveals a lot about yourself. It leads to good discussion and sharing. We also made mysteries of the rosary out of what you might call fun times in the Bible.

This was primarily a way of bringing Scripture into focus. This was our fourteen-year-old's idea. It could have been taken as disrespectful. But as parents, we have to be open to the fact that our children can help us with our faith. Parents have the idea that they have to feed the faith to the kids, and that they don't get anything back from them. That is not true.

If we listen, we can get remarkable faith lessons and stories from their eyes. Kids, as well as parents, have a story to tell. It's frightening sometimes. When you start discussing this, every parent can come up with something one of their children said or did that had a remarkable, though perhaps simplistic, religious meaning the parents hadn't glimpsed. But you can't do it if you aren't listening to them. We are so busy teaching the precepts of the faith. Many Catholic parents are more concerned that their kids are in mass on Sunday than that they have any real faith developing and operating in their lives.

Can you give another example of a faith lesson you learned from your children?

Yes. When our kids were very small, we went down to the inner city for mass. We were deeply involved in racial work and in the peace movement, and a community there met our needs. The Sunday liturgy was wonderful. The community was supportive. We would come out uplifted. But then we would drive home through the worst of skid row to get to the freeway. It would be about 11 o'clock, a very unlovely time on skid row. Men would be staggering and lying in the gutter. Some would be vomiting. They were terribly sad looking people.

Sunday after Sunday, the kids would comment on this. Why can't we help them? We'd say we do help them by giving them money here and there and doing other things. But our kids kept talking about this. One Sunday on the way home, Patrick, who was about four then, said, "I know what let's do next Sunday. Let's bring a loaf of bread, and when we come home, let's stop on the street and give each one of these men a slice of bread." I said, "Oh Pat, they need so much more than that. A slice of bread wouldn't go very far and wouldn't be much help." Typical parent again. We kept driving, and it got silent in the car. It was silent for a long time, and then Teresa, who was about seven, sighed and said, "Well, at least I wish they knew we cared." Isn't that a powerful statement from a seven-year-old?

You've written, "The more I work with parents, the more I discover a universal feeling of disappointment in the family observance of Christmas." What do you suggest to improve the celebration of Christmas?

I think Advent can be rich if it is not overformalized. Part of the problem is that families get so geared up for Christmas that they lose the spiritual side. It's not intentional. They really want to do something about it, but they can't. They're too busy with Christmas programs at school, shopping, sending out cards, and getting ready for everything.

It is unrealistic to say to families that they should do all kinds of hour-a-day rituals or prayers. I would suggest during Advent that they try five to ten minutes after dinner or before bedtime. And if they can't do it one day, they need not feel guilty. Families would do well to get out of the idea of ever more stimulation during Advent. There's a tendency to try to do more and more, when the kids need settling down. A walk together or meditation before the Christmas tree would be more appropriate.

We take turns leading a family Advent activity. It can be anything. We've done our Christmas cards as part of this. We'll light candles, write notes to relatives, talk about them a little, and say a prayer at the end. I like to see families give a religious dimension to decorating the tree, to making cookies, and things like that, even if it is just saying a prayer beforehand or singing a carol. We always have a blessing of the Christmas tree.

Another of our traditions is the Jesse tree. Every year since Teresa was a baby, we have used Jesse symbols we made of construction paper. The Jesse symbols are of Jesus' ancestors.

They include things such as Adam and Eve in the garden, Noah and the ark, Jacob's ladder, Moses in the basket or at the burning bush. During Advent, every night we bring out one of the Jesse symbols and talk about it. Then we put it up on the chandelier or the door jambs. Then every few days, we go through them as a family.

During November of Teresa's first year at college, I was getting the Jesse symbols out for Advent. I said to the men, who were watching a football game on TV, "Let's make a set of miniature Jesse symbols, just like ours, for Teresa." We sent them to her with an Advent card. She called, in tears, "Oh, Mom, I got the symbols, and I'm going to put them up just the way we used to." Later she told us some of the kids came into her room and asked, "Are those signs of the Zodiac?!"

Families are interested now, I think, in simplifying Christmas and expanding their concern for others. I suggest that the way to start is for families to get together and talk about the situation. Who isn't going to have a good Christmas this year? What are our responsibilities? How can we cut back? Let the family make decisions like that. In our family, we do not put mammoth amounts of money into a tree. We would rather take the extra money and help someone else get one. This kind of thing isn't necessarily the Christmas basket idea either. It is more a matter of cutting back on conspicuous consumption, because that can become Christmas.

What about Lent?

Lent can be a rich time for families today. There are a lot of things families can do and are doing. Telling what Lent was like in the past presents a challenge: How can we translate those ideas and practices into action today? We always try to do four things — a positive and a negative thing as individuals and a positive and a negative thing as a family. On the negative side, giving up deserts and some TV would be typical. The positive things have centered on reading Exodus. That's become a tradition with us.

When the kids were little, we used to have a living stations of the cross during Lent with four other families. We would put paper crosses on the backs of the kids. One of the fathers would be Pontius Pilate. Each kid had to go to his or her own mother at the fourth station of the cross (Jesus meets his mother). At the end, the kids would lie in the "tomb" like stacks of wood. The kids still talk about doing that.

We have our family Ash Wednesday ritual in the evening. One of the kids will set up a Lenten centerpiece beforehand. We used to call them shrines, but today's kids call them centerpieces, so we call them centerpieces. One year for a centerpiece, Teresa made a dessert, which is a Lenten symbol, out of cinnamon sugar. With the blowing out of the candles and the kids going by and eating the cinnamon sugar, you can imagine what that was like! We keep the centerpiece on the dining room table during Lent. Often it has a cross in it, but we use whatever the kids come up with. A friend of ours did it, and her son put a bull whip on the dining room table. She said she looked at that and thought, "Do we have to look at that all during Lent?" To the boy, though, it spoke of the sufferings of Jesus.

We'll start our Ash Wednesday ritual with a song. We'll sing something like "Lord of the Dance," or we'll have one of the boys play, "Let There Be Peace on Earth" on the trumpet. Then Jim or I will say a spontaneous prayer, "It's Ash Wednesday again. We thank you, Father, for bringing us together in this sacred season, etc." Then we'll start talking about Lent and how it came into being. Jim's a historian, and he'll tell some of the interesting historical things about Lent — the hair shirts, the public penitents, the public shriving of kings. Again, it's telling our story. During the meditation, we usually have more instrumental music. We will then start talking about what we want to do for Lent. As we do that, we write down things on pieces of paper and make a chain out of them that goes around the centerpiece. We continue in this way during Lent, reading Exodus, saying the stations and checking how we are doing on our resolutions. We sometimes invite other families to join us.

What experience do you have with small groups of families praying together?

If there is any message I would like to get over, it is that a support system of other families is important. When our kids were little, and we were deeply involved in a parish where there was a lot of social outreach, we found four or five couples with kids our children's age. None of us had much money, none of us had much family around here. We were in suburbia. Jim and I were doing some family prayers and rituals on a childish level, because our children were young.

We asked these couples if they would like to get together once a month to pray and talk about their faith. That's how we started, long before the prayer movement. It came out of social action, the social awareness of the 1960s. We met in our homes. We started by having a mass, but that got impossible. One time the celebrant, a friend of ours, said, "When are you going to be mature enough to have a prayer service yourself and not have a mass?" That did it.

After that, we would have what we called agape meals. We'd have a prayer service and a potluck. After the meal, some of the parents would take the kids for a little religion lesson. I even wrote a book for kids on the early church, with a little boy as the hero. I would read it every month. Of course, I was writing it as we went along. The kids would then go play while we adults would talk about some phase of our faith.

Of the five couples, seven were Catholics and three were not. We depended heavily on our Protestant spouses to lead us in Scripture. At the time, we Catholics knew nothing about the Bible. When our families were young, our spontaneous prayer centered on our careers and our families. As the kids grew, we prayed our way through the teen years. Later, we found ourselves praying for sick and elderly parents. Through it all, this has been a rich relationship. Now our kids are pretty well gone, but we still get together five or six times a year. I would recommend this kind of small group relationship to any couple.

What is the key thing to keep in mind about family prayer?

The experience you have as a child — and all kinds of data support this — is the primary determinant of your lifelong faith. You experience God only through people around you. You can't experience God through doctrine. You can learn doctrine, but if you are going to have an experience of faith, an experience of God, it will come primarily through the people closest to you, your family.

We know, for example, that at age five, a boy's experience and view of God comes through his dad. If his dad is distant, so is his God. If his dad is touching and loving, so is his God. If his dad is cruel, so is his God, and if his dad is absent, so is his God. Fortunately, he can grow out of this, although it won't be easy. The point is that the way parents make God a part of their lives is the most important religion lesson they can give their children.

Chances are the sacraments are already operating within the family. The idea is to let them come out. John Paul II summed it up well when he said, "Families, become what you are — a community of love." I think that is beautiful. And we can become communities of love. There are thousands and thousands of beautiful community-of-love families today, but they have to be more visible, more vocal, and stop being embarrassed about it.

8
Three Ways
to the Center

Ernest Larkin

**The Reverend Ernest Larkin is a Carmelite priest who has
become known for his teaching on centering prayer. He has
developed three forms of the prayer. He spends about half
his time giving retreats and workshops, the other half writing
and publishing. A major emphasis in his writing and teaching is poularizing the teachings of the two Carmelite
spiritual giants, St. Teresa of Avila and St. John of the Cross.
His books include *Christ Within Us* and *Silent Presence*. He
is also featured on two audio cassette series, *Centering and
Centering Prayer* and *Spiritual Awakening,* and a video tape
program on St. Teresa. He taught theology for twenty years,
including ten at the Catholic University of America, and did
continuing education work among priests in Phoenix,
Arizona. He is currently working out of Chicago, where he
was born August 19, 1922, and where he enrolled in a high
school seminary when he was thirteen years old.**

I was seventeen years old and just out of high school when I
went into the Carmelite novitiate. I was young and eager, and I
bought the whole package. That meant high ideals and, especially,
religious observance. Life was pretty much measured by perfor-
mance, and basically that meant physical presence at all the
exercises. As long as you were in the chapel, it was presumed
you were working at your prayer and spiritual life.

I have always been observant in my religious life, especially in the novitiate and afterward as a student. There were ups and downs, but basically I thought I was doing all that was expected of me if I was at chapel or recreation or study according to the schedule. We spend almost four hours a day in chapel, counting mass, meditation, and the divine office, which we said in choir. In the novitiate, we also recited the little office of the Blessed Virgin daily.

The burden of so much chapel prompted one of my class to opt out after a couple of weeks, with the remark that he had not expected that the Carmelite life meant living in church. Then and later, however, I took all this observance in stride. Even so, my prayer life was not that significant to me. It was not that influential. Prayer was one corner of my life, but all the rest was where I was really living.

Both before and after ordination, I lived a very ordered life. My assignments were in an academic world — on the high school level, in the seminary, and at Catholic University. Because I was observant, I was looked upon as a "good religious." But I was what I now decry as mediocre. In the language of spiritual theology, mediocrity is being a "good person." You do the things you are supposed to do, but there is no life inside and little growth. You look the same spiritually at fifty as you did at twenty-five. Everything is external, even prayer, and my life as a religious and priest for thirty years was all of a piece: that of a good servant, a good worker.

How did your prayer become more personal?

That came with the charismatic renewal in the late 1960s. The renewal was the last of a number of awakening influences in my life in that decade. I had gone to the seminary and got into a tight system at a tender age, with the result that I missed a lot of the normal experiences of an adolescent and young adult. The 1960s gave the possibility to people like me of having some of those missed experiences, such as having more independence, rebelling against the system, and getting involved in close relationships, especially with women; the last mentioned was the most significant. All my life, I had been a friendly person, but I was dominated by my role; I was always professional, hence aloof and distant. But in the 1960s, because of the atmosphere in the church which spilled over immediately into the academic world, I was able to live more personally and more freely, to start moving from role identity to a more personal and autonomous existence.

I think this had something to do with the way my prayer life was about to move. When I was first introduced into the charismatic renewal, I did not buy it. I was in on the ground floor, because this was 1968, and my contacts were some of the early leaders in the "pentecostal movement," as it was then called. I used to go to a lot of meetings, including national ones. But I was always the inquirer, the critic, and the seeker rather than a believer. But the contact affected may own prayer life, because I started to realize the possibility of a personal relationship with our Lord. Little by little, I was moving in the direction of being a more personally convinced Christian, a more prayerful person.

But there were conflicts. I had at the time the life-giving but giddy experience of falling in love. Yet, I was committed without recourse to what I was as a religious and a priest. I had to work through the emotional upheaval of separation when my friend wanted to move toward marriage and family. At the same time, I had other dependent relationships as well, and I was pulled apart by the conflicting demands, expectations, and advice of different people. I could not handle this all, because my background had made me a "pleaser" rather than an independent agent. Besides, there were the burdens of academic obligations and involvement in administrative tasks in my religious community. The result was a physical breakdown.

In January 1970, I had surgery for bleeding ulcers. My doctor said it would be good to get out of the academic world for a while, and I was lucky enough to find a berth in the new diocese of Phoenix, Arizona. The bishop was looking for a theologian to work with clergy and other adults in continuing education. I went there for one year, supposedly. I found a welcoming environment in the still infant charismatic renewal there. But again I was an outsider, not willing to put my nickel down. Every time I would go to a meeting, I would have a thousand questions.

In January 1972, I decided either to get out of the charismatic renewal totally or get into it with both feet. I decided to get into it. I had always loved the people in the renewal. They were marvelous folks. There were some kooks, too, and that was OK. I went through the "Life in the Spirit" seminar. I was prayed over. People were happy, because they wanted priests in the renewal, especially perhaps theologians, who might bring the added dimension of teaching to the movement. I, too, was happy to be among these enthusiastic Christians. I did not have any big conversion experience at my baptism, no fireworks, no sensation or experience when I was prayed over, other than a warm sense of being beloved by God.

Yet I can almost identify the point at which I had a whole new style and depth of relating to God. And it came through being prayed over and entering into the charismatic renewal as a disciple, as a believer. I closed off my theological questioning for the time being and followed the official thinking of the charismatic renewal, as it was represented by the leaders of the movement. I, too, assumed leadership roles, especially locally in Phoenix.

For the next three years, I was deeply involved in charismatic activity — prayer groups, talks, meetings. Eventually, we formed a covenant community, called "The People of Joy," and followed patterns set down by the People of Praise in South Bend and the Word of God community in Ann Arbor. I was one of the coordinators; I was also liaison between the renewal and the local bishop. My style of prayer through those years became much more personal. Jesus was real to me. I used to enjoy the prayer meetings very much. My individual contemplative, meditative prayer life, never particularly strong, was helped by my new involvement. I think my prayer life was more public than private. But it was very, very real, and I did grow in those years.

I was not able to pray in tongues in Washington. I recall my friends trying to "teach" me to pray in tongues, telling me to relax and utter a couple of syllables, as if to get started. I think they were on the right track, but the block to praying in tongues is our inhibitions. My theology of praying in tongues is simple. It lacks mystery totally. I think tongues is a way of expressing oneself in nonsensical language that one finds an authentic vehicle in prayer. After I got into the renewal with a personal commitment, I found it easy to pray in tongues.

I was now free enough and excited enough about God to talk "gibberish" and sing "gibberish," and find it meaningful. The words have no intrinsic sense; they are a nonsense language, finding their sense in the reasons of the heart. If the gift of tongues is ever a real language, that is an exception and a miracle. I am willing to admit the possibility of such a miracle, but I would demand that it be proven. Tongues is no more miraculous, no more supernatural than saying the Our Father. And that, of course, is supernatural enough, because it is the work of grace.

In 1975, I made a thirty-day retreat. Here was a new shift in my prayer life, a quantum leap of sorts. My prayer became experientially my personal relationship with God. I saw that everything hinged on my personal relationship with Jesus. I saw the hour I spent at the beginning of each day in quiet prayer as the most important hour of my day and something to which I should be faithful, no matter what. Through this request, I returned to seeing my daily contemplative prayer as central and the highest priority.

In those days, my contemplative prayer was basically scriptural, and I would reflect on the Scripture and/or just try to be present to the Lord. It was formless, without any good method or pattern. The Lord was quite real to me, and so the hour passed, although sometimes it was a marathon, and I was hanging in there. But it was generally rewarding. It certainly was an experience I thought important in my life. For the most part, as I recall, I was faithful to it.

But I suffered because I lacked method. That is where centering prayer came in Praying through centering came into my life about 1979, when my effort to be faithful to an hour of prayer each day was running into more and more difficulty. My daily prayer had become old hat; the prayer became more and more dry. I hope interior growth was there, but the aridities were a sign. At the same time, I needed techniques to support me though the wear and tear on the psychological and even physical level. Till then, I was just there, giving some Scripture to myself, then maybe looking at the trees outside to remind me of God's presence and his "gifting" the world, then engaging in dialogue with him, and so forth.

Even though I had moments of good prayer, the process lacked order; it lacked pattern. I can recall being easily moved to tears at times. I remember thinking, "Gee, that is really neat. I must be getting somewhere, because I can cry about my love for Jesus." I think now that some of those tears were authentic and some were sentimental. But without a method or theory, I had no way of measuring my experiences at the time.

From my retreat in 1975 on, there was a definite pulling away from the charismatic involvement. I had become sick again in 1975, long before the retreat, and I had to curtail my activism. I withdrew from the charismatic renewal little by little. First, I resigned my leadership positions. Then I stopped going to meetings, and eventually, by 1978, I had dropped out. I was still close to the charismatic people, who were always and still are dear to me, but I was no longer a card-carrying member.

The charismatic renwal does not speak to me anymore. It had done its good in me; it awakened me, shifting my thinking from production-oriented, achievement-oriented existence, from doing a lot of things, to a more receptive stance before God. It was providential in my life, and I am grateful to the Holy Spirit and to many people in the renewal for what I was privileged to receive through this vehicle. But I am not served by it any more.

I am turned off by what I consider its shortrcomings, especially its fundamentalism, its single issue stances, its lack of historical sense, its rejection of the complex and gray nature of human existence. I had been willing to live with those deficiencies as problems and deal with them as best I could; but I am not really willing to do that any more, at least in terms of being served personally by the renewal. I have, since 1979, cast my lot with the contemplative currents and movements in the church today. One such current is centering and centering prayer.

What is centering prayer?

Centering is basically a new language for the contemplative approach to life. The term was coined by Thomas Merton to describe moving beyond one's empirical self, which is our false self, the self that judges everything by appearance and by sense perception, into a deeper level of spiritual awareness and wholeness. Centering is getting in touch with your whole being, being in touch not just with the outside world or with your own psychic world, your own ego world, but also with the deeper reality we call our heart or center.

Following the lead of a friend and theologian, Father Tom Clarke, a Jesuit, I have developed in my own practice and teaching three methods of centering prayer. They are guided imagery, centering prayer as such, and consciousness examen. Guided imagery is a way of getting into depth contact with yourself and God by using images. The image in question is any symbolic activity, any activity that is expressive of your deepest will, your freedom, your deepest identity. Guided imagery is not just visual, nor is it just audio. It can be movement, such as dancing. It can be a gathering of many experiences, such as the liturgy or a charismatic prayer service. Somehow this imagery allows us to pull together our outer and inner selves. The imagery is a symbol. It puts together our consciousness and our unconscious, our outside and inside.

It is a natural way of praying, one might say, the most normal way of praying. Its most frequent expression today is scriptural prayer, in which one allows oneself to be swept up in some scriptural passage, such as a scene from the life of Jesus or an Old Testament story. You can, for example, identify with one of the characters. You listen to a passage in Scripture as being spoken to you by God or by Christ. For instance, you read or listen to the story of the woman at the well, and, as you do so, you become that woman at the well. You hear her responses as your responses. You let the story speak to you. You don't try to analyze it or control it. Rather, you let the story carry you wherever it takes you. It is easy to do that if you are relaxed enough, listening enough, and willing to be led rather than standing in judgment on the story.

How do you "become the woman at the well"?

That incident from the life of Jesus speaks to me very much. I have used it many times in my prayer. If I am going to use this story as the vehicle into my center, I open the Scripture to the fourth chapter of St. John's Gospel and read a few lines. I see Jesus moving through Samaria at Schechem, which is modern Nablus in the West Bank. As he is sitting there, I let him emerge into my consciousness. I try to let an image of him form there. I do not necessarily say, "What does he look like?" But I let an image form in my mind. I let it happen. Perhaps his face comes into view or the perspiration on his garments, dust of his tunic, or the sight of his feet worn and weary. I visualize him as he addresses this woman — who is myself. She has come there for a practical purpose, to get water. And I hear this man say to me, "Give me a drink."

This whole representation moves slowly. I do not press it. I allow the imagery to emerge out of me, not out of the book, not out of some picture I have seen. The imagery is best when it is my imagery, when it comes out of my history, my unconscious, my past. Those images will come if I am patient enough, quiet enough, and slow enough. And they translate the story into a conversation between Jesus and myself.

I see Jesus concerned and gentle and forthright with me. I hear myself say to him, "How come you're asking me for a drink? I'm not one of your people, and I'm a woman, a nobody." What does this language say to me? Maybe it says, "How come you are asking me, who is taken for granted by my peers, maybe also ill-equipped to do my job." A reflection like this may come forward in my thought. But mostly, I want to be there with him. Guided imagery as a contemplative form of prayer — like all contemplative forms — leads to presence to the Lord. I want to be present to him. If there are reflections, fine, but the main reason for the images is presence to the Lord. The story, if I listen to it carefully, evokes my story. I start realizing a little more that I am a person who is related to Jesus, and he is a person who is related to me, and my life in many ways mirrors that woman and Jesus.

In the years between 1975 and 1978, I was largely proving to myself I could do an hour of prayer every morning. I would hang in there no matter what. Many times, I would check the clock. But once I learned guided imagery and saw it as a method of contemplative prayer as valid as being attentive to the Lord in silence, which is the more traditional Carmelite concept of contemplation, new possibilities opened up. I started to structure my prayer. I would spend the first half of the prayer in silent attentiveness to the Lord (the second method of centering prayer), and then the second half of the prayer, I would use the liturgical readings of the day for guided imagery.

In those days, I always tried to stick to an hour. I do not anymore. Have I regressed? I don't think so. My total meditative prayer time still adds up to an hour or so, but I am not hung up on the time. My time frames now are about twenty minutes of simple attention to God in what I call mantric prayer, the second form of centering prayer, then about twenty minutes on guided imagery prayer, in which I usually use the Scripture; usually I offer mass at this time, and then after mass, spend time doing my journal, usually another twenty minutes. Sometimes I use other forms of guided imagery, such as nature, such as Lake Michigan, which I can see from my window. It is a beautiful image of God for me. I look at that lake and let it tell me things about God, and it does not disappoint me. It speaks eloquently of God at this point in my life. It's amazing.

You referred to your second form of centering prayer as "silent attentiveness to the Lord" and "mantric prayer." What is that?

The second method of centering prayer I teach is mantric prayer. I call it strict centering prayer, because the word *mantra* has been co-opted by some writers to describe this form of centering and no others. It uses the mantra or holy word as a focusing agent. Mantric prayer is a centering process in which I try to be both relaxed and alert at the same time in an attitude of total presence to the reality of God. I try to keep myself in that attitude by repeating a holy word or holy phrase rhythmically, synchronized with my breathing. The mantra has to be a short phrase, because I repeat it again and again with my slow breathing. Mantric prayer is thought-less, concept-less, image-less presence to the Lord. It is based on the premise that being near the Lord is enough. Mantric prayer does nothing for my imagination, intellect, or feelings. But it holds me at attention to the Lord, and that is what real prayer is, loving attention to him.

Being a Carmelite, I have always identified contemplation with this stance in prayer. The mantra is not part of our tradition; simple presence is the whole contemplative effort. So the mantric form of contemplation is most natural to me as a Carmelite. The only new element is the mantra itself, the holy word. This may not sound like a significant addition, but it is a sign something is going on. If you don't use a mantra, you are unmoored. If your attachment to the Lord is not strong enough to automatically and spontaneously repel distraction, ennui, and boredom, you will wander all over the place.

The mantric form of prayer brings order into contemplative prayer. I use the mantric form as an entrée into prayer. If I really want to pray — whether using guided imagery or using reflections on my life, which is the third form of centering — I find I best begin with mantric prayer. That gets me in touch with the Lord. From that vantage point, I can move into other contemplative forms as well, which in another setting, without that presence to the Lord, would be active forms of reflection or meditation and not contemplative at all.

How exactly do you use this mantra?

I use "Abba" as my mantra about ninety percent of the time. The other times, I use "Jesus." I say the mantra more or less continuously, not out loud but in my mind. I get in touch with the Lord in a brief act of faith, in which I identify the Lord's reality within me. Then I hold myself at attention by saying "Ab — ba," saying "Ab" as I breathe out, and saying "ba" as I breathe in. It is a simple and natural approach. The mantra does not call attention to itself. Eventually, you say the mantra unconsciously. It starts being said in you. You hear yourself saying it. This may sound strange, but it is true. This happens to me, not in any extraordinary way, not at all times, but as a consoling support, as part of my consciousness, almost part of my breathing at prayer.

What is the third method of centering prayer? You have called it "consciousness examen" and "reflections on my life."

Those phrases describe it rather well. In this form, I reflect on my life. I use the experiences of my life, which are part of me now, to reveal God to me. They can do that if he was really present and acting in certain past actions. I can retreive that presence by reliving the experience, now at a deeper level of my being, with more awareness of what perhaps at the time was not noticed at all or noticed only vaguely and without appreciation.

For example, I recall that this morning, I felt threatened by the prospect of having to give a presentation on prayer to a group. I recall how inept I felt, what anxiety gripped me, what fears assailed me. I had awakened frequently in the night and rose early, because I was worried and troubled. I remember that experience. It is part of my life. I bring all this to prayer and try to locate God's presence in the experience. Was he there at all? If so, why did those negative feelings assail me?

As I relive the sequence of events, I try to "taste" them. I begin to grasp that I was beleaguered, precisely because I was unaware of God's presence in the anticipation of that talk. I recall that in my prayer at the time, both formal and informal, I had protested that this ministry was his work. I recall having said: "Maybe you can use me better in my weakness than if I am confident and feel totally equal to the task." At the time, there was only dry faith, raw resolution, and no feeling of God's support. But as I pray about the experience now, I start realizing God was sustaining me through the ordeal. He was there, and my faith tells me he was supporting and sustaining me. I experience a certain quiet joy, peace, presence.

I am now able to recognize other dimensions of the experience, namely, the working of God in a situation involving conflict. I had been unaware earlier, too preoccupied to notice. But now I notice, and I identify that God was there, allowing me to rise above the situation and act in it. At the time, I was thinking only about my ineptness and fears; I was feeling only threat and anxiety. That was me not allowing a faith vision. In retrospect, I experienced the resolution of conflict by redoing the original episode. I say: "This is the Lord's work, and I am doing it on his terms." That brings liberation in the playback. In the prayer, I experience the joy of that liberation and gratitude for it. I get in touch with God that way.

All three forms of centering prayer are supposed to culminate in the presence of the Lord. Generally, I use them in patterns. I start with the mantric form and move into one of the other two. That is what I do when I am basically together. But if I am worried about something, or if I am overly tired, or if I am out of sorts, I will probably start out with either guided imagery or consciousness examen; they are easier to do if you are distracted or anxious. The mantric form does demand a certain amount of interior space.

What is the relationship of these three forms of centering prayer to meditation and contemplation?

Meditation, as the term is used in Catholic tradition, refers to a style of prayer that precedes centering prayer. Meditation is a form of prayer in which there is much thinking and imagining about God, but less contact with him. It is about God, about me, about people. It is not as much presence to God as it is figuring out, analyzing, making resolutions, making good responses. Meditation leads to contemplation. You come to the point where you know God, so you don't want to be thinking *about* him or even to be making affective acts such as faith and love and contrition toward him.

You just want to be with him. It is like two people who love each other. They don't want to be giving each other five reasons they love one another. They already love each other, and they want to be together in silence, perhaps enjoying together some reflection or some beauty before them. Meditation is one step removed from real prayer, because real prayer is contact with God. Meditation is like getting the stage set for real prayer. And the real prayer is contemplation.

The word *contemplation* has many senses. In general, it means presence to God, attending to God, contact with God, knowing and loving God, loving awareness of God. Those are all acceptable descriptions. The three methods of centering prayer are contemplative in thrust. They are contemplative in hope. A person who is an actualized contemplative is less dependent on any of the three methods than a beginner in the art. Contemplation in the true sense is not tied to methods. It is grace, gift, God's self communicated to us and experienced. It is where you are spiritually. It is God influencing your life, whether you are aware of it or not. These centering methods are helpful, because they make a person vulnerable to God; they keep one at attention; they provide order in your search.

What image of God do you have as a result of praying in this way?

God has become much more of a person. By that, I mean he is much more present to me precisely as a person and as other. I have, thank God, a deep sense of his love for me. When I am struggling with a problem or working through a moral decision, I can start with the realization that the Lord is there, and that he loves me. I can get in touch with him and feel that if I hang in with the Lord, I am bound to succeed, to come out with a good effect, because he loves me and is the Lord. The Lord is more real, he is more loving, he is more personal, he is more the desire of my heart. I do not like to miss my prayer. If I miss my prayer in the morning, my day is fragmented. My efforts at contemplative prayer have changed my consciousness.

I would have to say, however, that no image immediately springs to mind that describes God for me. Even a word like "Abba," which is a good word for me, does not do it. God is more like a pervasive influence, like a force. I do not know what he looks like. I do not know what he feels like. He is just there. I believe he is there. It is a matter of faith, but a faith based on experience. It is not a theorem. I just have to say that through prayer, God is part of reality. He is not the things I see, but he is in them.

Touching God on the deepest level — the spiritual level — is trans-historical. It is more than a metaphysical experience. It is something in the realm of faith and God, and, therefore, it is not measurable psychologically or physically. There is, however, an overflow. God fills the emptiness of our spirit. If God is filling that emptiness, there is bound to be an overflow of some sort or another. The overflow might be darkness in my consciousness, a kind of numbness or lack of feeling in my interior being. Or it might be light and warmth and felt love. Sometimes, I feel light and airy, precisely because I have been close to God. I have the joy of being a believer, the joy of being a disciple of Jesus, of having the experience of spending time with him. That gives me a light feeling.

Here is one specific experience I have had, usually in terms of the third form of centering prayer — finding God present in some past experience and then reliving that experience. When I have discerned God's presence in this way in an intense degree, I sometimes get a good feeling in my solar plexus. It is almost as if my solar plexus were an indicator light on the dashboard of my psyche. Is it an accurate pointer? Does this experience prove God is there?

I know this kind of experience is dubious, but when it occurs, I feel more sure, more joyful, and more peaceful about the Lord. I get a warm feeling, and I praise God. I have not had this particular experience much lately. But I do recall that I used to refer to my "solar plexus feeling" as a high point of discernment. It could be open to deception, I am sure, and I am glad God is greater, not only than any thought, but also any feeling we can have about him. The bottom line of all contemplative prayer, like the Christian life itself, is faith, and I am glad the search is on that level.

9
Raising the Voice,
Lowering the Bucket

Teresita Weind

Sister Teresita Weind is a pastoral minister at St. Catherine
of Siena-St. Lucy parish in Oak Park, Illinois, a Chicago suburb. She has concentrated on bringing new members into
the church through the Rite of Christian Initiation of Adults.
She also gives retreats and spiritual direction, and speaks
on racial understanding and black theology. She was born
July 6, 1942, in Columbus, Ohio, the third of eight children
and the oldest girl. She spent most of her grade school years
in two religious worlds, the Baptist church, which she attended with her grandparents, and the Catholic schools, in
which her mother enrolled her. In seventh grade, she was
received into the Catholic church. After graduating from a
high school operated by the Sisters of Notre Dame, she joined
that community and became a nurse. In 1969, she began her
ministry in the Archdiocese of Chicago, working for five years
at Cabrini Green, the city's biggest housing project, and, at
the same time, getting a master's degree in theology. She
then went on to six years at the archdiocesan religious education office. Music plays a major role in her ministry and
her personal life. "I live it and use it to express my inner
spirit," she says. "Music is my prayer, my speech, my theme,
and quite often, even a mode of stillness for me."

I entered the convent with a strong sense of prayer, because in high school, I had the good fortune of having Sister Mary Evelyn Jegen as a teacher. She had the sophomore home room at St. Joseph's Academy in Columbus, Ohio. She required all the girls to come in every morning with a prayer on a three-by-five or five-by-seven index card. It had to be our own prayer. As with any assignment, some took it seriously, and some didn't. It really appealed to me, and I did it religiously.

I really go back to that as the beginning of a structured form of praying. We couldn't copy the prayer. That was against the rules. I'm sure my own experience with my grandmother at the Baptist church was a major reason this appealed to me. As a child in the Baptist church, I had expressed prayers in my own words, but I had not written my own prayers. In my sophomore year, I wrote one every day. I found that after I moved to the next grade, making up prayers had become a part of me, although I didn't write them down anymore. I continued doing my own prayer every day, and by the time I entered religious life, I had a sense of wanting to pray, of thinking I knew how to pray. Prayer was something about which I wasn't anxious.

Another thing that helped was that we lived across the street from St. Dominic's Catholic school. I had the opportunity to worship with the sisters every morning in their convent chapel. During my high school days, I'd go over for mass at 6:30 a.m. Many times, I would stay for a little while afterward and do my own prayer. I walked to school most days. It was a thirty to thirty-five minute walk. On the way, I was aware that I was praying and composing prayers.

Can you recall any of the prayers you composed and wrote on the cards?

I wish I could, but I would only be manufacturing something I really don't remember. To the best of my memory, Sister started us with prayers of thanksgiving. We were to write something for which we were grateful. I didn't realize it at the time, but I know now she was developing an attitude in us to be grateful for life.

In the novitiate, we learned other forms of prayer. We said the Little Office, and we prayed Matins, Lauds, Sext, None, Vespers, and Compline every day. During that time, I developed a love for the psalms. In the Baptist Sunday school, I had memorized many quotations from the Bible, including portions of the psalms, but I didn't know from where these quotations were drawn. In the novitiate, I incorporated not only my memorized prayers, but also the meaning of that prayer, and this was especially true of the psalms.

We were also taught morning meditation. We were up at five o'clock in the morning, with meditation from 5:30 to 6:00. That was followed by Matins, which was immediately followed by Lauds. That was the morning prayer structure every day. Like everybody else, I had my periods of sleep during meditation. We weren't awake enough all the time to know what we were doing. We'd start off with good intentions, but often dozed. I remember, too, that for a while, someone read a passage from Scripture. We were to try to put ourselves in the story with Jesus, or reflect on some image from the reading. Those were good periods of prayer.

The turning point for me was Dr. Martin Luther King's assassination. That was a major, major conversion for me. I was in North Dakota at the time. The day he was killed, I was at Mary College in Bismarck. I was working toward my bachelor's in nursing. When he was killed, and there was all this attention on Dr. King, I was embarrassed, because I didn't know who he was. The novitiate at that time pulled us out of the world. We didn't know anything that was going on except for our immediate formation. It was a hard experience, because I should have known, but I didn't. People expected me to say something, and I didn't know what to say. I didn't know anything about the civil rights movement.

Fortunately, by the grace of God, I had a good friend, Father Dennis Kendrick, a Benedictine. He was a history teacher and was informed. Later, he helped me to inform myself. But at the time Dr. King died, I couldn't appreciate the man or what he meant. Dennis, who was in Chicago at the time, called me and wanted to know how I felt about Dr. King's death. He thought I would feel sad, but I didn't have enough sense to feel sad. He got books for me, and I began to learn about the predicament of all of us black people.

When you say you weren't aware of Dr. King, do you mean that literally or that you just didn't know much about him?

I had heard his name, but I really didn't know much about him. I remember seeing him on television once. And the reason this one instance stands out is because I violated a rule the day I saw him on television. We had a long corridor that connected the novitiate to the chapel. One day coming back from chapel, I was walking down this corridor, and I could hear the television. It was in the professed sisters' living room. As novices, we were not allowed in there, but I overheard the TV, and there was a report on rioting. I think it was about Watts. I stepped in to see what was happening. It jarred me, because I didn't know things like that were going on. At the same time, the television reported something about Dr. King. So, I had heard of him, but I really didn't know the significance of his life, or what he was doing about civil rights. I didn't know anything about the Montgomery bus boycott. I didn't know anything surrounding the great events of his life and his assassination. I was quite ignorant about a great piece of history.

Yet you say Dr. King was responsible for a major conversion within you. As you studied him, what did you learn from him about prayer and spirituality?

I saw in Dr. King, and I still do, the integration of prayer and service. Prior to that, prayer was a "part" of my life. It was a time, a structured activity. I got up in the morning, and I prayed. I prayed at noon and in the afternoon and in the evening. But it wasn't until I came to know what Dr. King was doing that I could see the integration of prayer and service. Everything Dr. King was doing grew out of his experience as a Christian and a minister. I could see that prayer was the foundation of his work for human rights. I perceived his rootedness in the word of God as the impetus, the inspiration, for all he was doing.

I liked that, and I was eager to learn a different approach to prayer, so it wouldn't be compartmentalized. In studying Dr. King, I saw his whole life was an opening to the God working within him. I saw, too, how this opening led Dr. King to work for the sake of others. I wanted to live that way. I wanted especially to serve people who were suffering under repression. It was a change for me, a total change in the way I approached my prayer, and in the way I would live my life.

Specifically, how did you pray after that conversion?

At first, I don't know if there was much change in what I said or the way I did it. When I look back on that as a conversion, I see it as the beginning of a change within me that took many years. I know my prayer and my life became more outer directed. Nursing is a helping art, but I wanted to help people in ways other than through my profession. I wanted all of my life to be helpful. In my prayer, I was asking God to use all of me — in the same way he had used Dr. King — to serve the needs of my brothers and sisters. I guess that prayer was answered, because when I came to Chicago in 1969, I came to work in what I now know to be one of the hardest places in the world — the Cabrini-Green public housing project.

There, I prayed with the people. I learned their simple prayers. Dennis, who was working there also, was good in helping me with that. "Just the way you address them is your prayer," he said. "Your reverence for people is your prayer." I began to want the way I met people and the way I addressed them to be a true resonance of any words I would use in prayer. I couldn't do one thing with the people we were serving and speak to God with different language that didn't carry what I was doing. In that sense, my prayer was changing. I think my prayer became simpler, too, because I was with a simple people, a poor people. I was praying for earthy things. When I was removed from the world, I was rather abstract in my prayers. But living in Cabrini-Green and suffering with the hungry and the homeless and the naked made my prayers concrete. I was praying for someone's next meal, for jobs, for concrete needs.

Based on your work among the poor and your prayer with them and for them, what is your experience of God's presence among the poor? Is he particularly present among them, as we often say he is?

Yes, I believe that is true. I really believe God is particularly present in the lives of the poor. I believe that on a lot of different levels. The first is the faith of the poor. And you can see it in their prayer, too. I would never go so far as to say this is universal, but the people who lived in Cabrini-Green had an unadulterated trust in God. There is so little for them to rely on, to fall back on. The security is not there in anything other than God. They can never count on tomorrow. Few people they know will come through for them.

There is a certain personality and character structure about being poor that seems to keep other people who are not poor at a distance. I keep looking at my own life, and sometimes I find that feeling present. We tend to back off from the really poor, because they are so demanding. Every need is urgent. We wear out answering urgent needs all day long. You might like to say to someone, "Put that on your calendar for next week." Well, with the poor, there is no next week. It has to be now! And their trust in God grows out of that urgency.

They have to know God is for them today. He is here today, or there is not God. They can't count on anything in the future. They have to have it now, or they don't have it. I found that made some of them obnoxious. They became what seemed to be self-centered. But in others, I felt a real faith was at work, a genuine counting on the Lord and trusting in him. In that sense, I think they kept God present. He wasn't somebody coming from somewhere. He was there, and, in that sense, God is especially present among the poor.

In living in Cabrini-Green, I learned another reason for believing in God's presence among the poor. The reason is this: I don't know how a lot of things happen for the people there, except that they were brought about by some miracle of grace. Sometimes there was no other explanation for events. For example, the hearts of people we needed to work with to help the residents would be changed. One day these people didn't seem to care, and the next day they would come around, and we were getting things the residents needed. I believe that's God at work, caring for his poor, his own.

I also feel God is particularly present among the poor because of what happened to me and the other ministers at Cabrini-Green. Our experience made us strip down to what is true. Poor people have a way of calling us to truth. Excuses don't hold up. They can see through the fake kind of excuses we give about what we have to do and what we don't have to do. Something has to be the truth, or don't say it to them. Our time was for them, or else we had to have a mighty good reason for doing something else.

I think that was the best thing that happened to me. I had to be true, accountable. I grew to know God because of that type of mirror in the poor. I was looking into the eyes of people in need. They were not fooling. And I had to examine myself and say, "Can I be honest and answer those needs, or am I going to shuffle?" In that way, I think God is particularly present among the poor, calling us to truth. I believe all God wants is for us to be true to ourselves. But so many things can get in the way of that. We find so many excuses to fool ourselves. Working among the poor highlights that. You're constantly in an urgent, emergency situation, and you have to respond truthfully or fool everybody.

Were there any incidents that occurred, either to you or to people you worked with, that showed how this particular presence of God affected their lives and their prayer?

Yes, one in particular stands out. I arrived about the time two policemen were killed in Cabrini-Green. We knew the boys who killed them. And we also knew their families. They didn't happen to be Catholics, but we had met them in our work. The mothers who raised these boys didn't raise them to snipe off policemen. It was a big test of faith in their lives when they realized their sons had gunned down two policemen.

I could see they were grasping for something to hang on to. It is difficult to raise a child in Cabrini-Green. And the parents had to face that their sons would be convicts for life. The parents hadn't done anything to bring this on. A lot of parents there are lazy — I wouldn't be embarrassed to say it in front of them. They are not doing a good job with their kids. They don't seem to care. But many — and these two families were examples — tried to raise their children right, to respect people, and certainly not to kill.

When this happened, I am sure the parents could have done all kinds of things. They could have disowned their children. They could have disowned their church. They could have gone on a rampage themselves and committed ever more crime, but instead they turned to God, and, in a humble way, asked themselves the question any parent would ask, "Where did I go wrong? What did I do wrong?" We were with them when they prayed to know the truth. They prayed for their sons. They prayed for a fair trial, knowing a fair trial was probably going to mean a life sentence for their children. They didn't blame, and they could have. They could have blamed the city for the circumstances in which they had to struggle to raise their kids. Instead, they tried to turn their lives toward God even more. They asked for help to get through this. In their simple prayers, they asked, "Let me hold up. Just give me the strength to hold out. I want to sit through the trial. I want to support my children. I need you, God, to be there." Seeing this kind of faith was formative for me.

We used to celebrate mass in the homes for the residents. We'd choose a different family every other week. In these huge, concrete buildings, families gathered around their dining room table. There was nothing fancy. Nevertheless, we were bound together by the sacredness of the mass: our belief that Jesus is with us. Being part of those experiences was good for me. They were also formative, because I don't think the people's simple faith was a faith of magic. I don't think they thought Jesus was suddenly zapped into the bread. They believed that in the gathering of their family and friends with us, God was present in their house in a very, very special way.

How has your black Baptist background affected your prayer and spirituality?

I feel happy that I had the experience of growing up in the Baptist environment. Black Baptists have an affinity for the Word of God that makes them feel pretty much at home with the Scriptures. As a child, I memorized portions of the Bible. Verses from the psalms were drilled into us. We children grew into adults with that same ease with the Scriptures. There was little or no Scriptural reference, and often people didn't know from where a text or story was taken. One lady recently told me she loves the story about the crossing of the Red Sea, because Jesus was able to do so much! Well, it wasn't Jesus — it was Moses. But it didn't matter to her. All these stories are together in the Bible, and Jesus could be Moses, or Moses could be Jesus. There was this lack of clarity about what was where. At the same time, people were comfortable with the Scriptures. I think that is peculiar to the spirituality of the blacks. There is a kind of fusing of all the Scripture stories. They may not know the details, but they seem to get the message, and they keep going with it.

I think black spirituality crosses the denominations of being Baptist and being Catholic. Black spirituality is spontaneity for life. There is also a deep love for music. I believe one thing the Catholic church has tried to drain out of us is the idea that music is prayer. While I was working for the archdiocese, I was trying to teach again that singing is praying. I met a lot of black people who wanted the singing to stop, so they could pray. That is not the way they were raised. That's not the tradition we have had in our black spirituality. Music is prayer. Singing is prayer. I find black people are trying to reclaim that now and feel proud of it. We can sing a song, and for us, that is prayer. We don't need to hear the leader of prayer say after that, "Now, let us pray." We've been praying.

There is also the freedom with praying out loud that is not present in the Catholic experience to the degree you find it in the Baptist. But some Catholics who are beginning to relax a little bit are recognizing that this is a part of our experience. I also have found from looking at my own life and from being with other black people, that God is real for us. We don't have a lot of abstract names for God. Mainly, you hear a lot of black people speaking about God as "my mother." Today, in their concern for sexist language, other people may speak that way too on occasion. But black people aren't thinking about equality of the sexes when they pray this way. They have grown up saying things like, "God is my mother, and she got me through this." That image is real for them, because it is based on the experience of the closeness of God. God is as close to them as a mother, so it is not surprising they would say of God, "She nursed me through."

You are a musician, and you pray with music. How do you do that?

I love music. I play the autoharp, which is a zither with a chord bar attachment. I learned to play the autoharp because it is easy to play and the sound is so mellow. The chord bars automatically do what a person does with a fret or a guitar. It sounds like a harp. I use my autoharp to accompany myself in singing and in leading prayer. It's a beautiful mood setter, because the mellowness of the sound of the instrument has a way of toning people down. It has its own quality for assisting with the centering process.

Music provides one experience in which I both know and don't know something about the transcendence we can have as human beings. When I am really into the music, I'm not focused on myself. I can forget about myself in the music. One of my favorite authors is C.S. Lewis. In what I think is one of his most beautiful lines, he says, "Only God himself can let the bucket down in us to the depths in us." I love that, and I think music is like God lowering the bucket for me. When I really get into a song, I don't know when the ropes are turning and when the bucket is being lowered. I just believe that in the experience, some prayer is going on. I would be the last person to try to describe it, because I don't know what's happening. I feel outside myself in some sense, yet I feel good, because I'm not really outside myself. I know I am singing. I know I am listening if someone else is doing the music. At the same time, I can let go. I am not preoccupied. That's one of the reasons I often use the autoharp to begin prayer. It's for me as much as for the people I am leading. I don't want to be tied up with myself. The music is a way of letting attention shift from me, of letting God let the bucket down, of letting prayer happen.

Tell us about one of your favorite hymns, and how you pray with it.

One I like very much is by Walter Hawkins. It's called "Jesus Christ Is the Way." It's simple, with a call-response arrangement. Call and response is somewhat peculiar to the black experience. It grew out of the days of slavery, when few blacks knew anything about the language in America. A leader would call out a line and teach the slave community the response. Much black music was written that way. This hymn draws our attention to Jesus Christ as director, as leader. It all focuses on us as we try to discern what we want out of life, where we are going. There is some self-attention, but what is fascinating about music for me is that it makes us remember who we are and where we are without being overly self-centered. While I can be thinking about myself, I am not preoccupied with myself. The hymn starts out like this:

> When I think about the hour,
> Then I know what I must do,
> When I think about what God has done for me.
> I will open up my heart
> To everyone I see
> And say, "Jesus Christ is the way."

One of the things we blacks have had to defend in our music is the frequent use of "I." That personal pronoun is used a lot in gospel music. It has "I" in it, not "we." But what is amazing is that I don't think it is a selfish approach. I don't think of just me when I am singing it. I don't think of "I," even though that's what the words say: "When I think about . . . when I think about what God has done." Somehow, we are able to get above or beyond or underneath that personal pronoun. We are aware that it is really applicable to all of us. When that is done with a full chorus, with different parts and people coming in at different times, it is a moving experience. And it's prayer. I don't need someone after that to invite me to pray. I just want somebody to say, "Amen."

As director of Christian initiation in your parish, how do you teach prayer to people who are exploring living their lives as Catholic Christians?

I approach it by trying to find out what they are doing already.

That's always my introduction. When do you pray? I have heard a variety of answers. I also like to find out how they pray. A lot of their prayers are one-liners: "Lord, help me." "Help me get through this." "Help me to stop this." "Lord, I pray for my family." They are simple forms like that.

I don't find that people, when they describe their prayer, are talking about a liturgical structure such as I learned as a novice. They are not even praying the psalms. Some, especially the black people coming here, say they pray out of music. They put on a record, listen to it, and that makes them quiet, then they can pray. If you ask them what they do while the music is on, they say they listen to the words and let whatever they feel go on during the time the music is playing.

I try to find out why people pray. Crisis is the most frequent answer. People pray when there is something they cannot understand or cannot change, or they can't handle. The second most frequent answer is beauty. They pray in response to birth, beautiful weather, jobs, favors.

I haven't yet found a lot of people praying just because they want to. That I try to teach. I try to teach them to pray because they want to pray, because they want to cultivate a relationship with God. I try to get them to want to listen to God's power at work in their lives. I develop prayer as a relationship built on the experience of friendship or some intimate bond. I also teach prayer as sacred time. I try to get people to set aside a certain amount of time for prayer. I try to impress on them they need not wait for the next crisis. I start with three minutes a day with most of them.

With this year's group, I've asked them to keep a journal of their prayers. That provides some feedback. It is also a nice way for me to see what they are doing, but that is not really the point. I guess this is based somewhat on Sister Mary Evelyn's discipline for us in high school. I guess you could say I have my own set of prayer cards developing here. At the regular meeting of the catechumens on Sunday, I use a planned prayer experience that always includes the Lord's Prayer, a psalm, a song, and some spontaneous prayer. I'm trying to teach that as a skeleton of the liturgy of the hours, the church's prayer. I also meet with each of them six or seven times individually for an hour and a half to two hours. These meetings are their private interviews. We get into more personal things at that time. How is prayer making a difference in the way they are living? It's been good to see that for some, it does become influential in changing their lives. Others haven't caught it yet, or it hasn't caught them, but I still think they can do it.

You are a trained nurse. As a nurse and as a person who has a developed sense of prayer, have you had any experience in praying for healing?

Modestly, I have. I have been a little skeptical about the more demonstrative healing prayers. I don't know why; I just am. But a few years ago, I learned to pray for the healing of memories. I have found that one of the most profound experiences of my own life. I have been faithful to the healing of memories prayer, and through it, I have freed myself, or been freed from, a lot of resentment I was carrying from years back. I learned this prayer at the Thomas Merton Center in Canada. They taught it as a night prayer. It was close to what we learned as novices as the examination of conscience for the night. Unfortunately, when I learned the examen, the emphasis was on the examination part. The emphasis in the healing of memories prayer is on the healing power of Jesus. That makes all the difference in the world in the way you examine your day and your life.

I learned the healing of memories prayer in the fall of 1979, when I was at the Merton Center for thirteen days. They told us to divide our life into segments of thirteen. That gave me roughly three years to cover each night. We were to find anything that was still hurting us in each of these periods, give it to the Lord, and ask him to heal it. I found many things still hurting as I went back.

We were to go backwards, so the first night, I worked on the period from 1979 to 1976. There weren't a lot of things in that period, but as I backed up further in my life, I came across many things I thought I had forgotten. I thought these things had been healed, but they were still there. I know from this experience that the healing of memories can be very, very effective. I have taught it to some catechumens, especially those still working through divorces.

One resentment I carried for many years was against my mother. I didn't like the life-style she was living as I was growing up. My father had died when I was two years old. My mother never married again, yet there were more children. I resented that. I thought I should have had a father, and I wished she would have married again. For years, it was hard for me to accept that, but I thought, nevertheless, that it was dead and buried. But I found through the healing of memories prayer that I had tucked it away in my mind, that it was still with me. I had never resolved it. I found it had its own way of showing up, even when I would visit her or when she would visit me.

I had a lot of responsibility when I was nine, ten, eleven, twelve years old. I had been thrown into it, or it had been thrown at me. My mother was working, supporting all of us. There was no father in the house. What I couldn't see was that there wasn't one thing I needed — and there weren't many things I wanted, either — that weren't taken care of. Nothing went undone. But all I could see, blinded by resentment, was that I had missed all the basketball games, all the football games, all the parties, because I was babysitting my brothers and sisters.

And, if I wasn't babysitting, I was working outside the house. I used to work for the sisters across the street and cook for them in the evening. When I got home after cooking for them, I cooked for my own family. Then it was time for homework, and my brothers and sisters always needed help with theirs. And after I helped them, I had to do my own. Well, it was one or two in the morning every night before I'd get my work done. I resented that. But I did not know I was still carrying that with me.

After I went through the healing of memories prayer, and after these resentments surfaced, a beautiful thing happened. I was able to see the good in all of it. When I was sick, my mother was there to take care of me. When I was in need, my mother was there to answer those needs. When I was hungry, I was fed. I had a lot of responsibility, but it didn't hurt me. I began to appreciate how faithful a parent I had had all those years, even while I had to be a surrogate parent myself. It was only because of the healing of memories prayer that I was finally able to make it over the hump from a negative attitude to a positive one. Finally, the thing that was most beautiful was to appreciate that the responsibility had taught me something, too. I'm none the worse for having learned to cook and clean and shop and do a lot of things that are now serving me.

You said Dr. King influenced you to turn outward in your prayer. How has this prayer affected your approach to social issues?

My prayer helps me to be more aware of what is happening around me. For example, I can go through the city and notice very little if I really want to. I can keep my eyes closed, have a one track mind, as if I were wearing horse's blinders. But prayer makes me want to see what is happening around me. I want to know what is going on in the lives of people, especially in this parish. I want to know who is hungry, who is without work, who might be depressed, who is in pain because of some abuse. I want to know, because of the way I want to continue the ministry and mission of Jesus. I believe that if Jesus were here now the way he was in Galilee, he would notice what was going on in people's lives. I see prayer as a means of continuing the ministry and mission of Jesus. It's trying to keep alive the presence of Jesus, who is Emmanuel — God with us.

Prayer is an impetus. It pushes me to keep noticing other people, and after noticing, it pushes me to give an appropriate response. I want to be of some help or healing or support or saying, honestly — and this is happening more and more — I can do nothing except pray. For example, I can't find a job for someone. The jobs aren't there. But knowing the person needs a job will make me pray that much harder. And if the person knows that, it will at least bring us together. That brings up another thing I want: To live in harmony with other people. I have found this desire growing within me. I want to work with others. I can see the situation is far too great for me, or anyone else, to handle alone. For me, prayer in action means trying to stay in touch with and get support from and give support to other Christians who are after the same end.

10
The Light
in the East

Bede Griffiths

The Reverend Bede Griffiths is a pioneer among Western Christians seeking to enrich their faith with the religious traditions of the East. His journey to the East began in England, where he was born December 17, 1906. Following World War I, Father Griffiths attended Oxford University and found it a disillusioning place for finding meaning. After school, he went to the country to live a simple life. This led to his conversion to Roman Catholicism, and for fifteen years, he lived as a Benedictine monk in England. Then in 1955, at forty-eight years of age, he went to India. He assisted in founding a Christian community that was open to the ideas and experience of the East. In 1968, he moved to another such community, Shantivanam ashram, in South India, and he has lived there since. In three books, he has recounted his experiences and explained how he thinks the traditions of the East can enrich Western Christianity. They are *The Golden String, Return to the Center,* and *The Marriage of East and West.*

How and why did you become interested in Eastern prayer and meditation?

I read the *Bhagavad Gita,* the *Dhammapada,* and the *Tao Te Ching,* three Eastern classics, when I was in my twenties, before I was a Catholic or fully a Christian. But when I became a Catholic, in 1931, and a Benedictine monk, Eastern thought faded into the background. In 1940, after I had been ordained a priest, I met a remarkable woman, Tony Sussman. She had lived in Berlin and was one of the first disciples of Carl Jung. She had also studied yoga under a Hindu yogi. She and her husband came to England and started a meditation center in London. She had many books on Oriental spirituality, and they opened a new world for me. I was fascinated. From that time I began to meet other people familiar with Eastern thought, and my interest in it grew. Finally, I went to India in 1955 after meeting an Indian Benedictine monk who wanted to start a community in India.

What fascinated you?

The primary thing was the emphasis on the experience of God. We emphasize that, too, in Christianity, but there are differences. In Christianity, we approach God through the liturgy, doctrine, the fathers of the church, the Bible, and most fundamentally, through Christ. We come to an experience of God in Christ and the Holy Spirit. But in Christian tradition, little attention is given to the body or to normal psychological process.

Indian tradition, on the other hand, is based in large part upon the physical body — in particular, on the physical postures, or the *asanas,* as they are called in Sanskrit, and the breathing, or the *pranayama.* There is also an elaborate psychology, which sees how the body is related to the soul and how the awareness of God develops. For me, the Eastern religions give what we would call a lateral or horizontal basis for contemplation. In the Christian tradition, we start with faith, hope, and charity, and that leads us to a supernatural experience. In the Oriental, we start with the body, with breathing, and with certain other techniques to open the psyche to the action of the Spirit.

How do you combine these two traditions in prayer?

We use a kind of yogic meditation. We do it in a sitting position, which must be relaxed and firm. The body and the mind must be relaxed if you're going to be open to God. Often in Christian prayer and meditation, tension is created. Kneeling, for example, is a position of tension, in my judgment.

In the Indian tradition, you always sit to meditate. It is a position I find relaxing, one that opens me to God. So, first we sit. Second, there is breathing. In Eastern tradition, the breath connects the body and the mind. If your breath is agitated, your mind is agitated, and vice versa. If you can calm your breathing, then you can hope to calm the mind, you can be open to the presence of God. The third aspect, the most fundamental, is the mantra, that is, the sacred word or words.

We have adopted the Jesus Prayer as a mantra. The Jesus Prayer developed in the Eastern church. It is supposed to come from early centuries. It was developed particularly in the fourteenth century with the Hesychast movement, which is the nearest thing we have in Christianity to the Indian tradition. The Hesychasts used the name of Jesus, and words they added to it, as a mantra. They also related it to their breathing, trying to realize the presence of Christ in their heart. In this way, the Jesus Prayer links the Christian and Oriental traditions.

I use the traditional form of the Jesus Prayer, "Lord Jesus Christ, son of God, have mercy on me, a sinner." I have done it for forty years. It is a constant resource. When I sit to meditate, the prayer begins of itself. If I am tired or distracted, my mind may wander, but it keeps coming back to the prayer. As I get less distracted, I become more concentrated and aware of the inner meaning of the prayer and the presence of Jesus. I'm trying to place myself in his presence and be open to the Holy Spirit. The Jesus Prayer is the heart of my meditation and what I try to give to others.

I have found that the traditional form of the prayer is too long for many people. They like to shorten it, in some cases simply using the name of Jesus. One brother in our community, who is expert in yoga and who also teaches this form of meditation, uses "Jesu Abba" as his mantra. He says "Jesu" as he breathes in. To him, this breathing in symbolizes the taking in of everything, the whole creation, in Jesus. As he breathes out, he says "Abba," and, in doing so, he gives the creation to the Father. Many people have found this technique effective. But mind you, these are only techniques. You are using methods — the postures, the breathing, and the words — to open yourself to the action of the Holy Spirit.

How exactly do you use breathing in your prayer?

I'm not as precise as some people in relating the words of my prayer to breathing. One method I have used for some time is observing my breathing. It is primarily from Buddhism. In Hatha yoga, which is Hindu, you emphasize controlling your breathing. You do deep breathing from the base of the abdomen, through the chest, to the throat. It is a total breathing. But in the Buddhist tradition, you let your breathing come naturally and you observe. I have found doing that helpful in my meditation.

One of the most striking techniques for saying the Jesus Prayer is in *The Way of a Pilgrim,* the famous book about the Russian peasant who taught the prayer. He did it in a specific way. His basic method was to begin by saying the prayer out loud. Then, he said the prayer quietly. Finally, the prayer was supposed to go into his heart, where it continued more or less on its own. His technique suggested, in a wonderful way, the internalizing of the prayer and becoming one with Christ.

I haven't used techniques much. I am always a little afraid of getting bound by them. I think one should have a sort of inner freedom. After I begin to meditate, the prayer often changes. It may turn into a form of praise, or thanksgiving, or petition. I want this freedom for variation, because I am trying to be open to the Holy Spirit, and I don't want to be bound by a formula. This allows my prayer to vary according to the state of my body and my mind.

Contemplative prayer requires great perseverance. Many times, you are tired or distracted, and you can't pray. Most people who practice this prayer complain that they don't feel they are doing anything. "I'm just sitting there wasting my time," they'll say. People with this problem must realize the prayer is not in the body or in the mind, but in the deepest center of your being, where you are not properly conscious. God is working in you there, even though you may not be aware of it.

One of the great spiritual directors — I don't think he is very well known today — was Abbot John Chapman of Downside, a Benedictine Abbey in England. He was a great contemplative, and many people asked him for guidance in contemplative prayer.

Almost all of them would complain that nothing was happening, and that they were wasting their time. His advice was: Never mind, put yourself in the presence of God by opening yourself to the Spirit of God. Leave it to him. Even if you go to sleep, don't be too concerned, because God understands. Don't stop the prayer and do something else. Give the time totally to God. That was his constant advice.

We Westerners seem to have become almost completely disembodied as far as prayer is concerned. How do you use your body in prayer? Do you sit in a particular way, for example?

I don't sit in *padmasana,* the lotus position. That is the ideal, but I came too late to yoga for that. My limbs are too stiff. I sit upright in a chair. I think for most Westerners, that is perfectly adequate. All teachers of prayer say the spine, the neck, and the head should be upright, because that gives you a kind of inner harmony. They also say this not only harmonizes your body but harmonizes you with the universe as well.

I also try to observe the sensations in my body and, in this way, become aware of it. As you say, most of us, and I was like that for a long time myself, are quite unaware of the body. Our prayer is all in the head. That is our great problem, The fathers of the church used to say: Lead the thoughts from the head into the heart and keep them there. I would add that the prayer should pervade the whole body, from the soles of the feet to the crown of the head. That is why the position is so important. I think growth in the bodily awareness is one of our great needs. I have found it very important for prayer. My mind is very active. When I pray, I have to stop the activity of my mind, become more aware of the body, and establish a sort of inner harmony in my whole person between the body and the mind.

Concentrating on the body, the breathing, and the mantra gives you a this-worldly starting point from the Oriental tradition. But Christians, you say, pray with Christ as a starting point. Aren't you going in two different directions at once? How do you combine the two?

Chiefly through the Jesus Prayer. As I use it as a mantra, I combine it with the breathing and the bodily position. That gives me the worldly dimension while at the same time centering me on Jesus with the Jesus Prayer. It is said that the name of Jesus has power, and that through the name, you become aware of his presence. To me, the whole prayer is a movement to my center in Jesus, and I would say, through Jesus to the Father.

If you include the Spirit, as I do, the prayer becomes Trinitarian. I always try to make my prayer Trinitarian, and one way I have of including the Spirit is through a method of yoga known as kundalini yoga. According to it, energy rises through various *chakras*, or centers, of the body. The idea is that as you meditate, you allow energy to rise through the different *chakras* to the crown of the head. Again, the whole body is involved. When the energy rises, it does so through the power of the Spirit. The Spirit is present in all creation, in all matter, in life, in the body. As the Spirit is awakened in my body, it rises up through the *chakras*. With this rising Spirit, I focus on Jesus and through him on the Father.

In all this, the prayer has two key elements. First, with the energy rising through my body, my whole being becomes involved. And second, because this energy is brought about through the power of the Spirit, the prayer has a basis for becoming Trinitarian. With the power of the Spirit, I focus on Jesus through the Jesus Prayer, then open myself to the Father. In this way, I am participating in the life of the Trinity.

What are these chakras?

They are psychological centers. Some people say they have a physical basis, and I think they probably have, but essentially, they are psychological centers. There are seven of them. The first is the physical base, which corresponds to the area at the base of the spine; the second is called the "vital," and it corresponds with the genital organs; next is the emotional *chakra*, which corresponds to the solar plexus; next is the heart *chakra*, corresponding to the will; the voice *chakra* is located in the throat; the intelligence *chakra* corresponds to the point between the eyebrows and is often called the third eye; finally, there is the crown of the head, or the *sahasrara*, which opens to the infinite transcendence.

The idea of energy rising through these centers comes from the fifth century A.D. in both Hinduism and Buddhism. It came from a movement called Tantra. Tantra means to spread or to weave. The idea is that there is a force throughout the world, and it weaves all the different centers together.

How much time do you meditate per day?

Our norm is one hour in the morning and one hour in the evening. I consider an hour basic. It takes quite a long time to get into the prayer. Most religious in the Catholic church have a half hour. That is all right, if you are ready for it. But if you have to fit it in with other duties, as most people do, you have to have time to settle down. I find it takes an hour to get deeply into the prayer. Otherwise, the danger is that your prayer will remain on the surface. You may be praying, petitioning, and thanking God, but you don't get to the deep center. That is the secret. How do you get to your deep center, where the Holy Spirit is most intimately present?

In your book, The Marriage of East and West, *you speak of reading the Bible, the Vedas, the Koran, and the writings of other religions in your community prayer. This led me to wonder, how many religions do you pray in?*

I pray in only one, really, because Christ to me is the center of all. While we read those other Scriptures, we always relate them to Christ as the center. To me, that is fundamental. Some people do get a bit muddled about this. Frequently, people who come to our ashram have been into Buddhist meditation, or Hindu yoga, or Taoist thought, and so on. They don't know where they stand. That is why I use the Jesus Prayer and try to bring everything into relationship with Christ. St. Paul. says, "In him dwells all treasures of wisdom and knowledge." The fullness is in Christ. When we read these other texts in our prayer, it is always in relationship to Christ, to the biblical revelation, and to the liturgical prayer of the church. I find that important. Otherwise, you get a sort of syncretism, mixing different traditions.

My conviction is that the church is being challenged today to encounter these Oriental traditions. We have never done it. We have encountered the Greek, the Roman, and the European, but we have never faced these deep religious traditions which must have a relationship to Christ. We have to find that relationship. At the same time, we must not lose the Christian faith to syncretism. Instead, we must discover the values of each religious tradition and relate them to our life in Christ. That is why constant meditation is necessary. It is the way we can relate these different traditions and try to see them in their unity.

Could you take a text from the Hindu Scriptures that you find meaningful, and relate it to your faith in Christ, and show how it has augmented that faith?

My favorite text, which has an obvious allusion to Christ, is from the *Svetasvatara Upanishad,* one of the later Upanishads. It goes like this: "I know that great person (Purusha) of the brightness of the sun beyond the darkness. Only by knowing him, one goes beyond death, there is no other way to go."

That is written of the cosmic person, *Purusha,* who is said to pervade the whole universe. By meditating on him, you go beyond death, as the text says, beyond the limits of this world, and you open up to the transcendent. For a Christian, that is obvious: It puts a new light on Christ. You are seeing him from a more cosmic perspective. Perhaps that is what I would emphasize most about the Hindu and the Buddhist traditions. They give us a cosmic perspective. They help us to see Christ as the cosmic Christ, the Lord of creation, who brings all things and all peoples into unity. This relates quite nicely to my favorite text from St. Paul: "It was his plan in the fullness of time to bring all things to a head in him, things in heaven and things on earth." I think the Hindu text helps us to situate Christ, to see him as the head of all.

Many texts relate to Christianity in this way. Equally fundamental are those concerning the Hindu concept of Brahman. Brahman is the name of absolute reality. It can be approached in two ways. One is from the point of view of creation. You look at the phenomena of the world — the earth, the trees, the sky, every-thing. You realize — and this is the spiritual experience — that behind all those phenomena is the one absolute reality, the Brahman. Recognizing this one behind the many is called *vidya,* which means knowledge.

The second way is to approach this absolute reality through the realization that it is manifest in human consciousness. There it is called Atman, the self or the spirit. The great insight of the Upanishads is that the two are one: Atman is Brahman. The source of my being, my consciousness, is one with the source of the whole creation. That is a deep spiritual experience. It helps me to see that the God present in the whole creation is also God present in my heart. Then as a Christian, I realize that the pre-sence of God in creation and in the heart is the presence of Christ, because he is the manifestation of God. Again, this gives a kind of cosmic perspective to the Gospel that I find remarkable.

What prayer do you have in your community besides the hour of personal prayer in the morning and evening?

We pray in common three times each day. After the hour of meditation, we meet in the church. The church is in the style of a Hindu temple, with an outer courtyard, where we sit on the floor for prayer. It also has an inner sanctuary, which is always kept dark. The idea of the sanctuary is that God dwells in the darkness, in the cave of the heart. We have the Blessed Sacrament there with a small light by it. It is impressive to look into this dark space for the Blessed Sacrament. We always begin our prayer with chants in Sanskrit, which is the sacred language of India and still has tremendous power and resonance. It gives at atmos-phere of prayer to the gathering.

We begin with the *Gayatri* mantra, the most sacred mantra in the Vedas. The meaning of it is: Let us meditate on the glorious splendor of that divine light which fills the heavens and the earth and the space in between, may he illuminate our meditation. It begins with "Om," as does all Hindu prayer. "Om" is like our "amen," a kind of sacred utterance. The mantra goes like this:

Om Bhur — Bhuvas — Svaha

Tat Savitur Varenyam
Bhargo Devasya Dhimahi
Dhiyo yo nah Prachodayat
Om Shanti, Shanti, Shanti

Shanti means peace, and we always end with that. That sets the tone of the prayer. Then we have a hymn in Sanskrit. The one we sing every evening is *Vande Sacchidananda*. It is a hymn to the Trinity written by a famous Hindu convert, Brahmabandab Upadhyaya, in the last century. After the chanting and the hymn, we read from the various Scriptures. We rotate the Vedas, the Upanishads, the *Bhagavad Gita* in the morning in the course of a year. At mid day very often, we read the Buddhist text, the *Dhammapada*. We have been reading the Koran, but I find it difficult. It is full of denunciation, although it has marvelous passages, too. We also read the Sikh writings, which we find extremely good. They are neither Hindu, Muslim, nor Christian, but somehow combine elements of all. In the evening, we use the devotional poets, including *Kabir*, who was half Hindu, half Muslim. We also read the poets of *Tamil Nadu*, the state in which we are located. We read these poems in Tamil, the local language, first, then in English. We link up with the local culture in this way.

After these readings, we turn to the psalms and the Bible. In this way, we relate all of these readings to the Christian tradition. Normally, we read the historical and prophetic books of the Old Testament in the morning, the wisdom books at midday, and the New Testament in the evening, in which I relate this background to the Christian tradition.

After that, we have a *bhajan*, a devotional song, in an Indian language. Its words and music are simple. Everybody takes it up and repeats it. It goes on for five or ten minutes. We always end with *arati*, the Hindu ritual of waving lights before a holy image. We do it before the Blessed Sacrament. We take camphor, light it into a flame and wave the light. The original idea, I think, was that by lighting the darkened image, you brought God to light. After we wave the light, each person takes the light to their eyes with their hands, symbolizing the taking of the light of Christ to ourselves. We end this rather beautiful ritual with a prostration.

How many people participate in this community prayer?

There are six community members, but we have a great number of visitors. Often in recent years, we have had fifty or sixty people at the same time. In addition, people from the village come. At a Sunday mass, we may have more than 100 people. At weekday mass, which follows the prayer in the morning, we may have fifty or sixty. We celebrate the mass Indian style, according to a rite which has been approved by the Indian bishops and the Holy See. It is a simple adaptation of the Latin rite. We sit, according to Indian custom. We wear a shawl instead of the ordinary vestments. We use *arati* and various gestures like it during the mass, but for the most part, it follows the form of the Latin mass.

During the offertory, we offer four elements, beginning with water. We sprinkle water around the altar and on the people, and then the priest takes a sip. This is a rite of purification. Then we offer the fruits of the earth, the bread and the wine, and eight flowers. The flowers, in addition to being from the earth, symbolize the eight directions of space. In the ancient traditions, a sacrifice was always offered at the center. This was a way of relating yourself to the whole cosmos. Then we offer incense, symbolizing air, and camphor, symbolizing fire. The idea is that Christ assumes the whole creation and offers it to the Father. In this way, the mass becomes a cosmic sacrifice. At the consecration, we wave the camphor lights and use incense, but that is about all we do as far as adaptation is concerned.

You don't incorporate any of the Oriental readings into the liturgy of the word?

No, that is forbidden at present. I hope in time that it will be allowed. The Second Vatican Council said more radical adaptation may be necessary. We are hoping that in time, we will get a more Indian mass. This is a beginning, really.

You say in your book that it is important for Christians to become familiar with Eastern prayer and spirituality. Why?

It can add a new dimension to Christianity. We hardly seem to realize that Christianity comes out of Palestine and developed entirely in a Western direction. All of the structures of the church, the theology, and the prayer are Western. We have only developed one side of Christianity. When we open ourselves to the Oriental, we shall see Christ not only with a Western mind and Western character, but also with an Eastern mind and an Eastern character. Then and only then will he be universal.

Western Christianity does not appeal to the East. After hundreds of years of missionary effort, only one percent of Asia is Christian. This is not because people do not want Christ, but because they cannot take the Western structures. Our Greek theology — with its persons, natures, substances, accidents — is completely alien to the Hindu and the Buddhist. They have their own metaphysics, with a profound understanding of the universe. If we can speak in their language, great change can take place. The same with our mass. It is beautiful and significant, but it is totally different from the Hindu way of worship. Theirs would be more spontaneous, with the beating of drums and more enthusiasm. If we could adapt to the Oriental mind and character, it would be meaningful for America and for the West as well as for Asia.

What would that dimension be? In your book, you seem to use various words to describe the Eastern dimension of prayer and spirituality — imaginative, symbolic, intuitive, feminine. Is it all of these?

Yes. The words *yin* and *yang* are also used to characterize the difference between East and West. The Western world has developed the yang, the masculine, the active, rational approach to reality. The yin is the feminine, intuitive, more passive, with a synthetic sense of the whole. It characterizes the thought of the East. The East and the West have each developed in one direction, and we are at the stage when the two halves can come together. If it happens, I think humanity and Christianity will be finding their fullness. America stands between the East and West and could be the meeting place for these two traditions.

You also us the phrase "symbolic thinking" to describe the way of Eastern prayer and thought. What would be a good example of this approach?

I think the New Testament is the best example. Jesus nearly always taught in parables. What is the kingdom of God like? He immediately gives images — like a pearl, like a leaven, like a seed. St. John's Gospel is a perfect example of a symbolic theology. You can see it in the different instances he takes from the life of Christ. During his talk with Nicodemus, he speaks of the Spirit being like the wind that blows where it will. He talks to the Samaritan woman about water that will spring up to eternal life. He takes the bread, feeds the 5,000, and speaks of the bread from heaven. He speaks of himself as the good shepherd and the vine. These are symbols. They give you a theology, one that is concrete. The Greek is abstract. You need both, but the concrete is primary.

In view of the differences in language, culture, religion, geography, and life-style, do you think these Eastern modes of thought, prayer, and spirituality can be transferred to the West?

There are problems, but young people all over the world are discovering Eastern traditions. We have people from all the continents coming to our ashram. They are all in search of the same thing — trying to experience God in terms of Eastern thought and meditation. Many of them leave the church, because they do not find meaning for their lives in the way the faith is presented in the West. They come to India — to Hindu ashrams, to Buddhist monasteries and similar places — to discover their bodies, to have psychic experiences, and to begin to become aware of God. After that, if they come to a Christian community, the Christian symbols begin to come to life for them. Some come back to the church as a result. I think this is a strong movement.

What about the people who can't go to India? What about the American nuclear family, in which there are children and mothers who work outside the home? More and more, they are one-parent families, and frequently they are caught up in what we call the rat race. How is what you are talking about going to reach these people?

You already have in America innumerable communities from the East — Hindu, Buddhist, Sikh, and others. My hope is that more Christian communities which follow these Oriental methods will spring up in America. Shantivanam in Kansas is a good example. A very interesting liturgy with many Oriental elements is developing there. The same is true of Osage Monastery in Oklahoma. Householders bring their families to these liturgies. It is from places like this that I would hope the movement could spread to America.

We spoke about alienation from the body. I would like to ask you about alienation from work, which seems to be a serious problem in the United States and perhaps in much of the industrialized West. How does what you are saying address itself to that?

This is a big problem. I feel the current system of technology is alienating. I am a disciple of E.F. Schumacher and his belief that "small is beautiful." I hope Western science and technology will begin to decentralize, developing smaller groups and smaller industries. We must also recover the relationship to the land. One person having hundreds of acres is not, in my judgment, the right method of farming. I think a great many people find real pleasure in working on the land.

Fritjof Capra, the physicist, in his fascinating book, *The Turning Point,* says we are moving out of a culture which was mechanistic and materialistic and moving into one which is organic and holistic. Such a culture relates the human being to the cosmos and to one's fellow human beings. This has the effect of making work human again.

I have tried at various times in my life to relate the Christian admonition to "pray always" to work, with the idea of making the work experience meditative rather than alienating. Do you have suggestions for doing that?

It is difficult in the current society. The Benedictine tradition is one of trying to make our work a means of prayer. But then, a Benedictine monastery is usually in the country. We're much nearer to natural surroundings and natural ways, although I must admit that in America, the monasteries usually have highly mechanized farms. I don't think that is conducive to prayer. Frankly, we are still a long way from making work more human and a means of prayer. I am hopeful, but we may have to go through a difficult period, maybe a catastrophe, before we can recover a more human, a more contemplative way of life.

What about the contemplative way of life you are living and the urgent problems of the world? Do you find a connection?

Yes. My conviction is that world problems cannot be solved at their own level. As long as you remain on a human level — and still more on the material level — there is no solution to the problems of the world, such as the conflicts between Jews and Arabs, black and white, Russia and America, capitalism and communism. Only when you go beyond the human and discover the divine mystery, which is present in the heart of every human being, do you get the necessary insight. Then you are able to deal with these problems. I think it is through contemplative communities and an awakening of contemplative prayer that an understanding and an answer to world problems will be found.

How would attempting to rise above the human situation in contemplation help us to deal with such an urgent issue as nuclear weapons? How is contemplation going to help keep nuclear weapons from exploding and killing us all?

It's a big question, no doubt about that. I honestly think the answer is to be found in the life of Jesus. He was faced with the Roman empire and its problems — slavery, economic oppression, and social injustice. He responded not by trying to face those problems in the concrete, but by the total surrender of his life to the Father and awakening a power, a spirit in the Roman empire which eventually transformed it. I think a similar transformation must take place today.

My hope is that it will come through small, contemplative communities springing up all over the world. As you meditate, you discover a deep, hidden power at work in the universe, which you haven't recognized. Once it is recognized and begins to act, the process of transformation begins. The victory of Christianity came only through hundreds of martyrs and terrible suffering, and, I think, we are probably going to have a difficult time in the next century or two. I believe spiritual power is eventually going to be stronger than nuclear power. That is my only hope.

How is the spiritual power going to be stronger than nuclear power?

We say the crucifixion of Jesus released the most powerful force in the universe. But it is a hidden force. It takes a long time, and people have to undergo a great transformation before that force can come into play and transform the world. It is our responsibility to help bring it about.

That force is the Holy Spirit?

Yes, the Spirit that is present in the church, but which Christians as a whole realize very, very inadequately. Contemplation is living in the Spirit, in Christ, in total surrender to the Father. That is the power of redemption for the world. It begins with individuals and small groups and spreads from there.

How must one pray and meditate to discover or bring about this power of redemption? What is the one thing a person must do above all else?

You must persevere. Many people get discouraged. They ask God for things, and they don't happen. They feel, what good is it? Or they do this contemplative prayer, and they feel they are empty, and that nothing is happening. Perseverance in faith is most necessary. You have to go on day by day, week by week, month by month, and then you will see your life will begin to change.

To me, the principal sign that your prayer is effective is that you receive guidance in your life. You begin to feel more and more that you are not an isolated individual, that you are not working in a haphazard way. You feel that some other power is working in you and through you, and your life is being shaped and guided. You are confident then that the same thing is happening all over the world. There is a power shaping human destiny, although it all seems chaotic, and we may all be blown up in a nuclear war. Yet, there is this hidden power always at work. It is the power of grace, of salvation. You develop an awareness of this as you meditate, but you have to persevere through discouragement and apparent failures, until you discover God is present, God is at work, and your life is in his hands.

11
Prayer as Life,
Prayer as Time

Juan-Lorenzo Hinojosa

Juan-Lorenzo Hinojosa teaches at the Oblate School of Theology in San Antonio, Texas. He is director of a program that prepares lay people for ministry, conducts programs for Mexican-American parishes, and teaches credit courses for seminarians and others at the school of theology. He also gives spiritual direction and conducts retreats and workshops, particularly for Hispanics. He was born June 24, 1946, in Bolivia. While growing up, he lived in the United States as well as in South America. During his childhood, three traumatic events occurred: His parents divorced, his mother died, and he attended a military boarding school for three years. He has a doctorate in spiritual theology from the Graduate Theological Union in Berkeley, California. He and his wife, Sarah, have five children. Dr. Hinojosa was interviewed while giving a summer workshop on Hispanic spirituality sponsored by Retreats International at the University of Notre Dame.

My prayer breaks down into two kinds. One I call prayer of encounter. This is prayer in which life and prayer are one. There's no distraction. Certain key experiences, often centering on events in my daily life, are prayer in the deepest sense of the word. I am thinking, for example, of key moments in my life that sent me in one direction or another.

Second, there is prayer as response. In it, life and prayer are not totally identified. Here, I am thinking more of my prayer time, or prayers we say as a family. My own "prayer of response" tends toward the devotional. It has a strong "heart" orientation. For instance, I find a lot of meaning in offering flowers to God. That is a sign of love. I always pray with lighted candles and incense. I find a prayer space meaningful, and for many years, we have had one in our home. When we have been able, we have consecrated a room as a sacred space for prayer. When we haven't, we have set aside a corner. We don't do anything in that space but pray. It has a table, candles, Scripture, possibly flowers.

Posture is important for me. That comes from experience with Eastern religions. My back must be straight and aligned but comfortable at the same time. In the prayer space, I have a Zen pillow or a low bench I put over my legs and sit on. My personal prayer tends to include Scripture. Writing is another key part of my prayer. I find it very rich. I dialogue with God about my life, and where I am, and where I am sensing God is.

Often, I reflect on my life as part of my prayer, what is happening currently as well as the past. I go back to my journals. That is a deep experience of prayer. It is especially satisfying when I am in a period of desolation and dryness and do not sense God's presence. Also, my prayer is now intertwined with my ministry. Anything I do, I pray. I do that, for example, with preparations for my lectures and classes.

My personal prayer also has a strong liturgical focus. I find the triduum, as well as the rest of Lent and all of Advent, to be very rich. These seasons play a big role in our family prayer. We have traditions around these seasons, especially Advent. I also find feast days satisfying and enriching.

As for my family's prayer, here is an example: From here, I am going to South America for three weeks to visit my father, who lives there and is ill. I haven't been there for about nine years. I am going to be separated from my family for more than a month. In addition, my older daughter is going to South America for about six months. We have never had this kind of separation. Before I left, we gathered around the table for our last meal. I intoned the prayer and included the reality of the upcoming separation, asking God to be with us as we went through it. As a result of the pain we were sensing, my wife and I started to cry. We experienced life in its depth at that moment.

We celebrate feast days of the children. We tell the stories of the saints they are named for. We celebrate birthdays. We bake the cakes. We celebrate all major feasts of the church. Celebration is central to our life and prayer as a family.

Personally, I need a regular time to pray. If I don't have this, I tend to lose it. I have structured into my day a half hour of prayer, usually before I get into the day's work, but I am flexible about when and even where. If I feel like going out and walking for prayer, I do. If I feel like staying within the prayer space, I do that. I have a certain ritual for entering that space. I spend a moment standing before it trying to recollect or center myself. Then I enter the space, usually in a prayer posture. I read the Scripture or other books I use as aids — for example, I like the exercises in Anthony de Mello's book, *Sadhana*. Sometimes, I write, which is prayer for me. Sometimes, I light a candle or go out and get a flower and bring it in to the prayer space. That is an act of adoration or worship.

I try to adopt an attitude of listening, of open awareness before God. Sometimes, I have moments of thanksgiving and praise of God. Often, there is a dryness, a lack of an inclination toward God and prayer. Sometimes, I reflectively listen to my life — current events, problems, people. Sometimes, I touch the mystery of God in my life. That leads to joy and happiness.

What have you heard recently in your prayer with regard to your life?

Lately, I have been bringing the situation with my father to prayer. He is quite ill. Should I go to South America? I can't really afford to, but, after praying about it, I felt I needed to be with him and the family, which is being strained by his sickness. I felt God's guidance with this problem. That's an example of bringing my life to prayer.

I also feel my prayer flows into my life and affects what I do. For instance, when I am to make a presentation, I ask the Lord to show me how to structure it and what to emphasize. If I am in touch enough with the process, I become aware of a sense which arises from deep within me that it should be one way as opposed to another. The nonbeliver would say it is intuition, but I feel it is connected with God. For example, last year, I gave the keynote here at Retreats International. I did a presentation on what it means to be a bridge person. In doing that, I tried to articulate my own walk with God and share it with people. I feel that's when I am the most powerful. Then I sense God's presence in what I am saying and in what happens to people as they hear me.

"Articulating my own walk with God" sounds like the other type of prayer, prayer as encounter. What experiences have you had that you equate with prayer?

I moved into adulthood in a downward trajectory, a movement into darkness. I had some bad experiences in a military boarding school as a child. My parents divorced. I was back and forth between the U.S., where my mother lived, and South America, where my father was. My mother died. I was filled with anger and resentment, and my actions became antisocial. I got into drinking heavily, breaking rules, and undercutting the system as much as I could. I had brushes with the police and got thrown into jail, in South America, for stealing automobiles in order to joyride.

I started to study engineering at a college in the U.S. and got into antiwar activities. Because I was active in the Students for a Democratic Society, the U.S. authorities threatened to deport me. I was on the fringe. I starting getting into drugs, mainly marijuana. I read Jean Paul Sartre and Albert Camus and other existentialists, and their philosophny on the meaningless of life resonated with me. I was living almost totally for pleasure. Drugs and experiences with women energized me. But even that wore thin.

I dropped out of school, moved west, found myself in the Haight-Asbury district of San Francisco with the counterculture. I was soon initiated into its major sacrament — LSD. The world had been closing in on me, but psychedelic drugs opened a new world. For three years, I did a lot of exploration with mescaline and LSD.

In 1967, that period ended with what I call my "mirror experience." It began a second phase, a period of searching. The experience is hard to describe. It was almost as if a mirror was put in front of me, and I saw my inner self, instead of my outer reflection. What I saw was disturbing. I saw a person who lived his life out of selfishness. I saw a person whose life had lead to a dead end. Basically, I felt that my own will or ego, had led me to this point. It was a moment of truth.

Once I saw *that*, with my inner vision, my life began to turn. I knew I had to totally re-vision my life. But I couldn't figure out how. Because my will had brought me to where I was, I felt it couldn't help me to move on. I began to search. This search lasted, perhaps symbolically, about nine months and was a period of intense spiritual activity. First, I looked among the Zen Buddhists. I tried to create a *zendo* in my apartment.

During this time, I also remember seeing *The Gospel of Matthew*, a film made by a Marxist. In it, actors spoke the words directly out of that Gospel. I was impressed. Later, I read some of the passages. A key one was the parable of the "pearl of great price," in which a merchant sold all he had to buy it. Another was the treasure hidden in the field. Another: "Seek first the kingdom of God, and all things will be given to you." Another was about the birds of the air and the lilies of the field. I now know that, in a sense, these passages and parables summarize the Gospel: Living your life with God means you must hand yourself over, and that must be done not on your own terms, but on God's terms, and it requires your all.

At the time, these passages impressed me so much that I took all my money — about $1,500 — and gave it away. I decided not to handle money at all. I felt I was guided by God in this, although I would never have put it in those terms. If you don't have money, you can't go places or do things. You are at the mercy of the wind, and I felt myself becoming like a sail that could be receptive to God in that wind.

I entered a heavily ascetical period. I limited my diet. I didn't eat meat. I was not eating vegetables, only grains. I limited myself to two cups of water per day. I continued my Zen practice, but a devastating thing happened. A friend of mine came back from Mexico with some peyote. Peyote, which contains mescaline, is the sacrament some Indians use in their religious rites. I felt it was right for me to take peyote, because it had somehow appeared. Circumstances were becoming symbolic for me. I went into an experience in which I sensed my ascetical practice had failed. My will was still leading me. I felt at the end of this dark, painful, and hellish experience that I had gotten nowhere. My practice, it seemed, had only built up my ego and hadn't touched my deep center.

I moved in with friends who practiced yoga. I took it up, though with little hope it would answer my search. I had a rich experience, although I reached a plateau which confirmed this was not the answer for me. Through various circumstances, I got to Hawaii, and there I had another experience, one that brought the searching phase of my journey to an end.

I couldn't sleep one night. I had a sense of excitement. I felt something was going to happen, and it did. I had a very unusual experience; in fact, I have never heard of anyone having an experience like this. I was in bed. I felt myself get up. I mean that literally. I *felt* myself get out of bed. It wasn't my will, my volition, or my ego, that got me out of bed, even though I did leave the bed. This was a strange experience, and I was afraid. I wanted to know if I could stop it, and I could. But I sensed that it was good, so I allowed it.

For weeks before, I had been trying to keep myself in shape, and I would try to run from the house where I was staying to a church several blocks away. I guess the type of life I had led, including my severe diet, had weakened me. Whenever I tried to run this distance, I would be exhausted by the time I got halfway. This evening, an autonomous force or power was leading me. It took me outside. I felt myself begin to run. The night was clear and beautiful. I felt I was the only person on earth. I ran. Running was different. It was totally synchronous and harmonious. I didn't feel exhausted. My body seemed to flow gracefully. I looked to my right, and there was the church. I had passed it! I kept on running, and I felt I could run and run and run.

I learned something from this experience, although it was primarily nonverbal, and it is hard for me to put it into words. It had something to do with God. It also had something to do with allowing myself to be used, with allowing a deep power within me to help me function in a way I had never functioned before. I felt myself begin to walk. I just let my legs carry me. I saw a cemetery, a Japanese cemetery. I thought I might be dead, or that I was about to die. I didn't know what I would find. An open grave? I was afraid.

At that moment, I turned myself over. Basically, I surrendered my life to the power, or God, or whatever I was experiencing. As a result, not only my everyday life, but also my death, became acceptable to me. I went into the cemetery. I walked out of the cemetery. I realized my life wasn't going to end right there. I continued to walk, and eventually I was led back to the house and into bed. I slept that night as I never slept before or since.

That marked the beginning of a new trajectory in my life. God entered it quite actively as a presence for empowerment and guidance. I began to sense that God did not want me to serve him as a loner. I had a sense that God was calling me to seek him as part of a community of people. I had been leading the life of a *sadhu,* wandering Hindu ascetic.

I began to discern what community to seek. My first inclination was to ask God, "Why don't I seek you as a Hindu?" I had a lot of resonance with yoga and the whole Hindu tradition. What came back to me was, "Well, you could do that, but. . . ." So, I searched within myself and asked, "What if I seek you as a Buddhist?" I had studied the teachings of the Buddha, and I was attracted to them. Again, the response was, "You could do that, but. . . ."

Then I felt this question coming to me: "What would be the hardest thing for you to do?" Well, immediately I realized the hardest thing for me to do would be even to consider Christianity. I had had very bad experience with the church, especially with the clergy. I frankly did not feel I had ever met a holy Christian. I did not feel what I would now call the Spirit of God was present in Christianity. I could make neither heads nor tails out of a God who was hanging on a cross, who was supposed to be human and divine. I was repelled by Christianity. Clearly, seeking God as a Christian would be hardest for me.

So, I said, "OK, I hope you know what you are doing!" Once I said, "yes," I experienced a profound peace. I felt something from outside of me which filled my whole being. An experience of peace and joy filled me and confirmed that this was the right decision. From that point, I began the adventure that is my Christianity — the seeking of God in this community. It has been a tremendously rich experience: the deeper I go, the wider it gets.

As I look back, I can say that what began there was a process of reconciliation. The words God spoke to me were, "Be reconciled." The first focus of that reconciliation was to be my family. The second was to be with society and culture. I was called to give things a chance. That included the church. I hadn't done that before. This focus on reconciliation continues to be strong in my life. I see myself as a bridge person, a person who puts things that have been separated back together. That is the focus of my work, my theology, my prayer.

What about your family prayer?

Since our children's birth, we bless them every night. We say, "May you know, love, and serve the Lord all the days of your life," or a similar blessing. Blessings are a very important part of our family prayer. The most intense times of our family prayer are during Advent and Lent. During these seasons, we try to gather regularly and share prayer, especially around rituals. The children love rituals. We frequently use the prayer space for this. We also use the Advent wreath and the creche.

The morning of Christmas is magical. It is the most beautiful experience. My wife and I stay up late preparing. When the kids get up in the morning, it's still dark. The Christmas tree lights are on. The candles of the Advent wreath are no longer purple, but bright red or white. We light candles around the creche, and, finally, we place the child in the crib as a symbol of Christ's coming among us.

We file into the room with the youngest leading and each of us carrying candles. Of course, the kids are kind of looking at their presents, but more and more, they have been able to focus on what Christmas is about. This year, they didn't even look all that much at their gifts until after our ritual.

We also have other family rituals, especially around Easter. On Holy Thursday, we wash each other's feet. We express our love to each other. My wife and I emphasize to our children that we as parents are their servants. In this way, we try to initiate them in the basic servanthood that is part of being family and church. On Friday, we have silence in the home from noon to 3 p.m.

We do a family passion play. After we read the Gospel account of the death of Jesus, each of the children goes around the house gathering religious art objects. We put them all in a giant box. We take the candle that has been by the Scriptures, put it in the box, and blow it out. Then we put in the Scriptures, close the box, and put a cloth over it. That becomes a symbolic tomb in our house for Friday and Saturday.

Sunday morning is a kind of magical time again. The place is beautiful. Candles are lighted. The cloth is now lying in front of the box. It is like a burial cloth that is no longer being used. The children look inside the box and see a candle buring and the Scriptures opened to the account of Mary Magdalene's experience of the risen Lord. My wife or I will take up the Scriptures and tell them the story — powerfully tell the story, not just read it. The religious objects are no longer in the box, but have been hidden around the room. The kids find them and put them back in their places. It's a fun time, but also a deep experience. Taking the objects down and putting them in the box symbolizes the darkness and death of Good Friday. Putting them back symbolizes the rebirth of the Easter experience.

As for other family occasions, recently we've begun to use a blessing cup ritual for special times. We have a special cup and say prayers, and then we share the cup. Sometimes, we also break bread and pass it with the cup. We don't call it eucharist; it's an agape, I suppose. It is a deep expression of our family being church. The children really appreciate it.

Is it true that family religious customs and rituals traditionally have been important among Spanish-speaking people?

Yes. The Hispanic culture has been deeply Christian. It is in the bones of the people, almost. People have *altarsitos* in their homes. *Altarsitos* are little prayer spaces where they have statues and candles. They are quite common and are important in many, many families. Some have grottoes outside with a little statue of Mary of St. Francis. These are symbols of a religious dimension to family life. For instance, for a young girl's passage into womanhood, families have a *quinceañera*. It is a religious event, in part, and there's always a mass.

Do Hispanic families still have home festivals to celebrate major feasts of the church year?

The Hispanic population is too diverse to generalize, but in traditional families, that is still the case. In such families, the *abuelita*, the grandmother, is central. She is usually the most devoted. She is constantly at church. Devotions and prayers such as the rosary are very much a part of this spirituality. Often, the *abuelita* passes on the faith to the grandchildren.

I find many people still resonating with the old ways. For example, *posadas* are big events in San Antonio during Advent. *Posadas* started as a religious act of the people, and the official church wasn't much involved. During the *posadas*, a young woman and man are dressed like Joseph and Mary, put on a donkey, and taken around to various homes. Traditional songs are sung along the way. At each home, Joseph and Mary ask whether they can come in, and people tell them why they can't, that there is no room. They continue from house to house, finally arriving at a place where they are allowed in, and there's a big party. It's quite a religious event.

Similar events take place during Lent. There are many passion plays. Someone plays the part of Jesus, takes the cross, and goes around the neighborhood. This ritual usually winds up at a church, where there is a reflection on the death of Christ. *Postorales*, plays which depict parts of Jesus' life, are very much alive today. In New Mexico, you have the *penitentes*. This is an ancient tradition involving a group of men, who gather for spiritual exercises during Lent. These often involve vigils and hours and hours of prayers in a cruciform position, culminating in the rites of Easter.

Baptisms, first communions, and marriages are occasions for big gatherings in Hispanic families. So are wakes. On such occasions, everybody in the family gathers. There is a strong sense of family and the spiritual. The great thing about these events is that so many people get involved. Take weddings, for example. It is not unusual to have hundreds of people taking part in different facets of the celebration. In some cases, people pay for a portion of the festivities. You have the *padrino* of this — the ring, for example — and the *madrino* of that — the cake, for example. All of this helps the couple put together the marriage celebration. Theologically, you could say each person is bringing his or her gift from the Spirit and sharing it. The result is a celebration of a marriage in Christ in a very deep sense. And, of course, the result is a tremendous festivity.

A striking image I have of Hispanic spirituality is that of seeing pilgrims walking on their knees at the shrine of Our Lady of Guadalupe. It seems edifying and bizarre at the same time.

The spirituality of many Hispanics, in particular Mexicans, tends to be very concrete, very tactile. Touch is important. They will touch statues, for example. They write notes, perhaps containing prayers of petition, and stick them in a statue. They believe there's power in places and things, and that they have an impact on life. That's the world view this comes out of. Touching something holy is an expression of that.

Pilgrimage is also important to Hispanics. A pilgrimage can be undertaken either because one wants to or because of a promise one has made. Thus, going to Guadalupe and touching the statues and symbols is important. It involves both the tactile and the pilgrimage aspect.

What does the church at large have to learn from the traditional Hispanic prayer and spirituality?

On one level, the Hispanic people still have a strong sense of the sacred. I think that has been lost among many other people. Hispanics can help the church regain that. They can do the same with the importance of touch. On the one hand, that can be seen as traditional or old-fashioned, yet at this time, avant-garde people in the church are talking about the importance of touch. The Hispanic experience can help the church at large regain this sense of touch. It can be important to get beyond our narrow spiritualism to a more holistic approach.

To what extent are the ideas and practices of mainstream Catholics in the United States aberrations? For example, I wonder about the idea of stripping the churches of much of their artifacts and symbols. Can there be a place for the visual and tactile? I know some churches that are hiding their candles. Maybe we are at a moment of stripping before we can recover these things in a new way.

What is the role of prayer and spirituality in the new movements coming from Latin America — the base communities and liberation theology?

I have had no experience with base communities that are solely Hispanic, but prayer in small groups has been central to my life for the last ten years. As a couple, we have had a small group of people with whom we pray, with whom we share our lives. The group we are in now has a few Hispanics and a number of Anglos, or non-Hispanics. For us, gathering with other people to share faith is constitutive of our spiritual life. It provides empowerment, support, and often a challenge or an inspiration. This is part of what I spoke of earlier — seeking God in community.

Our current group meets every other week, rotating homes. The hosts are in charge of preparing. We usually take the Scripture readings for the next Sunday and reflect on them beforehand. The hosts will give us focusing reflections on the readings, and then we prayerfully read them out loud. We share what they say to us, how they challenge us. Very often, that will move into prayer.

People often work through situations and problems in their life. It can get very personal, and the sharing can be deep. That is the richest part of it for me. For example, a man and woman are struggling because he doesn't have a job. He has been working for the church for seven years, and he has had a difficult time finding a position. They brought that to the group, and we prayed about it. This is a example of people bringing their lives into this small group.

We did that when we were deciding whether I would enter church work full-time. I gathered a group of about twenty people from our Sunday eucharistic community. We told them what we were thinking about doing and asked their help in discernment. Would they confirm this particular move? We have done that with three or four major decisions. Each time, there was a consensus. Each time, I felt I now had confirmation through the community that what I was considering was from God.

What about liberation theology? What affect has it had on prayer and spirituality?

The liberation movements have had a strong impact. Nothing has given me more of a sense of original sin than seeing the oppression of different groups and getting in touch with the reality of structural evil. The first time I got in touch with the fact that I was part of an oppressive group was a deep experience of prayer. Among other things, I realized structural sin has little to do with choice. It's not so much a case of choosing to sin, but rather a matter of being born into it. A situation of evil predates you, and you slip into it. In that way, it is like original sin. In a way, I think, that is what original sin is, although this is an expanded notion of it.

For me, the process of liberation is intimately tied up with conversion. Conversion isn't just an internal affair. It also involves becoming freed from all kinds of prejudices and barriers between oneself and other people and groups. The woman's movement is a significant example of this for me. The idea of liberation from structures is integral to spirituality. It dovetails with what I see as the central experience of spiritual life, *metonoia* or conversion. A big part of that is dying to the inauthenticities within us that block life. This includes sexism, classism, ageism, and all the things the liberation movements are denouncing and trying to change.

This process of *metanoia* tends to be painful, because you are dealing with a self-concept that must die. That is painful. Death is painful. Loss is painful. We have a certain investment in seeing ourselves as we are. *Metanoia* has two aspects: Turning from something and turning toward something else. In "turning from," people must often abandon what they believe to be true. A man dealing with women's issues must do that. So must an Anglo dealing with Hispanics. In addition, this "turning from" involves coming to the knowledge that one is part of the problem, and that can be even more painful.

In the second part of *metanoia*, people turn toward a new perspective. They might never reach the point where they would no longer be part of the problem, but at least they are moving toward becoming part of the solution. They would be opening new levels of their affectivity. They would become more sensitive to values they had not been in touch with before, or had suppressed. *Metanoia* has a strong structural dimension and social justice focus.

How is metanoia's *social justice dimension supposed to work?*

First, people become more enlightened as to their part in structures of oppression. They begin to see their prejudices, their darkness. This self-knowledge is freeing. Catherine of Siena said self-knowledge is the fuel of prayer. Second, as a result of this type of prayer and self-awareness, people attempt to change. Being involved in trying to change the structures of evil is a spiritual act. Often, that will include a prophetic effort. A prophetic stance frequently leads people deep into the paschal mystery, especially in terms of crucifixion. They often draw upon themselves the wrath of the forces that have not undergone *metanoia* and do not want change. This can lead to a total entry into the paschal mystery — martyrdom.

We are in an exciting time in the church's life, when the prophetic dimension is again present. Tertullian said the church was born out of the blood of martyrs. I believe that is true. We are in a major period of church renewal, and perhaps the church is being "reborn" in martyrs' blood. In Latin America, there are Archbishop Oscar Romero, the four women from the U.S. who were shot to death, and many others. They are examples to us of prayer and life becoming one.

12
Burning in the Bones,
Dancing in the Street

Tria Thompson

Tria Thompson is a dancer, choreographer, actress, giver of retreats, and teacher with the Fountain Square Fools, a troupe in Cincinnati, Ohio, that proclaims the Gospel of Jesus Christ through the performing arts. She has a master's degree in religious education and the performing arts from Loyola University in Chicago. She was born in Cleveland, Ohio, January 15, 1947. For seventeen years, she was a member of the Sisters of Charity of St. Augustine of Richfield, Ohio.

She has taught at the Institute of Pastoral Studies at Loyola University and was on the staff of the Institute in Creation-Centered Spirituality when it was at Mundelein College in Chicago. Subjects she teaches include body prayer, dance as extrovert meditation, liturgical spirituality, and the performing arts and social justice. She was interviewed while teaching and working in Chicago.

I find dance very prayerful. There's a lot of power in bodily movement. Unfortunately, Western spirituality has lost much of that. The body has been negated from prayer for a long time. Bringing the body back into prayer alarms some people. They don't realize the effect it is having on them. They'll be upset without knowing why. But even when it upsets people, dance is healing. That is one reason dance has played an important role in the rituals of most religions, including, for example, the religion of Native Americans. Even in early Christian times, dance was important. The early Christians used to dance on the tombs of the martyrs. Apparently, some people got carried away and got too sensual. That is a reason, I think, that fear of dance exists today. People think it is too sensual.

I don't think it can be too sensual, and I don't experience myself as being too sensual. Dance is incarnational. As Christians, we become God's Word when the Word is spoken in us. It is enfleshed in us. As I studied Scripture and dance, I began to see that dancing is a way of becoming God's Word. You take the creative energy of the word, and you become it.

You see that happening to the prophets. They had a call to prophecy, to speak God's Word, and in effect, to become God's Word. I relate very much, for example to the idea in Jeremiah that speaking God's Word burns your bones. At one point, Jeremiah says he went out and did what God wanted, he spoke God's Word. But Jeremiah is angry, because things didn't turn out as he expected. "I did it for you, but you duped me," he says to God. "You told me to go out there and do this for you. I went, and they all told me, 'You fool, you idiot.' They were throwing stones at me." Then Jeremiah says he isn't going to speak God's Word anymore, but, Scripture says, it "burned in his bones." And he does it again. He has to.

That's how I feel. Praying through dance burns in my bones. I cannot not dance. If I were censured for dancing, I still would have to do it. I believe I am called to do it. But it is not easy. And because I believe that art — in my case, dancing — is related to social justice, I have taken my dancing out in the street to reach people, to get God's message out. That has been hard at times.

In Isaiah, I find another idea that means a lot to me as far as praying through dance is concerned. It is the idea of being purified. You must be purified. You have to go through the shipwreck experience, through the fire experience, for prayer to grow. I don't think the shipwreck experience is easy. The pain of dancing, the pain of being misunderstood, is to me a way of purifying myself and strengthening my dance as prayer.

Then there's Ezekiel. He eats the scroll to become God's Word.

Eating it? Becoming it? Imagine! To me, dance is like that, because you are becoming God's Word alive. If I am not God's Word alive, I can't understand my reason for being. We are in the world to speak the Word, to incarnate the holy.

We are holy. I believe our bodies are holy. And because I believe that, I take my instrument — my body, which is a beautiful thing — and I say to a group as I dance, "Well, what do you think of your body?"

Christianity has always said the body is good, but we don't take it out of the realm of ideology and into the incarnational. Body images have been terrible. That's why people are afraid of their bodies, and why they are afraid of dance as a prayer form. People's reaction to seeing a dancer's body in front of them is going to depend, in large part, on the view they have of their own body.

We have to realize, as Psalm 139 says, that we are "fearfully and wonderfully made." For me, that psalm is a key to seeing the body as prayer. The psalm says, "You knit me in my mother's womb. I give thanks that I am fearfully and wonderfully made." That gives me a sense of wonder about the human body, and how it is formed. The first chapters of Genesis also convey this wonder and beauty. There you have a wonderfully mystical view of the earth and the universe. You also see this mystical view in Teresa of Avila and Thomas Merton. We tend to think of Merton sitting and writing, and that he was closed off from the outside world, but he wasn't. He was very connected to it.

That's what mysticism is, I think. It's being able to connect yourself and what you are doing with the fact that you are part of a bigger body, a bigger creation. You are part of the cosmos, you are part of the body of Christ. You're each a cell. Think of all the little pores in your body. You can't even see them, but they are all there, breathing in. If each little pore wasn't breathing, you would suffocate. The more in tune you are with loving your body, the more you can connect with what is happening in El Salvador or disconnect from the apartheid in South Africa. Those "pores" are being blocked. They can't get breath, and it makes the rest of the body sick. We are called to do something about situations like that.

When I teach dance, I am mindful of people's attitudes toward their body. The reactions are interesting. At workshops, people will say to me, "I like dancing, but I like praying the *other* way," or "I like *really* praying." Their attitude is: This is a nice thing to do, but I pray better praying the real way. Making the connection between prayer and dance takes time. That is why I like working with a group for a while. I see the wonder of people's development. I see them going from a closed fist to an open hand. It's amazing. It's so beautiful. It's God's work.

How do you prepare a dance as prayer?

The process of making dance as prayer is interesting. I do it several ways. Sometimes, I'll go in a studio or church and start moving with some inner beat. Or, I take a position with my body and feel it. Maybe I am in a particular mood. I may be sad. I may be grateful. I want to get in touch with that feeling, not just think about it. You have to feel in your gut, in your center. Movement comes from your center, from your pelvic area, from your stomach, from your lungs. So, you have to feel in those areas, if you are going to dance.

Sometimes, I will just sit. Sometimes, I will rock. Sometimes, I have religious feelings. Sometimes, I will "see" things, but more often, I have feelings. I know something more than knowing. It comes through the kinesthetic sense, which is movement awareness. It's a bodily sense, a sort of sixth sense. Sometimes, I just listen to the music.

I put in at least twenty hours of listening to any music I am going to dance to. That is my goal, but from time to time, people will come and want me to dance the next day, and so the improvisational skill takes over, or at least I hope it does. But when I want to work on a piece I really like to form, to have it be something good, I like to take time with it. When I am doing a dance by myself, I go through and feel it. If something feels right, I leave it in, and if it doesn't, I take it out. I also have my dance teacher look at it and have people critique me.

I have changed the way I work with a group of people as a choreographer. I used to write out all of the dance. But I found that people couldn't do the things I had prepared. It wasn't prayerful for them, and I would get frustrated. Now I go with the people who are there, see how they are feeling, try to do things that relax them, and get them to experiment and to feel the music with me. Sometimes, I will tell them to follow me until they can't anymore. In this way, people create out of their own experience and prayer. They create out of their being. Then, I will give them little techniques, such as turns or sitting or standing in a particular way.

A person might say, "I don't feel good in this part. I'd feel better doing that." So then we will change parts. There is a real interweaving. It's kind of like how I feel with God, like the creator and the created. There is a great deal of interchange. It's in and out, now you, now me, now me, now you.

In group dances, the most important thing is for the dancers to be with me and each other. We must all be connected. And not only that, we must all feel it. A key element in achieving this feeling is for people to let their defenses down and allow the Spirit to come through. A feeling occurs when you do that. You can feel your aura. You can sense it. Many people are getting into that kind of thing these days. Esalen, an institute on the West coast where they do healing and yoga, has for years done something it calls "sensing your aura." On holy cards, we have the saints with halos. That's their aura.

Moving and sensing people being with you, and breathing with you, is profound. It's very moving, to the point of tears. I say to people again and again, "I can't tell you how to do it, but when we do it, you'll know it." And I want you to keep praying that you'll be able to let go and feel it in your gut rather than just think it with your mind." When that happens, it is so wonderful. And it happens! Many times, the feeling is "that's incredible!"

If dancing is becoming God's Word, how do you dance the Scripture?

I have danced to the Our Father, the Magnificat, and many other passages from the Bible. I did a dance for the Women's Ordination Conference to a Magnificat that had been rewritten in feminist language. To me, it was a great honor. I'm very much into Mary. Who was she as a woman? So it was an honor for me to dance her canticle in a language that wasn't sexist, especially as I was going to try to become that language. And not only that, I was able to do it in front of these women, my sisters. I felt gifted to incarnate its meaning. I recorded the text beforehand and played it during the dance. I particularly remember the words that said something like, "The proud will be put into the dust, and the lowly will be lifted." This suggests the cycle we go through: To be holy, to be holistic, we all have to pass through being lowly and being raised.

What did you do in the dance to communicate the message of the text?

It is important for people doing dance as prayer to realize you cannot be literal. I don't take every single word and try to act it out. For example, take the "poor." I don't ask myself, "How will I be poor?" Rather, I more or less try to get into a movement pattern.

The music was playing as I entered and began to dance the Magnificat. Then I sat with my legs crossed, with one knee under my chin and the other leg around it. That is a dancer's sit. Then I did a contraction. In a contraction, the movement comes from your pelvis and your stomach. It's a sharp movement in which you pull in. I was sitting on the ground and contracting, with my arm coming down while my leg was going up. Now, why did I pick that movement? Well, because it felt to me that was what I should do. I didn't approach it by saying, "Of all the movements I know, what movement will I start out with?" I try to expand my movement patterns and phrases with dance lessons. I go at least twice a week for a lesson. I do that to give the body more vocabulary and to have it feel itself into different positions and to experiment on different levels.

But, back to the Magnificat. After going through the beginning contraction, I went into a yoga position which is called the "cat." You do that while you are sitting with your buttocks on your heels. You come forward and touch you head to the ground, and then you reverse the movement. During the words, "My soul proclaims the greatness of God," I went to one knee. As the words, "My spirit rejoices in God, who gives me freedom," were spoken, I did some *sisonnes* — runs and jumps with both feet that end by landing on one foot. Then I did a couple of jumps left to right with my arms stretched out to the congregation to sort of ask, how can this be?

I incorporate mime into some of my dances. Mime and dance are different. Mime is a much more focused energy movement. Dance is more of a pattern and keeps moving constantly, whereas mime concentrates on focused movement and illusion. I incorporated a little mime into this Magnificat, because I was dancing to a script. I wanted some connection between the script and the dance, so people wouldn't get lost.

I did some movements about breaking shackles and trying to get people to listen to the needs of others. That part was more mime than dance. During the words, "Sharing your bread with the hungry," I went from an up-on-my-toes position — that's a *releve* — to the ground, rolled over, and came back up. I continued moving and went into a *tableau* here and another there. A *tableau* is stopped movement, sort of like a frozen picture. I also remember trying to "pick up" the big burden the poor were carrying. As I carried that load, it became lighter and lighter. Then I raised the burden up around my head, and the movement kept going up and up. As I did that, I did a *pirouette,* which is a fast turn on one foot, with an *arabesque,* which is an extension of one leg behind your body. Then I went into an *attitude,* which is bending the leg and moving it around the body.

The movement was from burden to lightness. The words were about the poor having been formed by God, and great things having been done in them, and that God was expecting great things from me. The words "God expects great things from me" were in the text a couple of times. At those times, I ran toward the congregation with outstretched arms, lifting my sternum high and looking up and around.

I love to have eye contact with the people I am praying with. I strive for that, because I think it is important. It is very healing. I think, too, that it draws people who are watching from being passive to being actively with me. I can feel if I am connecting with them.

After the burden was lifted, the movement got technical. The last part of the narration was something about "when you come to serve the Lord, prepare yourself for a journey." I contracted down to the ground, did a few turns, and went off.

How would one begin to learn, or learn to appreciate dancing as prayer?

In my beginning workshops, I start off with breathing in unison. Many people are out of touch with what it is to breathe, to really breathe. Doing it together helps them to learn that again, while, at the same time, developing a sense of unity.

With beginners, I also teach a circle I borrowed from the Hopi Indians. It is a prayer circle, which for them is a form of healing medicine. The person who is ill sits on a painting in the sand, a sandpainting they call it. The rest of the group forms a circle around the sick person and breathes on that person. I have everyone come and link arms around each other's waists. Then I teach them to do a *demi-plié*, a movement that starts with the bending of the ankles and knees without throwing out the buttocks. Then you push up with your feet, and you unbend your ankles. Then you push up through your calves, and you unbend your knees, and up through your thighs, and then you push yourself all the way up until you are straight. You tie it in with your breathing. When you breathe out, you go down, and when you inhale, you lift up. We do that for a minute or two, until you can sense that you are one breath with the person on either side of you in the circle.

The more tense you are about it, or the more you are thinking about it, the more difficult it is to get the sense of oneness. I usually keep going until I sense that everyone in the circle can feel that all are in tune. And then at the end, all raise up on their toes, doing a *release*. You have a center right under your sternum. That's where your diaphragm starts. It is a strong center, and if you lift up in there, you can stand on your toes a long time. In this way, you are holding each other up. You are also holding up the circle, and by extension, you can feel yourself holding up the whole world. It is healing at every level.

I ask people to go home and practice the *plié* and the breathing. If they do, each time they come back, the circle will be stronger.

The awareness of breathing and dancing as one becomes strong. And it is. Something in it is very, very holy and healing.

I also use folk dancing. I use a lot of Hebrew folk dances, because they come out of our tradition, and they were used in ceremonies for religious worship. Concentrating on walking and skipping can be helpful, too. Skipping is a hard one. People forget how to skip after they are six years old, and it is hard to get back, because it requires a laterality of the body. Laterality of the body is what you do naturally when you take a step. If you take a step with your left foot, your right hand will swing forward. If you take a right step, your left hand will swing forward. But when people start thinking about it, they can't do it.

Also, people are always looking at their feet. I am always telling beginners not to look at their feet. If your head does not trust your feet, and it must look at them all the time, your body is out of shape. You start going down. But if you can keep your head up and say, "I trust you, feet," you cannot believe the movement you can go through. Keeping the head down leads to sensory deprivation. I have worked in a hospital, and I know studies have been done showing that the more your head is down, the more you close out the world. I work on lifting people's faces up, holding up the diaphragm, and getting the body oriented to hold them up. It's amazing what is in our body that we don't listen to or appreciate.

Take the positions we have for prayer. We seem to have only two: Kneeling and sitting. Well, about fifty other positions could be used for prayer. I have people lie on their stomach or back or sit in a cross-legged position. If a position is painful, as the cross-legged position might be, I tell people to remember that the saints had pain in their bodies, too. I also tell people to breathe through the pain and pray through the pain, because there are places in the body or on the earth that are in pain, too. I am not talking about going to the point of being masochistic or pulling a muscle. But you can learn to listen to your body for pain that is good for discipline and stretching and for pain that can hurt you. But people tend not to do that.

I have people go through fifteen or so different prayer positions, one being standing with the fist raised to God. I try to get them to feel what they are feeling when they stand like that. What are you feeling physically with your fingers folded into your palm? What are you feeling with your muscles tensed? What mood is evoked? Then I have them take that fist and embrace it and see what happens.

There are all kinds of discoveries to be made with our bodies. I learned that from doing aikido and judo and the other martial arts. If someone is coming at you with power, how do you redirect that power to save yourself and to redirect the person without hurting him or her? You take the energy the person is throwing at you and change its direction. It is possible. And I think it is holy. I think that is prayer. In the martial arts, you symbolize that in a prayerful and ritualistic way. Any aikido or judo class I ever took part in was prayerful for me: how you prepare yourself, how you bow before your opponent and your instructor, how you center yourself, how you meditate, how you energize yourself and focus on what you are going to do. These things are stressed with reverence.

As for an intellectual framework for prayer, I very much like Meister Eckhart's thinking. He has four paths of spirituality. There is *via positiva,* which is yourself in creation and your awareness of creation. There is the *via negativa,* which is to let go, let go, embracing both the goodness of darkness and the evil of darkness. The third path is the *via creativa,* which is the breakthrough experience. It is sort of like Ira Progoff's and Carl Jung's "aha!" experience. It is a peak experience. And the fourth path is the *via transformativa,* which is concerned with social justice. It is interesting to sort through Eckhart's thinking in answer to the question, what happens when you embrace the clenched fist?

How do you relate dance as prayer to social justice?

We started doing it as a result of my class in dance as extrovert meditation. The students didn't want to quit after the class was over. The first thing we did in the social action area was to go to the soup kitchen at the Catholic Worker house and dance grace at an evening meal. Then somebody asked me if we would dance at a nursing home. In ways like that, we started to connect with what was happening in the world. Later, I had students bring in newspaper articles about situations they would like to consider for dance as prayer. Out of that, we started improvising daily themes based on what was happening. We asked ourselves: How could we become like the situations, and how could we help heal them? We tried to put together dances that would do that.

We first went out into the street on behalf ot the equal rights amendment. We went to Springfield, the Illinois state capital. After we prayed, I led a march around the capitol. I had a tambourine in one hand — we called it Miriam's tambourine — and a Hebrew horn in the other. I went around the capitol once by myself. Then two of my students joined me. The third time around, five students joined us. More people joined each time until the sixth time around, there were about 100 people. It kept building. We went around six times, because we patterned our demonstration after Joshua bringing down the walls of Jericho. He brought the walls down on the seventh time around. We went around only six times, because were making a statement, saying we would be back to go around the seventh time if the amendment wasn't passed.

Before we went to Springfield, we did a demonstration here in Chicago on "isms," including sexism and racism, and how they divide people. We did that on the sidewalk in front of St. Peter's Church in the Loop. It is so interesting because of people's reactions. Sometimes, they will say we are crazy or are communists. Sometimes, they will call the police. On this particular day, we went inside the church to pray. We had clown makeup on. As we went in, no one noticed us. But after we had prayed and started to leave, people saw us in our makeup, and they went hysterical. They went up to the church office and reported us. Some people even came up and grabbed us.

Students in my Prophetic Players class spend a lot of time out on the street. The idea of the course is to familiarize oneself with the Scripture and relate it to the world. I have the students read the prophets and Walter Bruggemann's book, *Prophetic Imagination*. I have them identify how they feel themselves as prophetic and how they feel their experiences as prophetic. For example, we have taken poems from women in prison and dramatized them back to these same women. That was an extremely moving experience.

I have people from different walks of life praying together. I believe it is a prophetic experience. We do what the prophets did, saying, "We will not put up with a particular thing or situation any longer." We stand out on the street and say that. We put our bodies on the line.

The stations of the cross have been a powerful experience for the students. When we do this particular street liturgy, we prepare at home, putting on whiteface and black costumes. We travel from our homes on public transportation. When we are wearing whiteface, which we use for mime, we can't talk. Everyone is coming from different places in this way. They are scared to death. Some, even those from Chicago, have never been on an elevated train before. As soon as you put on whiteface, people notice you. So, here they are on the train or the bus with whiteface on, and people are looking at them and coming up to them. And they are not allowed to talk. This is part of the process.

When we meet at our destination downtown, we come together and do the prayer circle. At times like that, it is very healing, very centering. Then we go out to the various sites or stations, for example the International Harvester offices or the El Salvadoran consulate.

After we have a street liturgy, we talk about the experience. What happened? How did they feel? Did they feel resistance in themselves? What kind of resistance did they meet from other people? Was this political resistance? How does the experience relate to the particular prophet we are studying? We also examine Johannes Metz' ideas on politics and religion. When he was in Chicago, he said, "To speak of being political and religious is redundant, because if you are one, you are the other." We try to make our experiences in the street living examples of that idea. The final challenge to the students is: How are they going to take their experiences and form their own troupe someplace else? Two of them are now doing this kind of thing in Toronto. To me, doing this is the incarnation of Eckhart's fourth path of spirituality, the *via transformativa*.

To me, Prophetic Players and street theater embody four main elements of liturgy: gathering, telling the story, breaking the story or breaking the bread, and sending forth. Time after time, I experience this as a religious experience, as a priestly experience. For example, a couple of days ago, we demonstrated against apartheid in South Africa. First we gathered at the South Africa consulate here. We came together with picket signs and leaflets to help tell our story. The story we had to tell had two parts. First, there is what is happening in South Africa. On the other hand, there is the Gospel story. The two conflict and, therefore, we protest apartheid, because it is contrary to human dignity. We broke the story by miming it and by giving out the leaflets, and, of course, with the signs people could see. Finally, we sent people forth and invited them to carry our message with them. We also invited people back to tell what happened. The counselors from the South African delegation came down, and they were very upset about the demonstration.

I feel called and blessed to be able to do things like this, because I think they are so important. For many years, the arts and justice have been separated, it seems. But there is a trinity that must go together, I think. Spirituality connects social justice and the arts. The arts connect spirituality and social justice. And social justice connects spirituality to the arts. We need those connections. We need them because the art form is a way of healing. And what is amazing about it is that you can, with the art form, help bring about the healing.

For instance, last year I did a ritual drama with a man on the estrangement between the sexes. The man and I had not been hitting it off very well. There was some animosity between us. The ritual drama incorporated Scripture and poetry. We had all the women to one side of the room, the men to the other.

At the beginning, I was bonding with the women, hugging them and clasping their hands. He was doing the same with the men. Then he passed toward the women, going by a table in the center of the room, and I did the same, moving toward the men. When he saw the women, he sort of backed off, and when I saw the men, I did the same thing. Then he knelt on one side of the table with his back to me and faced the women. I knelt on the other side of the table, facing the men.

At this point, the narration was about "though the body has many members, it is one." He put his arm back behind him over the table, and I did too. We were groping, but we couldn't touch each other. We went around the table and did a deep contraction. We then turned toward each other. At this point the narration was about "when one part of the body is crushed" — and we contracted — "then we are all crushed, and when one part of the body is healed, then we are all healed," and we both raised up and made eye contact.

Then we reached across the table toward one another. There was a candle in the middle. We touched the candle, and together, we lifted it and put it back down. While we were doing that, we intensified our eye contact. We continued eye contact as he went toward the women and I went toward the men. We started to enter the "new world" of men for me and women for him. Then we looked back at each other and did a sort of "OK." We ended up with him being among the women and me being among the men.

To me, the experience was healing. It said, "This is the way we want things to be between men and women. We want them to be healed. We don't want a split between them." And we did it in the art form. And I felt it personally, too. I felt differently about that man after we did the ritual drama.

One, year during a big Holy Saturday demonstration here, Bill Kurtis — who used to be a television newsman in Chicago and later was with CBS — interviewed me. He asked, "Why are you wearing all this makeup, and do you think that all this is really going to help?" I was amazed when later I heard what I said. I was really into the idea that the world is broken and needs healing. And, I was saying I believe art is the way of healing. Our body is a wonderful work of art. It makes us all artists, and we can express that art spiritually and in justice. And that's the whole Gospel message: To be beautiful, to be holy, and to be just.

13
Praying
for Healing

Francis MacNutt

Francis MacNutt was among the first U.S. Catholic priests to become involved in the contemporary practice of praying for healing. At the time, 1967, he was a Dominican, teaching homiletics at his community's house of studies, Aquinas Institute, then located in Dubuque, Iowa. He found out about healing through prayer from Protestant ministers, whom he came into contact with through his work in preaching. He was born in St. Louis April 22, 1925. After serving in the army in World War II, he received a bachelor's degree from Harvard, a master of fine arts degree from the Catholic University, and, after joining the Dominicans in 1950, a doctorate in theology from Aquinas Institute. He has preached on healing and prayed for healing around the world and for years practiced his ministry at Merton House in St. Louis. He has written three books, *Healing, The Power to Heal,* and *The Prayer that Heals: Praying for Healing in the Family.* Since marrying, he and his wife, Judith, have carried on a prayer ministry from Largo, Florida, where they live with their two children. The interview was conducted in Fulton, Missouri.

If my prayer is unusual, it is not in the contemplative sense but because of what happens when I pray for people, asking God to heal them. Once I entered the Dominican order, my ideal was to become a saint. In those days, I constantly read lives of the saints. Miracles of healing characterized their lives. I wondered why healings took place with St. Teresa of Avila or St. Dominic and all the other saints, and why there weren't more now. That was a big question for me. I read those books avidly to find out more. We were told healings were rare. We were told we were not to aspire to be a saint in the same way the saints were, but in more ordinary, everyday ways. Yet, we were expected to read books about the saints that celebrate their lives. It seemed like a star system. That was the first reason I began to wonder if there shouldn't be such healings today.

The second reason came later, when I was dealing with suffering people who came to me for help. Many good people were suffering in ways that didn't seem redemptive. For instance, many people suffered from mental depression or anger they couldn't control. I was confessor and spiritual director to many sisters. Many of their problems were not moral in the sense that they had done something wrong and could solve their problem by going to confession and repenting. Nevertheless, in many instances, there was a moral connection. For example, you can't get rid of depression by willing it. Some people I counseled were tempted to commit suicide or had attempted it. So, I wondered. People were bringing all this unhappiness to my doorstep and asking, what does God think of this? Why did so many people who had dedicated their lives to God have this load of unhappiness? That didn't seem to make much sense; there had to be a better answer than to tell them their depression was the cross God gave them to carry.

I started reading psychology to try to understand this better. The more I read psychology, the more I discovered a kind of determinism. The basic tenet of psychology is that you have to love yourself, before you can love others. And before you can love yourself, you have to be loved into being. But where does that come from if it isn't given from the beginning of a person's life? Hosts of people in our society weren't given that love from the start. Their parents may not have been able to give them love, or had even abused them. It seemed people like that never had a chance. They seemed to be left out. I said within myself, "That's not fair."

And that's what these suffering people were telling me: "I've had an unfair life. I was cheated. Maybe you're happy. Maybe you had good parents, but my father used to beat me. My uncle sexually assaulted me. So here I am, a mess at age fifty. Can you help me?" I found psychiatrists gave a certain amount of help. But I also found that badly wounded people never get well, generally speaking. You can medicate them and keep them out of harm's way, but they don't get cured. I couldn't fit their sad lives in with basic Christian ideals about being filled with love, joy, and peace.

Consequently, when I heard through my contacts with Protestant ministers that some individuals were praying for healing, I said I would like to meet them and find out more. I met a woman who routinely prayed for people in hospitals; she claimed they were healed. As a result, in 1967, I went to a Camp Farthest Out — a kind of six-day family retreat — in Tennessee. About 700 people were there. Many of the people I met, Protestants, were doing the things we members of religious orders were supposed to be doing — like talking about Jesus with one another.

That was one thing St. Dominic did. We were supposed to do the same thing, but mostly, we didn't. I had discovered about rectories and monasteries that it was easy to discuss theology or what was happening with the bishop. But rarely did anyone talk about Jesus. That was reserved for your conference with your spiritual director. That was a very private thing, and still is. You talked formally and publicly about Jesus when you gave a sermon, but, by and large, a discussion with a group of priests was recreational. I often wondered why we never talked about Jesus.

At this Camp Farthest Out, I met hundreds of people who thought nothing about sharing with me what Jesus had directed them to do. They considered it normal to bring Jesus and their religious experiences into their conversation. What impressed, too, was that they were pretty normal people. They weren't ultra-pious types who were talking about Jesus all the time. At this camp, they were sitting at tables eating and talking about their experiences of the Lord and how he helped them with this or that. Though it was a new experience for me, I realized this was a part of our Catholic tradition.

I also realized that if what they were saying about healing was true, it could solve the pastoral counseling problems I was dealing with. Often, with people who came to me, I was not able to help on a very deep level. I was just helping to keep them alive by caring about them. I had several people tell me they hadn't committed suicide because they were afraid of disappointing me if they went that far. Keeping people alive is good as far as it goes, but it certainly isn't the same as healing them, is it? I would have been glad to send them to someone else, but where do you send them? So, praying for healing made a lot of sense — from many points of view. It seemed to aim toward the ideal of what Christian life is about. I was enthusiastic when I first heard about it. I tried also to be critical, to see if it was true. If it wasn't true, it wouldn't help people and would only raise false hopes and make things worse. I was impressed by the speakers at that camp, like Agnes Sanford, who were thinking-type people and not ostentatious. She was restrained, reserved, Anglican. Yet, she was praying for healing and believing in it.

By the time I went to my first Camp Farthest Out, I had read a couple of books on the baptism of the Spirit. I couldn't figure it out theologically. How did it fit in with baptism and confirmation? Nevertheless, I felt that what happened as a result of this baptism of the Spirit was what we Catholics were talking about as the Christian ideal. The disciples were given a power of the Spirit at Pentecost. The people who believed in baptism of the Spirit were talking about the same phenomenon. That's why I went. I wanted somebody to pray, so I would experience that. And I was prayed for at the camp.

It was a curious experience. Four counselors were assigned to pray with people. I ended up with the one who was an Episcopalian priest. His group prayed on the assumption that you had not received the Spirit before. When they prayed for me, I didn't experience anything different, so they told me to believe I had received the Spirit. I responded by saying I already believed I had received the Spirit in confirmation. Then they asked me to pray

in tongues, because for them, that was the initial evidence for
the baptism in the Spirit. I prayed in tongues, but still I didn't
have any experience to go with it. It was like praying the rosary,
something I did in faith. But when I prayed in tongues, this group
was delighted, as if I had succeeded in finally receiving the Spirit.
And I said, "Wait a minute. What I'm looking for is an interior
experience of the presence of Jesus, something different from
what I already know." I was confused by the whole situation.

An hour later at lunch, I shared that with Agnes Sanford. She
said that if I would like her to pray with me, she would be glad
to do so. I said yes. She said she sensed they shouldn't have
prayed for me the way they usually do, assuming I had never
received the Spirit. It was pretty clear I already had, she said. She
felt we should pray for the release of the Spirit that had been
given in baptism, confirmation, and ordination; that sounded
right to me. She prayed for me the next night with a couple of
friends. This time something happened. I was swept over with
joy. There were waves and waves of joy sweeping over me. And
I laughed. After that, I was convinced praying for healing was an
ordinary thing priests and ministers ought to be doing. So I started
doing it.

The first person I prayed for was a sister. She had been in a
mental hospital. She had been referred to me by her psychiatrist
for spiritual direction. She had had six months of shock treatment
and was in terrible shape. I'd go into the hospital and sit down
and talk with her, but she wouldn't say anything. She would stare
into space and wouldn't respond. It was a triumph to get her to
say anything at all.

A year later, when I first prayed for her, she was at her community's motherhouse. I was nearby giving a priests' conference,
and I phoned to see how she was doing. She asked if she could
see me. I told her I had learned about inner healing and asked
her if she would be interested in having me pray for her. I wasn't
sure what to expect, and I was kind of hoping she would say no.
She was a real mess. Suppose nothing happened? I prayed for
her, and she cried. It was the first sign of emotion I had ever
seen in her. And her life changed at that point. It was a deep

change from unhappiness to the beginning of new life. That was in 1968.

I saw her again about ten years later at a workshop, and she was really different. She came up smiling, and I didn't recognize her. I didn't know who she was until she told me her name.

So, I was led into praying for healing by a concern for the Gospel and the things that happened during the time of Jesus and the early church. In those days, there was healing, but we weren't seeing it much now. How come? The other thing was my concern for people. I figured that if something like this worked, I had better find out about it; it could mean the difference between life and death for some of my friends. Because it was a spiritual thing, it was supposed to be our business, the business of priests and ministers.

The experience with Agnes Sanford, then, is one you would describe as a release of the Spirit?

Yes, that is the way she prayed for it. She also prophesied that I would help a great number of people by using inner healing and combining it with confession. And that happened. I helped encourage hundreds of priests to get involved in the healing ministry.

After the release of the Spirit, my prayer life changed, altghough not so much in the contemplative aspect. I began praying in tongues, especially for healing. Several times, the tongues have been interpreted, and at least three times, people who knew a foreign language recognized what I was praying. Now when I pray with people for healing, I pray in tongues most of the time if the people I am praying for are not put off by it. I don't pray in English very much, because praying in tongues is quicker, which is a consideration when there is a crowd of people waiting. The results seem to be about the same.

Praying in tongues happens to different people in different ways. My internal experience is that my part is to be free enough to make up a language — as it were, to just go along with it. The faith aspect is that this really is some kind of language, and God is using it in some way in my spirit, not in my understanding.

Paul talks in 1 Corinthians 14:3 about how his Spirit is somehow praying. As I understand it, the Spirit is using tongues to pray through me and to escape the limitations of my own intelligience — my own prejudices and lack of knowing how best to pray. The times my prayer in tongues has been interpreted, or during the three times it was directly translated, something was going on that I didn't realize. When I am praying with somebody, I don't know everything about him or her. But God does. If I turn this over to the Spirit, the Spirit will pray for whatever the person needs. So, in intercessory prayer, which is my main use of tongues, I turn my prayer over to the Spirit to help the person with God's power and wisdom, so far beyond my own.

A number of people not only pray in that way, but they also tell you they *know* the experience that God is praying through them. It is interesting if you ask a crowd of people, "How many of you experience God praying through you while you are praying in tongues?" A large number do. A certain number also say they experience something rising up from inside them. It is like a river of living water coming up from within. It seeks expression. Sometimes you can see that when you are praying for somebody for the baptism of the Spirit. You can see their lips quivering, and they are almost afraid to give it utterance. Finally, they do, and it's like a gusher of praise.

As soon as I found out about healing, I began to share it with other priests and with people in general. Because I had a Ph.D. in theology, I became known as someone who could talk about divine healing, but who was also somewhat respectable. At that point, I was executive director of the Christian Preaching Conference. Every time I had a chance, I would speak about the baptism of the Spirit and healing, because I realized they were important if we really intend to preach the whole Gospel. At preaching conferences, I would tell how the baptism of the Spirit had changed the preaching of Protestant ministers I knew. I was invited by all kinds of groups. Many were Catholic prayer groups, where priests weren't involved. I would encourage the lay people to keep going, even when some church leaders questioned their orthodoxy, as happened in those days. I was also invited by groups such as the Full Gospel Businessmen, who had never had a Catholic priest address their meetings. Later I was invited by groups of Catholic priests, too. Eventually, I dropped the work I was in to pray for healing and teach about it full-time.

My healing ministry continued to grow. Healing attracts people. We found at the Notre Dame conference of the Catholic Charismatic Renewal that the seminar on healing was usually the best attended. In part, that happens because people are sick. Sometimes church leaders — even those involved in charismatic renewal — interpret the interest in healing as looking for the spectacular — for bread and circuses — that people don't want the real guts of the Christian message. In part, that may be true, but I think the continuing growth of interest in healing results from the vast need for it.

You said that on three occasions when you were praying in tongues, it was determined you were speaking another language. Tell us about one of them.

The most dramatic — the most extraordinary — involved a woman I had known for a long time. We went to the same high school. She was born Protestant. She was a brilliant person, an honors graduate in college. She became a Mohammedan and a Sufi, which, as I understand it, is for Muslims really interested in prayer. When I would return to St. Louis, we would have coffee and talk. I was always trying to convert her and gave her Teresa of Avila and people like that to read. She was never too impressed, although she liked Thomas Aquinas. She became curator at an art museum. She wanted to deal more directly with people, so she went to work at a center for disturbed adolescents. At that point, I started telling her about inner healing. She was interested but skeptical. She said if it was really that good, the scientific world would have heard of it by now.

About five or six years ago, I was visiting the city where she was then living. I called and asked if she would like to get together. She said she would be happy to, but that she had broken her leg and was confined to a wheelchair. I said I could probably stop on the way to the airport. I did. We had only about an hour to talk. I was thinking to myself, there she is sitting in a wheelchair, should I offer to pray with her or not? Finally, it was time to go, and she rolled away in her wheelchair to phone a cab. I was kind of asking in prayer, Lord, should I do this or not? It seemed I should.

When she came back, I said, "You don't have to do this, of course, but I'd feel terrible if I didn't at least offer to pray for your leg." She said, "You know, Francis, that is not my real problem."

By this time, she had left the Sufis. "My leg is not my real problem," she said. "I really want to know God. I'm really searching, and I'd appreciate prayer for that." That was a much better reason to pray. I went over to her and put my hand on her head and prayed for that. I asked if it was all right to pray in tongues, because this was one of those cases where I didn't know exactly how best to pray. She said that would be fine.

I started praying for her in tongues. After about thirty seconds, she pulled my hand away and said, "My God, Francis, what are you doing?" That confused me, because she had given me permission. I said, "I don't know, what am I doing?" And she said, "You really don't know, do you?" And I said, "No." And she said, "My God, that's amazing." I said, "What's amazing?" And she said, "you're praying the Shahada." And I said, "What's that?" She said, "You don't know, do you? That's the prayer we learned like you learn the Lord's Prayer. It's our basic prayer." She said I was praying it in Arabic. I was very surprised.

Then the cab driver was at the door — just at the worst time. I had to go to the airport. As I was going to the door, she said something else was happening. She said something was being rearranged in her body and in her leg. She said she thought she could walk. And she got out of her wheelchair and walked. She was totally healed of her broken leg.

When I got home, I wanted to find out what the Shahada was. I talked to her on the phone. Later, she wrote me a letter with the Arabic on one side and the English translation on the other. It is very much like the basic Hebrew prayer, "The Lord our God is the one true God. Holy is his name." I left out — and this is interesting — "and Mohammed is his prophet" and went on down to the next line, which was about the compassion of God. It was extraordinary.

Dramatic things like that happen when I pray in tongues. I

don't know how much of it is because of praying in tongues and how much of it is because of praying in the power of the Spirit. The most dramatic things are the healings. Last night, for example, we prayed for about seventy people. As far as I could judge, with three or four exceptions, something happened to each person. Some seemed to experience a total healing. Others, like a little boy who was flown down here from Minnesota, showed improvement.

I don't know the name of this boy's disease, but the problem centers in his spine. As I understand it, the nutrients aren't coming through his body to the muscles. The result is that his arms and his legs are weak, and he isn't able to move them correctly. His legs aren't able to hold up his body. This infirmity is supposed to get worse and eventually is supposed to kill him. But through the prayers of his parents and others, it hasn't gotten worse. He also has a curvature of the spine. Usually when we pray for that, the alignment at least improves and, if we have time, it completely straightens out. We prayed for that last night, and his spine seemed to straighten out. As far as his parents could judge this morning, the spine was straight. As for the muscles, things like that are hard to check out. They are going to take him to a doctor and have his spine x-rayed.

People are always wanting to know how much is psychosomatic. I'm sure some is. If eighty percent of sickness is psychosomatic, that's what you're dealing with. I don't see that as a putdown. Yet, we have had a number of bones grow — for example — in people who have had a foot damaged by polio. That's not just psychosomatic. Last year we prayed for a woman who, because she had polio, had one foot that was size five and the other that was size seven and a half. We prayed for her, and in ten minutes, the smaller foot grew to a size seven and a half.

In 1974, at Camp Farthest Out in Iowa, I had my first experience with a person who was possessed, a woman from Brazil. She was of Portuguese-Indian parentage. Her father had consecrated her to Satan when she was in her teens. She was to be a priestess of Satan. There was a blood sacrifice and so forth. When I met her, she had burn marks all over her arms. They were like tattoos and were in patterns. She had done this with cigarettes. She had been in and out of mental hospitals.

I thought she needed inner healing, but when I prayed for her for inner healing, nothing happened. She was a sad-looking person, although hauntingly beautiful, too. She was about thirty years old and married. She would go to cemeteries and sit. From time to time, she said, she heard voices that told her to put the burn marks on her body. She told me this was satanic.

I didn't have much experience with this kind of thing at the time. I believed in the demonic, but I didn't know what to do about it. A minister at the camp had done a lot of praying for deliverance, so I turned her over to him. Also, I was a speaker at the camp, and I didn't want to stay up all night and be too tired the next day. Plus, I didn't know how to work this out with the church law regarding permission to do an exorcism.

What happened when the minister prayed was pretty dramatic. She was falling to the ground and looking at me in an imploring way, like, "Won't you take over and help?" I was thinking this was a demonic ploy to get me out of speaking at the camp by wearing me out. The minister and his group assured me they could help her, so I left, even though she was pleading, "Please don't go." I felt too that it wasn't her crying out, but the demons were causing her to do it.

As it turned out, the minister and his group were unable to do much. At dawn, there was a knock at my door. It was the woman. She said, "You are the only one at the camp who has the power to help me. This is caused by the satanic priesthood, and you're a priest of God. Don't you believe in your own priesthood?" She really put it to me. She seemed to be desperate. She told me she had gotten away from the group that was working with her by telling them they had been successful, although they hadn't been. She said she did that because they didn't have the spiritual power to do the job. They sent her to her room with two women who were to stay with her all night.

She tried to cut her wrists, but the two women prevented that. She was going to leave the camp, she said, and wanted to let me know I had failed. She had telephoned her husband, and he was on his way to pick her up. She shook me up quite a bit. I wondered, too, if she might be appealing to my pride. But I decided maybe I had better do something. I told her I would meet with her the next day. I said I would try to do my best if she would try to do her best.

When we met the next day, she said she knew her trouble went back to the time she was consecrated to Satan. She had been consecrated to a particular demon. It was important to get the name, she said, but she couldn't remember it. All she could recall was that they clipped a verse out of the Bible and pinned it to her. And said it was from the book named "Jup. Jup? Is there such a book?" She had an accent. I figured she was talking about the Book of Job and told her to look through that. She came the next day, she had found it. This is fascinating from a scriptural point of view, because the verse, "He is torn from the shelter of his tent, and dragged before the King of Terrors" (Job 18:14). In the older translations, "King" and "Terrors" are capitalized, making it a reference to a being. In some more modern translations, there seems to be a feeling that demons don't exist, so it's in small letters and used as a metaphor. But there is a "King of Terrors." Footnotes I had read said it was a Ugaritic god of death.

Anyhow, I expected something violent when we prayed. I took it in steps. I asked her first to give her life to Jesus, which she did. Then I asked her to renounce evil and go to confession, which she did. This woman was a Catholic and occasionally would go to mass, but she would be in torment and usually had to leave early. Next I said a simple prayer to bind up the King of Terrors, and I commanded him to go in the name of Jesus Christ.

The whole process was very quiet. She just said, "It's gone." Then I prayed for her for the baptism of the Spirit. After that, she prayed in tongues, and she interpreted her own tongues. The interpretation was: "Just as Satan has used you as his priestess, I shall now use you for my greater glory." The whole thing took about an hour and a half. It was very beautiful and very peaceful.

I saw her a year later, when I asked her to speak to a group of Dominicans. She was leading a normal life, but she couldn't remember much of what had happened to her during the deliverance. The demonic had taken such control over her that it apparently blocked out her own person and her memory.

In addition to deliverance, you pray for other types of healing. What are they?

Inner healing is one of the most important of all the things I do. Inner healing is emotional healing — the kind of thing for which a person would ordinarily consult a psychologist or a psychiatrist. It is concerned with areas of our lives where our emotions somehow control of us. We can't control them, and we need help. The most common is depression. Many people are mildly depressed or, as Henry David Thoreau said, "lead lives of quiet desperation."

If you go to a place such as Latin America and return, you sense that most of our country is suffering from some kind of depression. Praying for inner healing is different with each person. The ideal way to do it is to sit down and talk with the person and listen, as you would during a counseling session. You might talk for forty-five minutes and then spend twenty minutes praying with the person. There should also be a chance for follow-up. You might have to pray for a year with a person for complete healing to take place. Sometimes, though, it is relatively instant.

Spiritual healing is a lot like inner healing, and they are not always easy to differentiate. A common example of the need for spiritual healing is when we cannot forgive our enemies. Yet forgiving enemies is a basic commandment Jesus taught. Humanly, it is difficult to forgive our enemies. If a person has a difficult time doing that, I ask Jesus to pour into the person his love, his forgiveness, his understanding of people. The idea is to help people do what they can't do.

I think that is the whole message of Christianity. The law is not enough. We need a saviour at every level of our being. I think this is a hidden key to the Christian life: The ideal that Jesus calls us to is humanly impossible. The great commandment before Jesus came was to love God with our whole heart and our whole soul and to love our neighbor as ourselves. Loving our neighbor as ourselves is impossible enough. But Jesus gave, beyond that, a *new* commandment to love one another as he loved, which includes loving our enemies. But you don't see most

Christians doing that. It is a major area in which they need healing.

In addition, there is physical healing, but the most important is inner healing. It's hard to talk about, because the subject is so vast. It goes all the way from praying with somebody who is in a mental hospital suffering from a profound psychosis to praying with somebody who has ordinary problems. For instance, one of my problems has always been an excessive shyness, a basic fear of people. That is pretty common. God has helped me a lot with that. It seems each of us has what we have traditionally called a "predominant fault." It's the thing we brought to confession every month, yet it never went away. That's the area where healing can take place in all of us.

There are many different gifts of prayer. Some people, for example, have the contemplative gift of pryaer. They are gifted with the "prayer of quiet," as St. Teresa of Avila called it. I think the idea of prayer as a gift is a key to understanding it. St. Teresa and other saints spoke of prayer as being a gift. You can prepare yourself, but ultimately, God has to reveal himself to you in one way or another. I think people have a single concept of what prayer is like. When they talk about the prayer of Jesus, for instance, they think of his going up the mountain to be alone. But if you think about it further, a good deal of the prayer of Jesus was out among the people healing them, prayer the kind of prayer I am talking about. It was public, and it was intercessory — asking his Father to heal poor, wounded humanity.

Because of these various gifts of prayer, I always try to work in a team. That way I will have the assistance of friends who have gifts of prayer in areas in which I do not. For instance, in praying for inner healing, we often don't know what went wrong in a person's life, or what we are dealing with, say, from the person's childhood. It may be blocked from the person's memory. In cases like that, some people have a gift of knowing things that happened in the past in a way they could never know humanly. I like to pray with Judith, because she has the gift for this kind of spiritual discernment. She will stop and ask God in silence what's wrong with the person. Usually, God reveals to her the problem.

What is your gift of prayer?

People tell me I have a lot of faith. I'm not sure I think of it that way. It just seems to me pretty natural that people ought to be healed. I have a basic sense that God loves people, that he is good, and if we ask for help, he will hear our prayer and answer. Jesus said a lot about faith in prayer for healing.

One of the things that struck me about five years ago was that the object of faith in the Gospels usually has something to do with healing. I read through all four gospels to check it out, and it is true. It surprised me. When something is specified — such as Jesus saying "Woman, your faith has healed you" — the object of faith is healing. It is not the Trinity, although the Trinity is the great truth of our faith and is more important than healing. I know that. But as a practical problem of faith, healing is stressed a great deal in the Gospels. I would say my gift of prayer is along the line of having the faith to believe God does heal through prayer.

What percentage of persons that you pray for are healed?

In general, though it is hard to verify this without a scientific study, I would say about seventy-five percent of the people we pray for for physical healing experience a change. Most of that is improvement rather then complete healing. A certain number of total healings are relatively instant — say, in five minutes. Some take much longer. For some types of physical problems, the percentage is higher than seventy-five percent, say, closer to ninety percent. For instance, I have had considerable success in praying for arthritis and bone problems. There are other illnesses where quick healings are relatively rare. Like a paraplegic. Things like that require a creative miracle. A nerve tissue doesn't grow back if the spinal cord is severed. Medically, that's it. Healings in ailments like that are more difficult and more rare, obviously.

Right now in Florida, we are praying with a young man who is a quadriplegic. He is about twenty years old and was racked up in an automobile accident. When we started praying with him, he had no feeling from just below his neck on down. He had feeling on the top of his shoulder, but from his bicep on down, there was nothing and no movement. In a way, I always hate to see somebody like that come forward, because healing doesn't happen as commonly and as instantly. I prayed with him for the first time about six months ago. He felt something going on, but there wasn't any discernible change.

The next time, I wanted to check to see if there was a change. So we put a little mark on his chest marking the level at which he could feel. After we prayed for half an hour, that went down an inch. The next time, it went down another inch. The next time, it went down three inches. The next time, it started going down on his arms. Now he can feel from the top of his bicep to his elbow. I have prayed for him now about six times. That kind of progress is encouraging to me, even though it's slow and gradual. On the other hand, with a bad back, I am surprised if there is not at least an immediate improvement; if we can pray for half an hour, there is often a total healing.

What is the success rate for praying for inner healing, spiritual healing, and deliverance?

I think they should all be 100 percent. But because of our own obtuseness and other reasons, it is less. I would estimate that eighty percent of the persons I pray with for inner healing whom we can work with for a period of time are healed. The same is true of spiritual healing. Deliverance is more difficult to estimate. Many different elements enter in, such as the person's willingness. Moreover, in all prayer for healing, the degree of spiritual growth in the one doing the praying is a major factor. If we were closer to the Lord, much more would happen — and faster.

When praying for healing, do you ever have the feeling that power is going out of you or through you?

Different people in the healing ministry have different experiences of this. Some feel that a great power goes through them. I don't. But it must go through me, because I feel drained afterward. I feel really tired. Also, the person I am praying for usually experiences heat, a lot of heat. Further, about one of four or five people being prayed for will feel a current going through them. It's very gentle, not like electricity. If you have your hand on the person's head, that person will feel it go through him or her all the way to, say the lungs, if the lungs are the problem.

Where does praying for healing fit in with the rest of the healing arts, such as medicine and psychology?

I see it as complementary. I wouldn't hesitate to go to a doctor or a dentist. In our old terminology, I see it as a supernatural way of healing. But God uses the natural, too. He heals in all these ways. Healing through prayer is a special way of either speeding up the natural processes or, in some cases, going beyond them.

What do you say to the skeptics who don't believe healing takes place through prayer?

There is evidence. They should examine it. If I am talking to a group of doctors, and there are skeptics, I say, "Let's take some of your patients, and let's pray for them, and you check it out." Then they can see we are not talking about theories.

Do you think every Christian has his or her version of the gift of prayer for healing?

Yes. Healing is not to be understood in a narrow sense. It is more a question of praying for things we need to be human, to be redeemed and saved. We are getting into praying for healing of relationships more and more. Healing of marriages, too. More and more, I see praying for healing as not only something respectable, but also as the basic reason Jesus came. If we didn't need the power of God, the law would be sufficient. We wouldn't need a savior. I think most Christians don't fully understand the depth of what that means. The notion that people can do everything by themselves, or with a little encouragement, is widespread. But it is not true. That's Pelagianism.

In traditional terms, we need grace. We are talking here about grace. There's a gift aspect to reality that you cannot earn. Sometimes it is given when you don't ask, as to Saul on the way to Damascus. But the ordinary way is that you have to recognize God as a loving father and be dependent, declare your dependence on him in prayer. Christ is our lord and savior. I don't think the charismatic renewal has gotten that point across to the main body of the church in sufficient depth. There is an essential Christian understanding here that has been rediscovered in greater depth. It is essential. We aren't just talking about praying for healing for a sick person here or there. We are talking about that we can't live without grace. We can't live without God's help.

14
The Prayer
of Peacemakers

Philip Berrigan and Elizabeth McAlister

Philip Berrigan and Elizabeth McAlister personify the Catholic peace movement.

Along with his brother, Daniel, Philip Berrigan has been active in the antiwar movement since 1961. His first public demonstrations were for civil rights. From there, he moved to protests against the Vietnam war and his current target, the nuclear arms race. Among his many protests, he says the three most notable — and also the "most expensive" — were the destruction of draft records at the Customs House in Baltimore in 1967 and in Catonsville, Maryland, in 1968, and the damaging of a component for a nuclear weapon in the Plowshares Eight, which he discusses in this interview. He says he has been arrested at least fifty times, but he is not certain exactly how many. He was born October 5, 1923, fought with distinction during World War II, was ordained a Josephite priest in 1955, earned two master's degrees and has taught high school and college. His writings include five books.

Elizabeth McAlister is serving a three-year prison sentence in the Federal Correctional Institution in Alderson, West Virginia, for her part in a protest against nuclear weapons at Griffis Air Force Base near Rome, New York. In this action, which she discusses in this interview, she and a group of peace activists damaged a B-52 bomber Thanksgiving Day,

1983. She became involved in the peace movement about 1965 and "simply grew with it." She committed her first act of civil disobedience in 1970 and has been arrested about twenty times. She was born November 17, 1939, and joined the New York province of the Religious of the Sacred Heart of Mary in 1959. She has a bachelor's degree and a master's degree in art history and taught eight years at the college level. Seven of those years were at Marymount College in Tarrytown, New York.

Philip and Elizabeth married in 1969, and they have three children. Of their years together, they estimate they have spent six apart because of prison terms. Since 1973, they have lived in Jonah House, a community of peace activists in Baltimore.

What role does prayer play in the lives of veteran peace activists like yourselves?

Phil: During a three-year stretch in prison for protesting the Vietnam war, I began to see prayer in a new perspective. Dan, who was locked up with me, and I came across a book called *Resistance and Contemplation* by Jim Douglass, who is a dear friend of ours. His thesis is that resistance and contemplation dovetail, and that a contemplative life is essential to resistance. Without contemplation, he says, Christians can't carry out their basic obligation to resist evil and do good.

At the time, Dan and I were working with about fifteen prisoners, studying with them, praying with them, and actively organizing with them. We studied Douglass' book, and, I think, went through it about five times with these men. Some were in prison for resisting the draft and some for other reasons. The prisoners went on to do acts of resistance in federal prison against the Vietnam war. Some were treated harshly by the authorities because of it.

Out of the study and work with these men, I began to see more clearly that prayer presents us with a yin-yang situation. On one hand, the relationship with God seems biblically ordained to perfect our relationship with other human beings, and, reciprocally, the relationship with other human beings is meant to perfect, our relationship with God. I began to see, too, that the oddest things can be contemplative — things you hadn't thought of as prayerful before. For example, going up against prison authorities because they are unjustly handling prisoners, or exposing them to bodily injury, can be a contemplative act. On the other hand, praying for the strength to stand up for helpless prisoners who are being beaten, say, by a goon squad, is essentially an act of resistance, though it is contemplative, too. Prayer works back and forth and has to be discerned that way.

We've experienced the same thing in our community life. Most people seem to find commmunity life extremely hard. First, you run into a diversity of people, and, second, the culture educates you to look upon the nuclear family as the be all and end all. I think the Bible focuses on the larger family, holding that the smaller community is meant for the larger human family. The result is a tension that often has to be worked out during prayer.

We were not formed by our religious training to do this — at least not in the areas of justice and peace. Both Liz and I come from community life and long years of community training. But we were not trained to work in community with people who are about the essence of the Bible — justice and peace. We were not trained to live with them and to support them and to be supported by them. To do that, you have to be able to deal with other folks nonviolently and justly and decently. That is a little hard to come by from time to time. In such a situation, the yin-yang role of prayer is important.

Liz: If I were to describe the role of prayer in our life and work in one word, I would pick "central." Prayer is central to our work in resistance and in justice and peace. And in the community, I would say it is omnipresent. It may not be the formalized prayer of kneeling in a chapel with the lights low and the candle light flickering and the Blessed Sacrament exposed. But there isn't any carrying on, and holding on to sanity and focus, it seems to me, without prayer.

As Phil says, it takes effort to try to understand one another in community, especially when the going gets tough. You have to try to understand where this or that one is coming from. You have to come to terms with some of the human differences and the ways we rub one another wrongly. You have to both accept people and challenge them. The ability to do that is the result of prayerful reflection.

We live in a community with eight adults and three children. That's plenty of human diversity to deal with on a day-to-day basis. This is also a house that has people coming through it. That gives you more diversity. Some of them are very thoughtful and call ahead. Others drop in out of the blue, and your schedule goes to the wind. Pretty soon, you wonder — am I using my time well? Reflecting on that and putting it in perspective is a process of prayer.

Raising children requires prayer, too. I don't know how one would be able to do that without a lot of prayer, because if anyone tests one's nonviolence to the hilt, it can be one's children. I think the level of child abuse in this country is clear evidence of the lack of prayerfulness.

The community prayer is rooted in the Bible, although you could distinguish a whole variety of prayer. We try to read the Bible alone and together, trying to hear what it is asking of us. The summons to act comes to us both individually and as a community out of the Scripture. The effort to discern *how* we act is prayer over the Scripture and prayerful reflection about the times in which we live.

Out of that process, we decide to act, to resist in this, that, or the other way. This is the process we have used to go against the powers in this country. For example, that is how the various Plowshares actions have come about. We have gone into well-guarded facilities such as a plant or an air force base and symbolically damaged first strike weapons. We go in at the risk of our lives.

The whole process of enabling each of us to do that is a prayerful one. You don't enter a guarded facility because you are arrogant enough to think you can do it. You do it because you are summoned to do it, because you act in obedience to God's command. I had to come to grips with seeing it that way before I could act. I had to pray for the faith to believe this was God's will for me. I had to pray to overcome the fear of acting. It would not come off without a highly active prayer life.

At what point did you realize you had to resist, and what role did prayer play in that?

Phil: Sometimes it seems unfortunate to assign prayer a role or a compartment in one's life and works of justice and peace another. If one is a Christian — that is, trying to be one — one prays and acts against injustice, whether it is personal or systemic. I learned that from my family, from friends who nonviolently resisted public evils — violation of civil rights, Vietnam, the struggles against the calculated exploitation of the poor, the proliferation of nuclear weapons. I also got it from prayer itself, the sacramental life, and the Gospel.

The Lord stressed "deeds" and "works" — what Mohandas Gandhi would call "conduct." Prayer helps to develop a selfless spirit for conduct, for deeds, for works. But it is no substitute for them. In turn, resistance clarifies my weakness or lack of nonviolence, sending me back to God for help, for more clarity and strength.

In light of all this, I began to understand the need for resistance in the early 1960s, after encountering in the deep South the vicious racism accorded blacks by whites. This sense deepened with experiences at Selma, Montgomery, New Orleans, and Atlanta as well as with reading and prayer. It deepened further with the U.S. escalation in the quagmire of Indochina, with prison, and with the nuclear roulette we are playing.

Liz: God can speak in some people directly. There are others, like myself, to whom God must be more pointed. It took a friend pointing his finger at me and saying, "What about you?"

The time was April 1968. I had been present for much of the trial of the Baltimore Four (of which Phil was a member). The trial ended with a conviction shortly after Easter. A couple of weeks later, I was asked to meet with five people in New York City at the apartment of mutual friends. George Mische was in town. He explained that another action was being planned in Catonsville and reviewed the plans. Then with great drama, he pointed his finger at me and said something like, "What about you being part of the action community?" I don't remember his exact words. The finger is what I recall most clearly.

I looked behind me, around me, squirmed, stammered empty rationalizations, and finally agreed to think about it. The days that followed were critical. It was a totally new idea to me. Only a certain type of person did an act like that, and while I could understand and explain the act, I wasn't that type of person.

The Book of Revelation (2:17) says: "I will give everyone who seeks to be faithful a white stone, and on the stone will be written a new name, known to none but the one who receives it." I began to understand the summons George had delivered as this stone, this call to fidelity and to action. His words and his pointing finger had such power for me because they corresponded to some urgings with me I had been deaf to or refused to listen to until that time. The invitation, the stone, was a new identity, and I was convinced the time had come to heed that call or lose the sense of meaning and direction in my life.

There was a stumbling block, however. It had become clear to me during the Baltimore Four trial that is was not sufficient to act. It was also essential to be able to explain it. As Peter says, "Be always ready with your defense whenever you are called to account for the hope that is in you, but make that defense with modesty and respect" (1 Peter 3:15-16). I was not able to explain the hope except with borrowed phrases and then incoherently, stumbling. The idea, the identity was new to me.

I came to understand that a seed had been planted in me, and it needed silence and care to grow before it could withstand the pressures of public exposure and trial. I did not go into the action of the Catonsville Nine, but waited. The next time, I was able to say "yes" with clarity and peace.

What are the Plowshares actions?

Phil: We have taken the name and inspiration for them from the famous passage in the second chapter of Isaiah — it's in Micah as well — about people beating their swords into plowshares.

In the first of these actions, eight of us, including Dan and myself, damaged two Mark 12-As, manufactured at the General Electric plant in King of Prussia, Pennsylvania. It is a prime first strike weapon that is retrofitted into our Minuteman ICBMs. Later actions were against elements of the Cruise and Pershing II missiles, the Trident II submarine, and the MX. On Thanksgiving day, 1983, Liz and a group acted against the B-52 bomber, which is used to launch the Cruise missile from the air. That was at Griffis Air Force Base at Rome, New York, east of Syracuse. Shortly after that, a priest friend of ours and a group acted against a Pershing II launcher at an American base in West Germany. And one Easter Sunday, 1984, eight women and men disarmed Pershing II components and a Pershing II launcher-carrier at Martin-Marietta in Orlando, Florida.

You say that in preparation for these actions, you went through a prayer process. Would you describe that?

Liz: The process has been one of trying to discern how we stand up against these weapons. We had determined to have "A Year of Election, 1980·" The idea was that every day during 1980, people would be at the Pentegon saying "no" to nuclear weapons. No matter who won the 1980 election, we felt it would mean little unless there was a radical change in our nuclear weapons policy and production. Therefore, we organized a protest with groups coming into St. Stephen and the Incarnation Church in Washington, D.C., for a week at a time. Each working day, these groups would spend some time at the Pentagon in a manner most reflective of who they were as a community. One or two of us would be with them.

The idea was not to put in as many hours at the Pentagon as possible, but rather to work with each group on community building and understanding the issues and our responsibilities. In this way, they would be strengthened as community and strengthened in their commitment to continue resistance when they returned home. Most of these groups, if not all, were coming out of a spiritual base.

That was our main focus for the year. But early in the year, one of the members of our community learned of the possibility of getting inside the General Electric facility at King of Prussia and getting to the warheads and doing a disarmament action against them. He laid that before the community. I would say there was an instantaneous affirmation that this idea was what we ought to be doing. From that moment, it was a matter of bringing together a community that would do that kind of an action.

Phil immediately said he would participate. That meant I wouldn't, because we have a commitment that as long as possible, we will not both be in a risk situation simultaneously. One of us would stand aside to be with the children and carry out the activities of the community.

In considering the Plowshares actions, the groups come together at intervals for a couple of days at a time. That coming together was in prayer. The prayer time included a scriptural reflection and a liturgy. Bread and wine were shared, and people who shared in the bread and wine committed their lives — their own body and blood — to the service of humanity as best they could.

These gatherings would also include a consideration of the question, "Where am I in my own life?" This would be a kind of life-sharing to help people get to know each other and their values. In this way, they would know they could count on each other to act in a certain way — for example, to be nonviolent in any situation they might meet during the action, including dealing with the police, the courts, the public, and any anger and hostility. Life-sharing is important for developing trust with one another and as a community. After such gatherings, people returned to their lives and work.

That coming and going is essential. We could meet for a week or two and plan on going right into the action. But the time together becomes so intense that you risk psyching up one another. There's a danger that one or another might not really be committed to the action. Therefore, it is necessary to go back to the context of one's own life to think things through. "Is this something I really want to do, or am I just being empowered by this community to be and do something I can't carry on my own?" That would be the process.

Phil, how did this process work in the Plowshares Eight, the first of the Plowshares actions?

Phil: We met for a period of about nine months. It was on and off several times. It was a new idea. People were risking long jail terms. It was slow going. Once or twice, we didn't think it was possible. We had trouble finding a floor plan of the plant. Finally, we got one from a General Electric phone book that was in the vestibule of the plant. That gave us a general idea of how production moved and where the final product emerged for shipment to Amarillo, Texas, where it is stuffed with a thermonuclear package.

We didn't have much more information than that. Some people didn't think it was feasible, and several refused to join us because of that. They thought we were going in blindly and presumptuously. But a few hung in and continued meeting, and finally, the group solidified with eight people.

Of those, six were from a Catholic background or still looked upon themselves as Catholics. That has been a general rule through all of these Plowshares actions, a general rule in risky civil disobedience. For some mysterious reasons, those who are most inclined to risk their freedom, and sometimes their life and limb, in doing acts of resistance have been Catholics. There have been other Christians, too, but I would say more than half have been Catholics.

And you don't know why that is? I was hoping you would be able to tell us.

Phil: I can speculate, but I don't know that I can pinpoint any thing definitive. Liz and Dan and I have pondered this over the years. It might be a view of the Scripture. It might be that we did the stations of the cross more frequently. It might be the view we have of the eucharist as a re-portrayal of the Lord's passion and resurrection.

In any event, our gatherings prior to the Plowshares Eight action were essentially prayerful. We tried to project a biblical view of prayer. We took the view that we didn't want to undertake this action on our own authority. We didn't want to do it because it seemed right subjectively. We looked for a higher authority than that. We looked to the example of our Lord and the prophets. In doing so, we discovered, on the one hand, that prayer is a private thing. For example, our Lord used to retire for prayer privately, and he would pray mostly in secret. He says in Matthew's sermon on the mount that when you pray, you should go to your room in private and pray to your parent in heaven.

And yet, prayer is also very, very political, because when Jesus taught the apostles, to pray in the Our Father, he told them to say, "Your will be done on earth as it is in heaven." That's a heavily laden political statement, because to register God's will upon this earth would be to create an order of justice and peace. That's a central biblical theme. God is determined to make this world into a place of justice and peace, despite our resistance to that.

Prayer is essentially linked with that central theme. We kind of rebel against the privatized way prayer is handled so commonly in the Christian churches. We say it is essentially linked with social and political justice. When we are praying seriously and biblically in obedience to the way Christ taught us to pray, we are praying for the victims, we are praying for the starving children, we are praying for those who are being victimized by war. In prayer, we are preparing ourselves to call attention to the official crimes that cause such frightful loss of life and misery and suffering, even on the part of innocent children.

I have just been going over a few things on the hunger crisis. I came upon some really harrowing stuff on the relationship between the arms race and hunger in the world. UNESCO, for example, says 40,000 to 42,000 children die daily of hunger-related disease. The figure may go as high as 50,000. The unbridled arms race, which is costing the world about $700 billion a year, causes that. The Vatican has taken that position, saying the arms race causes the poor to starve.

Prayer is about these things, and how we transcend our selfishness and weakness and become the person for others. Whatever discomfort we are having emotionally and psychologically pales before what many other people are enduring out of sheer deprivation or as the result of living in the most frightful dictatorships and facing savagery and butchery. That is the view of prayer we are trying to cultivate, not because we like it, but because a higher authority says that's the way it should be.

I would like to ask each of you how you personally pray, and how you prayed during the Plowshares actions you were involved in.

Liz: In a variety of ways. There are times prayer is just breathing. There are times it appears to be close to thinking. There are times it is feeling what is around. There are times it is acting — for example, labeling the Pentagon or sitting in front of it as some kind of barrier between it and the work it does. I cannot hear St. Paul say we are to pray always and think there is just one way to do it.

We make the trip to Syracuse a great deal, because our brother and sister-in-law live there, and I am making it more frequently these days because of my court case. There are sections of the mountains in Pennsylvania and in New York state that are magnificent. Sometimes, prayer is just seeing those mountains and feeling the praise they are.

What was your prayer before the Griffis action?

Liz: In our first gathering, we also reflected on the biblical mandate to beat swords into plowshares. It seemed to us this was a mandate to alter our relationship with these weapons, to be subservient to them no longer, but to take a stand against them. The sense of those phrases from Scripture was that the people, not the nations, would beat swords into plowshares. In these verses, there is a beautiful juxtaposition of the nations and the people, but it is the people who will act. That was our reflection together on the first retreat.

We also talked about who we were, beginning a convenanting process. We used the term "convenanting" and explored what it meant biblically. What was God's covenant with his people, and what happened to that covenant? How does that affect us now?

The next major reflection we needed to engage in was sensing and learning to trust in the Spirit in these actions. This requires going back a bit to explain: The Plowshares Eight never got the hard information they needed so they could go into the action with a sense of confidence. There was some uncertainty as to what they would find once they went into the room where the warheads were supposed to be.

That dimension of uncertainty was the point where they had to make the leap of faith and trust that if this was what they were summoned to do, they would find open doors. And, in astonishing fashion, they walked into the room and there, in front of them, were the warheads.

That kind of thing was true for every subsequent action. People did their homework, but there were things that, without being undercover agents, we were not going to know, no group was going to know. After we had found out all we could, we would reach a point where we had to decide: If this is what we're supposed to do, the Spirit will open the doors. Are we prepared to make that act of faith?

The next main reflection was coming to grips with our own fears and understanding that the antithesis of fear was faith. We did a scriptural reflection on the fact that the Bible uses the formula "don't be afraid, have faith; don't be afraid, trust in me" eighty-five times. We understood, or sought to understand, that fear wasn't going to go away, but that with faith, we would be able to act in spite of it.

These were the main elements of our prayerful reflections. In addition, each of us had to do his or her own soul-searching, and come to grips with all the elements, and be able to say "yes" to the other members of the group and to himself or herself.

What then was your prayer as the action unfolded?

Liz: The thing that set it off for me — and I think for some of the others as well — was the reflection that we engaged in just before the action, coming to grips with the possibility that one or more of us might be seriously hurt or killed in this action. Looking at death in such a direct way makes everything, including life, much more real.

I found myself with thoughts like this: "I don't want to die. I'm not ready for this. If this is what God wants of us, we'll be protected, and we won't die. That sacrifice is not being asked. Still, at some point it may, and it might be now. So, I might be walking very, very deliberately into death. But I believe if it happens, something very good could come of it, and I am willing to embrace that. But am I? I'm not so sure."

I didn't try to resolve this ambivalence. I couldn't. I just tried to be with it and remain open to whatever might happen, in spite of being very, very afraid. I needed a calming, and I found that being aware of my breathing helped to do that. It was not a psychological calming. It was a calming in the Spirit. The quotation, "I believe, help my unbelief," became the words, if there were any words, of my prayer. By the time we reached the air force base, I was calm and ready to go through with it.

We had a long walk — at least half a mile, if not a mile — from the point we entered the base to the building where the B-52s were. It was early morning and still quite dark. It was cold and windy. When we arrived at the building, we could see lights on inside. We didn't know what that meant. We were prepared with crowbars to open the doors, but they were not locked. They were wide open. We walked in. With the lights on, it was like broad daylight inside and, sitting there, in front of us, was this huge B-52 bomber.

I was incredulous that it was there all by itself with nobody around it. And there wasn't, not a soul. As I looked at it, I thought of the people in Vietnam and their experience of this bomber. To tell the truth, my first whacks on it were retaliatory for the Vietnamese people. Only then did I begin hitting it with the idea of transforming it. Between blows, I was looking at the door in the hangar, expecting guards to come in the M-16s on us. That kind of illustrates how the sense of power of the place we had penetrated was present to me at all times, until we were finished.

Others in the group got into a deep celebration of what they were doing in the process of doing it. I was amazed and deeply gratified by that, but that was not my spirit. I remember Vern Rossman took the first whack at the bomb bay doors and, in that hollow place, the sound of metal on metal was such that I thought the whole base would be in there in a moment. "Vern, muffle it, muffle it," I said. But nobody came running in the doors, and we all got into it. No one came near us for an hour and a half after we were finished. That was our experience of having the doors opened.

There were seven of us. Three went directly to the B-52. The other four went to an adjoining area in the same building where we had half expected there might be component parts for Cruise missiles, but it turned out there were engines for the B-52s. They damaged five of those engines. We did spray-painting, pouring of blood and hammering, mostly around the bomb bay doors and the fuselage just above them.

Phil: They could have done damage inside that hangar for an hour and a half. But you can't fall into an orgy of damage and destruction, lest you destroy your symbol. The symbol says: All of us have a responsibility for these weapons. They destroy the relationship with the neighbor as long as they continue to exist and we threaten to use them. Because they destroy the relationship with the neighbor, they seriously compromise, if not destroy, the relationship with God.

In relating the symbol to the biblical mandate to beat swords into plowshares, you are suggesting to people that we all have to take responsibility for these weapons. We made them. We have to unmake them if we are going to survive on this planet. If you go into maximum destruction, the weight and clarity of that symbol is destroyed. If you do that, the authorities will aptly charge you with vandalism or aggravated terrorism. As a result, what you are trying to say to sisters and brothers in this country will be obscured.

Liz: We were in the hangar hammering, spray-painting and so on for fifteen to twenty minutes. We stood on the tarmac outside the hangar for an hour and a half, praying, holding banners, singing, waiting. . . . We went out to meet arrest and assume responsibility for what we had done. We were seriously tempted to go back into the hangar and do more damage. We talked about that, but concluded: We have an agreement with one another about what we would do by way of damage. We need to stick with that agreement, because that was our covenant. We have been protected from any harm in this action. How would we feel if, on the instinct of the moment, we went back in, and someone was shot. We accepted what we had done and used the rest of our time otherwise.

What was your prayer afterward? Were you thankful?

Liz: Yes, I had a deep sense of gratitude. I felt what we had done was God's will, this is what we were called to do. I felt that if we showed the least modicum of openness to God's will and willingness to submit to it, miracles would happen. What we were able to do at Griffis was nothing short of miraculous. I thought, why is this so hard for us, when the Lord makes it so easy if we give him a chance?

Phil, how do you pray and, second, what was your prayer as you went into your Plowshares action?

Phil: As a member of the Jonah community, I participate in two formalized periods of prayer we have each week. On Sunday morning, we have a Bible study period, perhaps about an hour and a half. Someone does a presentation, then we have a eucharist. That is for people living at Jonah House, plus friends who come in rather frequently.

On Wednesday evening, we also have a presentation from Scripture. The relationship to current life and death questions is always apparent. The connections are made. We try to exhort one another to be more faithful, to be more simple in our living, to be more just in community relationships, and to be more sensitive to nonviolent ways of resistance.

Apart from that, we operate under a kind of freely chosen mandate to carry on our spiritual life, or reflective life, individually. I tend toward meditation on the psalms and the New Testament. I do some Scripture reading every day. We earn our living doing contracting — painting, carpentry, and roof work. We try to limit work, so we are relatively free to do justice and peace work when we need to. For example, we will stop work to participate in a demonstration in Washington, or while Liz and Karl Smith, who is also involved in the Griffis Plowshares, go to Syracuse for a pre-trial appearance.

While working, I try to stay as reflective as I can. Some of this work is rather mechanical, particularly when painting inside. I try to do some praying while I am doing that. I go through the Magnificat and the Our Father.

I have always been affected by the New Testament's teaching on prayer, particularly Luke's passage that says, "Do you not think God will give the Holy Spirit to those who ask her or him?" That to me has meant the request for the advocacy of the Holy Spirit to strengthen us is perhaps the final, ultimate petition of prayer. We ask the Holy Spirit to be with us as our guest. In other words, we ask for the promises of Christ regarding the sending of the Holy Spirit to be fulfilled. Personally, this means a great deal to me. I can think more clearly, and I am more inclined to be more generous, if I do some solid praying requesting God to send his Spirit and that he not abandon us.

Liz and I were greatly moved by a great book by Jacques Ellul, the French theologian. He spoke about hope in a time of abandonment. He went through the Scripture and found a series of cycles of abandonment and presence of the Holy Spirit within our midst. He cites these modern times as a time of abandonment and affirms that the only way to end it is to plead with God to send the Holy Spirit. As part of that, people must try to be faithful in their own lives, particularly publicly and politically.

I find that plea for the presence of the Holy Spirit is a very important petition of prayer. The presence and power of the Spirit can transcend our cowardice, our weakness, and our self-indulgence, and can supplant our feeble efforts.

And what about your prayer before your Plowshares action?

Phil: There were six or seven gatherings or retreats. The last one was four days in duration. I would say it was pretty much an open question as to whether we were going to do it or not. The formation of subsequent Plowshares groups, it seems to me, was much more solid, because they knew more about how to prepare spiritually, psychologically, emotionally, and politically. We were groping, because we were the first. The big question during the final four-day gathering was, is there any possibility that we could do it?

The question of faith Liz brought up was pretty abstract to us at the time. We didn't understand how that would come into play. We didn't understand that if we took every measure we could to damage these hellish weapons, God would more than complement our efforts, and would, in effect, open the doors and allow a person to go through the maze of a large plant and find the right door the first time. We didn't understand that. We floundered with that, and only after a lot of gut-wrenching and a tremendous amount of discussion did we come to the conclusion that we should try. Then, we had to work out all the contingencies. For example, if it got to physical resistance on the part of the administration of the plant, how would we act? We decided that if it came to physical confrontation, we would stop the action immediately and perhaps do a token blood pouring or kneel in a circle and pray.

As I recall, the eucharist we shared the night before was a great turning point. The readings had to do with Isaiah's prophecy of beating swords into plowshares, and the beatitudes. Something apt and serious was said on the relationship of those two scriptures: That these weapons stand between us and our neighbors. These weapons literally have our name on them. They might be used to such an extent that the neighbor is going to be destroyed by them. We are commanded to love that neighbor. We and our children, in turn, will be destroyed by the weapons of others. That's the predicament of the present time. Both of those Scripture passages, one from the Old Testament and the other from the New, are completely nonviolent visions of how human beings ought to act.

Jacques Ellul says in a little book on violence that everything depends on the fifth commandment and on the pledge that we not kill. Everything in the Scripture and in morality and ethics revolves around that one command. The reason is that our sisters and brothers are made in God's image. That is the only image of God we have. We are commanded not to kill, and that command cannot be obeyed until these weapons are disarmed. It cannot be obeyed until we greet one another without weapons in our hands.

At that eucharist, people in the group played back and forth with these two Scripture passages in an insightful way. That seemed to calm the fears we had. We got up very, very early the next morning, because he had an hour's drive to the plant, but everyone seemed calm and peaceful and even humorous on the ride.

When we were able to carry out the action, and the police came and hauled us off, we were exuberant, because we realized that after more than 6,000 disarmament talks, a little disarmament had happened. We realized that the Scripture was true: that *nations* will disarm only if the *people* insist that they do. President Dwight Eisenhower realized this, too. He said he hoped we will see a day when the cry for peace from the people is so insistent that governments will have to step out of their way.

This crowd of "friends" we have in Washington — I call them that rather humorously — would have to step out of the way if people in this country insisted on peace with any sort of concerted and serious voice. They couldn't hold their power. They couldn't govern the country. They would be helpless. Gandhi recognized this in his dealings with the British in India. We could do the same thing here, but we are not at that point yet.

15
A Dying Man's Prayer

Geno Baroni

This interview was not part of the original plan for this
book. But, along the way, Monsignor Geno Baroni entered
the picture in a dramatic way. He called us, saying he was
suffering from a serious cancer and was looking for someone who might pray with him. Could we suggest some
names? We did.

As time passed, the thought of a man praying while suffering from a cancer that would take his life haunted us, so we
asked him if he would consider being interviewed about it.

He cautioned that he was not an expert in prayer, as were
the other people we were interviewing. Unlike them, his expertise was elsewhere. He had not written books on prayer,
not even an article, he said. What's more, he was just learning
to pray for the cancer, and he wasn't sure he would have
anything to offer that others couldn't do far better. Nevertheless, he said that if we were willing to risk not getting anything
worthwhile, he would be happy to oblige.

The interview took place Sunday afternoon, March 11,
1984, while Baroni was being treated for cancer at St. John
of God Hospital in Brighton, Massachusetts, a Boston suburb.
He died a little more than five months later, at age fifty-three,
on August 27, 1984, in Washington, D.C.

Baroni's expertise was people — people working together
in coalitions. He was a national leader in solving urban and
neighborhood problems. He tackled these problems through
coalitions that crossed racial, ethnic, cultural, and religious

lines. His list of accomplishments in this field is long. His highest position was that of assistant secretary of the U.S. Department of Housing and Urban Development, a post he held from 1977 to 1981. He was nominated by President Jimmy Carter and confirmed by the U.S. Senate. In that job, he became the first Catholic priest in U.S. history to serve in a cabinet-level position. Before that, he was founder and president of the National Center for Ethnic Affairs, an affiliate of the U.S. Catholic Conference. After leaving the government, he was a special assistant for community affairs of the Archdiocese of Washington.

He was born in Acosta, Pennsylvania, October 24, 1930, the son of Italian immigrants. After ordination and four years as a priest in his native diocese of Altoona-Johnstown, he came to Washington, D.C., in 1960 and started working in a black parish, St. Paul and St. Augustine. There, he got involved in inner-city poverty and housing programs and served on human relations and economic development groups. The *Washington Post*, in an editorial marking his death, said:

> "There were more than a few racially tense moments in the Washington of the 1960s, and when friction became particularly severe and potentially explosive, the word would go out quietly from President Lyndon Johnson, Walter Washington, the chief of police, or whoever else needed information, advice, and help to round up cool heads for heated neighborhoods: Check with Geno, the priest of the streets. Usually, a ride up and down the rough-and-tough blocks of Fourteenth Street Northwest would turn up a gathering somewhere in which you would spot the short, round figure of a white man of the cloth, touching bases as well as hearts among a group of black people."

He was appointed executive director of the Office of Urban Affairs of the Washington archdiocese, a position he held from 1965 to 1969. During this time, he founded several non-profit housing groups, including the Urban Rehabilitation

Corporation, to rehabilitate housing with federal funds. From 1968 to 1970, he served as program director for the Urban Task Force of the U.S. Catholic Conference, where he was instrumental in establishing the Campaign for Human Development, a national self-help program and anti-poverty agency of the U.S. Catholic bishops.

There were many other groups, struggles, honors. Summing up, the *Post* editorialized:

"All of us who had the good fortune to know Geno Baroni will miss his special insight, his concern for the neglected and the powerless and his unswerving faith in the ability of people to get along with each other."

Lately, much of my prayer has involved reviewing my life. At fifty-three, I look back, and I see that life has always been a surprise for me. Becoming a priest was a surprise. Getting involved in all the things I did was a surprise. As I look back, I see myself as an activist. Now, there's another surprise. I'm in transition. I go from being an activist to being a "passionist." I don't like to use the word "passion," because it is presumptuous of me. But I am dealing with moving away from an active life. With that, I am also having to move away from an activist motivation, from an activist prayer.

Since I have been ill, and particularly more seriously ill, I find I want to say some prayers out loud. I never did that before except, of course, for public prayer. I am now saying my personal prayers out loud. I do that with prayers such as the hours, the Magnificat, the Memorare, the psalms, the Lord's Prayer. I'm not sure why. I think hearing it may do things. It breaks the silence. I am less distracted. It is more meaningful. There is something about verbalizing the prayer. I find myself doing it more and more.

Do you think you might feel it increases the possibility of the prayer being heard or answered?

I thought about that, but I think the motivation is more one of trying to make the prayer efficacious for me. I found I got more out of it. The words, the voice, surround me. I can hear the prayer. That seems to help.

Do you have a set pattern of prayer?

No, not really. I'll do something in the morning and usually at night. Sometimes during the day, I will try to get myself relaxed. It depends on the pain level.

You say you are in transition from being an "activist" to being a "passonist." How did you become an activist, and how are you changing?

I think of a passage in the Scripture about Jesus and Peter. Jesus is saying, "Feed my lambs, and feed my sheep." They go through it three times. At the end of that, Jesus says something like, "When you were young, you did your thing, but there will come a time when you will be taken aside, and you will no longer be doing your thing." I forget exactly how it goes, but in my own mind, that text epitomizes my kind of transition.

Whatever spiritual life I had was geared to scriptural passages such as the Good Samaritan or "I was hungry, I was thirsty" in Matthew 25. They became driving forces. So did the social teachings of the church. As a result, I could see Christ suffering in people who were hurting. I worked that way. I prayed that way. You could even say I prayed that way with the newspaper. I would read about an eviction or some other incident and many times I would be motivated to get involved. That involvement was not only my activity, but also my prayer. I put the two together. I did that with a lot of things. And I judged myself a lot by saying, "I didn't do this, and I didn't do that." Like the priest in the Good Samaritan story, I walked by. I ignored. I got out of it. I often felt I should have done something, because somebody was hurting.

This activist side of me goes to my core. It goes back to my childhood. I came out of an immigrant, coal mine background — very tough, very, very tough. I was born in a strike barracks because my parents had been kicked out of the company house. My family was Italian-American. I wouldn't say they were particularly religious. My father didn't care whether I became a priest or not. My mother never said anything about it. But they cared about people.

I remember a poor old guy in my hometown. My mother used

to say about him, "There but for the grace of God, go I." He was
a bachelor, a guy who lived by himself and slept with the goats.
He'd pee all over his pants. I would have to get him clothes, or
invite him to our house, or take him food, and the kids would
all laugh and think my mother was crazy.

If I ever was healed, if I ever experienced salvation, it was in a
black parish in Washington, D.C. After I was ordained a few years,
I was having a hard time in my diocese, Altoona, Pennsylvania.
By 1960, I had gone through a couple of difficult pastors. I don't
know if it was my fault or theirs, but I was blaming myself. The
bishop said I was working too hard and told me to take some
time off. I spent a month at Madonna House, Catherine de Hueck
Doherty's place in Canada. I was very attracted to the community
there. I liked the idea of having a support group like that, and I
came close to joining it.

At the time, I thought I was a big failure. I was thirty years old.
I had worked hard. I was involved, but I was very shy, very backward. I wanted to do something, but dealing with the priesthood
was difficult for me. I hadn't done anything major. I had started
a credit union in one parish and a Labor Day mass in another.
I got involved in a steel strike in Johnstown. But I was an unknown
quantity to myself. I didn't know what I was going to do. I guess
I was in the middle of a nervous breakdown. I felt confused, and
I wanted a change. I started seeing a psychiatrist, and he recom-
mended I see a Catholic psychiatrist in Washington who had
been working with priests. I was torn between going to Madonna
House or going to Washington to see the psychiatrist. Finally, I
came to Washington.

The chancery put me in an almost all black parish, St. Paul
and St. Augustine. They said it was the only place they had. It
was a courtesy, a place for me to stay. That place was the beginning of my salvation. I didn't even belong to the parish in a sense.
I was just in residence, but I started to help out. I dealt with the
people who came to the door. I didn't know a city from a street
car. I began to see people. It was incredible! A mother with kids
who had just been evicted, for example, was not uncommon.
What was I to do? I was making fifty dollars a month. I'd find

out where you could find a food order. I started to get involved in things like that. That began to affect me as a priest, as a person, in my relationship with God, in my prayer everything.

In addition to these tragedies, I also saw beautiful people. They were part of the parish. They were struggling. They worked hard. They were people of great faith. My involvement with that parish lasted ten years. During that time, I became a super activist. I became involved in the Reverend Martin Luther King's march on Washington. I became involved in Selma. I became involved in the neighborhood, which was supposed to become a "target area" for Bobby Kennedy's juvenile delinquency program. And, in time, I didn't need the psychiatrist.

Specifically, how was this situation your salvation? What healing did you experience?

It came through two groups. On one hand, the parishioners taught me great struggle, great faith. Most of the rank-and-file parishioners had tremendous faith. On the other hand, a lot of the tragedies I worked with involved people who weren't necessarily members of the parish. They were people who lived in the community. I developed an awareness of Christ struggling and suffering through these two groups. That meant my work, my vocation was to serve and respond to that situation, to that suffering and struggling Christ.

The tragedies were endless. One spring night — it was still chilly — a nun called me, for example. She said she saw a woman and three kids running around the streets. They had been evicted and had no place to go. What should she do? I said, "Put her up in the convent." She said, "Oh no, we can't do that." I said I would see if I could scrape up some money and put her in a cheap hotel. I did a lot of that, but I also got turned upside down doing that, because one time I put a mother and five children in a cheap hotel, and she got raped. That drove me crazy.

At the time I was helping this woman with the three kids, Washington had a rule against a man living with a family getting welfare. If you got caught, you got thrown off the rolls. This woman's husband had gotten out of jail, and he had come to visit her and the kids. He was caught, and she was dropped from

welfare and eventually evicted. A reporter from the *Washington
Post* had asked me to call her if I came across such a case. I did,
and she wrote about this woman. Well, the next day, the woman
became completely disoriented. There was a story about her in
the paper. She had to be committed to the psychiatric hospital.
Three days later, she died. All hell broke loose. There were more
stories. The Congress — Washington didn't have home rule at
the time — had a bill before it about this man-in-the-house rule,
and there was a lot of agitation on Capitol Hill. In all the hubbub,
this woman and her children epitomized Christ's suffering for
me. She was hurting. She was suffering her own passion and
death.

Out of that came one of the first groups I helped form. It was
called the Coalition of Conscience, a group of Protestants, Jews
and Catholics. We began to raise holy hell about the legislation
on the Hill. We tried to keep alive the idea that the system had
to be changed. Meanwhile, I saw poor people every day. Sometimes I did better than others. There were times I should have
done better than I did. There were times I wanted to skip it. I'd
think, "You, again." But I couldn't skip it. I just couldn't. And so
I got involved. I would take you to the hospital if you swallowed
a box of sleeping pills, or if your child was sick and you needed
to go to the hospital clinic to get a prescription. I would go. I
would go to court with people. I would get upset and angry. I
would get angry at the injustice, and I would be grief-stricken in
terms of Jesus and the suffering.

I looked upon it as a kind of work of creation, of furthering,
with God's help, what he had started. Trying to do something
about these situations — that was my meditation, that was my
prayer. I'd say, "Lord, let me respond to whatever comes up today
as a Christian. Help me. What do I do with this stuff?"

*That was your activist style and activist prayer. In this transition,
what are you moving toward?*

The transition for me now is to move away from concentrating
on seeing Christ suffering in other people. I guess I did that to
the degree I was a Christian. The issue for me now is that I have
to see that Christ is suffering right here, in me. It was always over

there. Now the hard part is, how do I identify with the great mystery of Christ's suffering and death? How do I deal with my fears in the middle of the night? I know God loves me. I know I have to keep pushing that. I also know love — perfect love — overcomes fear, but the fears are there. What's happening to me?

I am having a hard time turning God's love around and focusing on myself. That's not easy for a kid who used to struggle with questions like, am I lovable or am I loving? I am certainly not lovely. I do want to be lovable, and I do want to be loving. First, I have to know God loves me. As a kid, I had trouble believing that. Why should God love me? Now I have to drop all the projects, drop all the activity, and concentrate on myself. I'm by myself most of the time. Is there a new vocation for me? I used to pray, "Lord, help me to help the Smiths, to help the Joneses, help me to do this, help me do that, to start this, to start that."

With that kind of prayer, I got involved in all the D.C. issues — human relations, civil rights, welfare, housing. I started a big community center in Washington. It became a place for a lot of things to happen, and a lot of people to come. I became director of urban affairs for the diocese. I went to the U.S. Catholic Conference as a program director for the urban task force. I started the Campaign for Human Development and the National Center for Ethnic Affairs.

There's one thing I still want to do: To set up a self-help development institute. There's no place in the United States where you can learn self-help development.

Tell us about your cancer.

I first had cancer in 1973. I had surgery, a tumor in my mouth was taken out. I had cancer again in 1980. This time it was in my neck. I had a radical lymph node cancer. It was taken out, too. This is my third cancer. It was discovered in July, 1981. I had just come back to the archdiocese from the government, from the Carter administration, where I was assistant secretary of Housing and Urban Development. This cancer is called peritoneal mesothelioma. It's a rare asbestos cancer. There are lots of asbestos cancers — thousands of them, and there are going to be millions, I guess.

This is a rare one, because it is in the abdomen. The doctors think it is caused by asbestos. The researchers are trying to pin me down on where I came in contact with asbestos. That's hard, because it usually takes thirty to forty years before it shows up. The actor, Steve McQueen, had this kind of cancer. I have had surgery. The cancer caused a bowel obstruction, which was very painful, and that had to be removed. When they found this cancer, some doctors told me I had six months. I asked one doctor what he would do, and he said he would go to Lourdes. So I did. I took my mother and my sister. I had never been to Lourdes before. It was a good visit. We also went to see my relatives in Italy.

Did you pray for healing?

After I got this last cancer, I got myself into a dilemma. I wondered, is this God's will? Is it his will that I accept this? If so, I shouldn't ask for healing, should I? But God doesn't will evil, does he? God's will is love. Jesus healed. People touched him and were healed. I began to look into healing prayers. I went to a few healing ministries. I even conducted one healing service — back at my old parish in Washington — and sometimes I think that if I get well enough, I might like to do more of that.

I was anointed many, many times. I found some interesting things. I found that a lot of priests don't know what to do with a cancer patient. I don't know if that was because I am a priest, or if it is true in general. They would come in and anoint me and run. They didn't know what to do. They would just take the ritual and go through it. The Assumptionist priests, with whom I stayed when I first came up here, have taken time and really prayed with me. That has been really helpful.

When I got this cancer, my reaction was: Good Lord, am I finished, or is there something else for me to do? I began to catch myself doing life review. I grew up over there. I was a priest over here. I was a priest over there. I got involved in this, I got involved in that. I began to find myself trying to put the pieces together, trying to make connections. I also began to sense the need for more physical healing. I wanted to be healed inside. I got involved in a cancer therapy group. There were eleven people in it, all with cancer. Three are still living. It was a secular group, but we did a variety of meditations, using techniques such as guided imagery.

I began to feel that the toughest healings, in a personal sense, stemmed from some kind of rejection. I have dealt with some of these. Maybe I'm still dealing with others, although I don't worry about them so much any more. I have to let go of a lot of stuff. I've just let go. When I let go of things, I start to think I should accept this cancer as God's will, but God's will means love, means action. I should respond to my own needs the way I used to try to respond to the needs of others. I ought to call around. I ought to call Richard Bloch's cancer hotline in Kansas City, or get hold of the cancer experts in Houston. I realized my doctors didn't really know much. They just said it was very rare. Should I accept that, or do I call around?

I would start looking. But then I would become passive again. That's the way I have been — active and passive. I guess I have to be patient. At least that is what somebody told me, to be patient to find out where I am. When I first heard that, the word *patience* hit me like a thunderbolt.

One person who has helped me a lot here in Boston is Henri Nouwen, the spiritual writer. He's at Harvard, and he comes to see me about every other day. In a sense, he is giving me a retreat. We talk, and we pray together. That has helped me with this transition. Now, most days I don't finish the newspaper. None of my friends can believe that. They can't believe that by now — mid-afternoon — I wouldn't have finished the *New York Times* and be on the phone calling people and saying, "What are we going to do about this or that?" But now I don't finish the paper many days. I've let go.

Some of that comes from being in hospitals. I've had roommates I was up with all night. I had no choice. They were in bad shape, far worse than I am in now. I got a whole different perspective in terms of the transition I'm in.

I find talking about this difficult, in a way. I can be very articulate and very glib in my field, but when I get on this turf — prayer — that's something else. I didn't go to meetings to learn to talk about prayer. I didn't develop the vocabulary and the lingo. I had a mindset, a framework, a context, and a content of what I thought was my prayer, my work, and I cooked my own recipe.

But now, I have moved into a new area. I still don't know the lingo. I've looked at a lot of books. I'm looking for a new framework in moving from one lifestyle to another. That's where I am, in that transition.

How have you used imagery in your prayers?

In the cancer support group, I learned techniques for trying to relax, and then, in my imagination, to take myself somewhere — to the ocean, the mountains, or a meadow. I would take myself somewhere and meet somebody. One childhood image was very strong for me. I grew up in a mining camp in the rolling hills of southwest Pennsylvania. Now, in my imagination, I put myself back there. I put myself in those hills with Philip.

Philip was a kid I met in high school. He happened to be Catholic. We were two of a kind, on the shy side. In high school, I didn't do anything. I wasn't anybody, didn't make waves, never got elected to anything, never did any big deals. I was an ordinary kid struggling along. Philip was killed in an airplane, his own airplane, a couple of years ago. He had six children. His family owned a resort. I had performed his daughter's wedding in April or May, and two months later, I conducted his funeral. I began to realize that Philip was my oldest friend, going back to fourteen years of age — from fourteen to fifty. He was somebody I always went back to. We would go off walking through the woods. We would go fishing. We'd just talk, philosophize about anything — life, the world, God.

When I began to look for a partner in my imagery, it was easy for me to go back and walk the meadows with Philip. Philip and I would be in a meadow. There would be an old house up ahead. We'd walk up to that house, and we would go inside, and we'd look — and then the inside of the house would become me, my body. We'd walk around, looking for the place the cancer was. That place would be a big room with doctors and nurses and x-rays. And they'd all be looking, watching the battle, and wondering, are you winning or losing?

Sometimes I translated the image of walking through the house with Philip, or looking at my cancer, to other images. I would meet somebody else. As I was going through one of the rooms, or part of myself, I would have my little light — you know, "this little light of mine." I'd meet Jesus, the divine light. That would become part of my meditation, part of my prayer. The divine light is within us, within me. I'm part of the divine light. I'm related to the divine light. I'm a child of God.

What would you say to Jesus?

Come with me. This is a temple of the Spirit, and it's hurting. I'm hurting. I'm hurting. I'm in pain. Jesus, help me to know your victory, your promise, your hope. Jesus, I love you. Jesus, love me. Jesus, forgive me. Jesus, help me. Jesus, I hope in you. I want to share the divine light. I want to be with you. I want to know you. Don't forget me. Meet my friend, Philip. Give me patience. Take me day by day. What am I supposed to do? Am I supposed to stay at Georgetown Hospital? Am I supposed to go to Sloan Kettering (a cancer hospital) in New York City? Am I supposed to go to Boston? Am I supposed to fight back? Help me with the fear. Help me with the doubts. Your love overcomes the fear and the doubts. Your will is your love. Are you taking me to another place? If so, help me cross over, to find peace. Help me to know your will, your love. It goes on and on and on.

What do you find Jesus saying back to you?

I am the way. I am the truth. I am the light. Have hope. He smiles. I say, "Can we hold hands? Can I be with you?" He smiles. I say, "Will you give me patience?" "Yes." "Will you give me hope?" "Yes."

What else does he say?

That prompts me to think of the things he hasn't said! "Come, now's the time. This is it." He hasn't said that, at least not in terms of now, this minute. This vocation, yes. This suffering, yes. It makes me wonder if I have to surrender more. The support group I was in had two or three psychiatrists in it. They would always be talking — in secular terms — about the issue of when you give up. When do you say, "The doctors say, 'This is it. There's nothing else that can be done.' " I have tried to translate that into the spiritual realm by saying, "Jesus, is this it? If so, I'm ready to go."

Once, I had a dream. It only goes so far, though. In the dream, there was a beautiful sunset. I was coming up on the sunset. All of a sudden, I realized I was in a place of harmony and peace. There was no conflict. I felt relieved. There was no fighting within me, no back and forth tearing me apart. I didn't really see any people, but I knew I was in a peaceful place where there was justice. I could almost hear music. I was getting closer and closer, but then I woke up, and I was in a bad sweat. I had taken Demerol or morphine, because I was hurting. I had had a couple of shots. Man, I was deep into that dream. Later, my reaction to waking up was, "Damn! I wish it were over." I wished I was there — wherever there is. I wished I was there.

The dream was so vivid. Now, I go back to that dream in different ways. I want to put Jesus into the dream. I want to see Jesus with the backdrop of the glorious sun. I want Jesus and Philip and me to go walking across the horizon.

But that may not come for a while. Cancer can be a long struggle. Or, if it gets into the pancreas, or some place like that, it would only be three months. I met Ruth Stapleton, President Carter's sister. She died in about three months. I don't know if it is going to be fast, or whether it is going to drag out, or if there is going to be a healing. I'm in a position where all three are options yet, and I don't know which way I'm going.

One day I said to the doctor, "Hell, the treatments just about put me under." I told her I was going to be dying of malnutrition, because I couldn't eat as a result of the medicine I was taking. But she said the tumor had been reduced at least fifty percent by the treatments. She said she wasn't promising anything, but there were good signs and that if we got enough treatments, we might be able to get it down to where it was controllable. The doctors don't use the word "remission" anymore. So, I don't know. I'm right in the middle. I'm right at the crossroads. Some days I say, "Good Lord, I've got to get ready. Yes, I'm getting ready. I'm ready. Help me to get ready. Help me to deal with it — the final struggle."

Some days, I think I have it all together in terms of God, and I feel the fear is gone. I feel close to God. On other days, it gets away from me. When you are taking thirteen pills as I am, the medicine puts you up, and it puts you down. One medicine makes you high, one makes you low. Sometimes, it seems it throws you to kingdom come. There have been times I refused medicine, refused chemotherapy, because I didn't think it would do any good. Once the doctors came to me and said, "We have this medicine — it's a poison — and we want to give it to you, but we don't know if it will do any good." I said, "Why should I take it? The poison is worse than the disease." I still have that dilemma, too. How long should I take treatment before I surrender and say, "This is it." I may be close to that, but I don't know.

One thing I pray for is for God to help me put this in a one-day context. I can't handle more than one day at a time. I can't put it all together in terms of what's going to happen in April, May, June, and July. I just don't know.

In thinking about myself, I am reminded of a man I visited who was very sick with cancer. After I anointed him, he started talking. He had had chemotherapy, drugs, surgery, radiation. He was up for more chemotherapy, and he shook his head. He told me he had come to see there was only one final healing, and that that final healing was not going to come through drugs, radiation, or surgery. That final healing was going to be death.

I found out he was afraid to let go. His wife was outside his room talking about plans she had, what they were going to do next week, and how the doctor had this new kind of surgery. He shook his head, but he was afraid not to go along with the doctor, not to go along with his wife. I talked to his wife and said, "Maybe it's time for John to let go, maybe it's time to say goodbye." I told his son the same thing. I told the son to tell his father he would care for his mother. I told him to tell his father that the grandchildren would know about him. I told the family to start this conversation. Don't just let it happen, I said. Don't just wait it out. Too often, I have seen people not dealing with it, not accepting it, not making arrangements. Once this family went through this process, he died within forty-eight hours. He was able to let go.

I have often thought, is that the way it is going to happen with me? I prayed about that and said, "Jesus, help me with the final healing." With me, the final healing is death, too. But I need to work more on that if it's right around the corner. I know it is inevitable, but we have a great denial system. I think it is really built-in. One of the doctors said to me, "Well, you've got cancer, but you could go out on the street and get hit by a truck." But I never believed I was going to be hit by a truck. It was always going to be somebody else. Until you get a death-threatening disease, you don't think that way. It's always going to be the other guy.

Would you say you have experienced healing as the result of your prayer?

There are days I find a calmness and a peace, and the fear is gone. But I don't know if I would call it healing. It is not universal. I can't say it holds up all the time. I go up and down. There are times I believe things are forgiven, and I have overcome the rejections. Most of the rejections are gone now. But one or two keep popping up, come back on me. Then I think, well, maybe I'm not healed from that rejection.

I've never gotten used to the language of healing. Maybe a couple of months from now, if that's possible, I will be further along. This is a whole new thing for me. I came here — it will be three weeks on Tuesday — and I thought I was going to stay three days. I thought once I got over the nausea and I started to eat, I'd get out of here, but here I am, day after day after day. I've been here in Boston since Christmas. I didn't realize it's been that long, but here it is, March. I was going to do this in March and that in April, and I have had to begin canceling things and not scheduling things. I almost canceled this interview. I came very close. I thought I shouldn't go through with it, because I didn't know how I was going to be. If I got a pain attack, and I'd have to get a shot or something. I'd have wasted your time coming up here. I would feel bad.

In what way has prayer helped you most in your fight with cancer?

I think it creates a context of putting you in God's presence. It connects you to God. It relates you to God. It reminds you of God. It makes you know God's love, makes you know God's forgiveness. You remind yourself of the promise, the victory, the hope, the resurrection. You see this situation is temporary. You come to realize Jesus is love, love, love, love. That is always helpful. There are times I wish I could pray, but I can't stay with it. So I just say, "Lord, you'll have to accept me as I am. Lord, you created me. Here I am, good and bad. Please help me."

There are many people suffering from cancer. I'm sure a lot of them are trying to pray, too. What is your advice to them?

I feel a little presumptuous in answering, because I am just learning myself. I just wonder sometimes what happens to people who don't believe. I find myself saying, "Lord, what about these people who don't know about your love, your forgiveness, your goodness?" Wow!

As for advice about prayer, I would suggest you get someone to come and help you pray. I suggest that because of the ups and downs. Some days you won't feel like praying, and then it is good if someone is there to help. Of course, you can't always do that. At night, for instance, people can't come, and you are usually alone. I've had all night sessions when I couldn't sleep, when the sleeping pill didn't work or wasn't strong enough. Sometimes during nights like that, I am able to pray pretty well. Some nights, I can't. Lately, when I have nights like that, I have been trying to let go. I'll say, "Okay, Jesus, I surrender. Help me. I'm in your hands. Take care of me."